Praise for *The Elements of Negotiation*

"Keld Jensen's new book *The Elements of Negotiation* is a great read. The book offers practical advice together with insightful and thoughtful reflection about how to be successful in negotiations. The 103 elements outlined by Jensen really will help you manage all your negotiations so that the outcomes will be effective and longer lasting. I thoroughly recommend this book for all the negotiators out there . . . both experienced and inexperienced practitioners."

Clive Rees, PhD in Commercial Relationships
Vice President, International Chief Procurement Officer
Executive Director Global Supply Chain Unit
Fujitsu

"Step aside, Chris Voss—there's a new master negotiator in town. Keld Jensen introduces groundbreaking strategies in his latest book, redefining the art of negotiation to the highest level of our times. Discover why top negotiators are turning to Jensen's innovative SMARTnership approach for results that benefit all."

Werner Valeur
Entrepreneur with multiple exits

"In my professional life, I have sought methods and techniques that not only improve my negotiation skills but also enhance my understanding of human interaction, which lies at the core of every negotiation. *The Elements of Negotiation* by Keld Jensen is a great representation of some of these methods.

The book is not just a collection of tactics; it is a compendium of wisdom, conveyed by an author who has clearly dedicated himself to mastering and sharing the art of negotiation. From the fundamental elements of nonverbal communication to the advanced strategies for emotional intelligence and adaptation, Keld outlines a path to negotiation that challenges the traditional view of winner-vs.-loser dynamics.

Through Keld's lenses, negotiation becomes an exercise in SMARTnership, where the true value lies in collaboration and mutual success. This perspective has over the years influenced the way I conduct professional negotiations myself.

One of the aspects of Keld's approach that I particularly appreciate is his emphasis on preparation, understanding, and respect for the other party's perspectives and needs. This methodical approach to negotiation underscores the importance of building relationships based on trust and mutual respect – an approach that has proven to be invaluable in both my professional and personal life.

I highly recommend *The Elements of Negotiation: 103 Tactics for Everyone to Win in Each Deal* to anyone looking to improve their negotiation techniques. The book is not just a guide to negotiation; it is a guide to achieving a deeper understanding. The essence of negotiation lies in the ability to understand and appreciate the people we negotiate with.

It is this insight that makes *103 Tactics for Everyone to Win in Each Deal* essential reading for anyone aspiring to achieve more meaningful and productive negotiations."

Lars Krull
Head of MBA,
Aalborg University (Denmark)

"Unlock the mysteries of negotiation with Keld Jensen's comprehensive guide. From dissecting every element to outlining winning tactics, this book offers clear steps for mastering the journey toward conscious competence and avoiding common pitfalls. Gain confidence and expertise in the art of negotiation."

Mark Bowden, best-selling author on Human Behavior
and Advisor to G7 leaders

"Do we even need to introduce Keld Jensen anymore? As one of the most prolific negotiation authors globally, his publications have reached nearly three million readers. He consistently ranks among the Top 30 Negotiation Gurus and teaches in some of the most prestigious eMBA programs worldwide.

As a negotiation professor at McGill University in the Desautels Faculty of Management, I have trained thousands of students across our BCom, MBA, and executive education programs. I am committed to providing an excellent learning environment to my students, which has been recognized with several teaching awards. I am always on the lookout for practical negotiation books that both students and managers can utilize to enhance their skills.

The Elements of Negotiation: 103 Tactics for Everyone to Win in Each Deal is not merely about making deals; it's about mastering the multifaceted elements of negotiation. This includes managing information, behaviors, emotions, language, and tactics, avoiding common pitfalls, and more. This book serves as a periodic table of negotiation, encompassing all the essential elements one needs to know. It provides comprehensive knowledge essential for achieving personal and professional goals.

Every page of this book is a treasure trove of actionable insights. Each element of negotiation is explained with clarity and is supplemented by concrete examples, providing readers a practical understanding of how to apply these tactics in real-world scenarios.

I firmly believe this is one of the finest books on negotiation available today. It is perfectly suited for students and practitioners eager to acquire extensive, actionable knowledge on negotiation."

Jean-Nicolas Reyt
Associate Professor of Organizational Behavior
Desautels Faculty of Management, McGill University

"I recommend this book to be read at least twice and keep on the desk as a reference, an Almanac of negotiation.

Keld's book is a masterpiece, transforming the art of negotiation into a precise science. Drawing on decades of experience and research, Keld provides readers with an unparalleled roadmap to navigate the complexities of negotiation. With eloquent details and a clear roadmap, he effortlessly guides readers through the intricate elements of negotiation, breaking down each component with ease of explanation.

What truly sets this book apart is Keld's ingenious use of the periodic table as a metaphor for negotiation dynamics. By likening negotiation elements to chemical elements, he brilliantly illustrates the diverse array of strategies and outcomes possible in any negotiation scenario.

As I delved into the book, I found myself deeply reflecting on past negotiation experiences, inspired by Keld's thoughtful insights. His meticulous attention to detail encourages readers to explore their own negotiation styles and adapt them for greater success.

From understanding emotional intelligence to making strategic adjustments, this book is essential for anyone aiming to excel in negotiations, whether novice or expert. It serves as both a comprehensive guide and a source of inspiration, offering valuable lessons for every stage of the negotiation process."

Tarek Amine
Principal Vice President and Chief Supply Chain Officer
at Bechtel Global Corporation

"Just like chemical reactions, negotiations require a delicate balance of elements to realize the desired result. In his new book, Keld is the expert chemist who teaches us how to identify and deftly mix and adjust these elements to achieve optimal results in any negotiation. A must-read for anyone looking to become a master negotiator."

Laurie Ehrlich
Chief Commercial Counsel
Datadog, Inc.

"While working at Google, you come across a number of internal and external personalities, and having a sound negotiation skill baseline is critical to any person's success. If you thought negotiation was all about power suits and stern faces, think again. Keld Jensen brings his *103 Tactics for Everyone to Win in Each Deal* to life in a book that is rejuvenating the fun in negotiations, packed with clever tactics and insights that will have you thinking differently in a negotiation – and maybe even enjoying the process. Keld's ability to turn "kew" negotiation themes into resounding examples brings individual's mindset from an avoid negotiations mentality to a lead negotiator. These elements of negotiation are valuable to all industries and experiences."

Jim Daly
Head of North America Deal Pursuit
Google

THE
ELEMENTS
OF
NE GO TI A TI ON

THE
ELEMENTS
OF
NE GO TI A TI ON

103 TACTICS
FOR EVERYONE TO WIN
IN EACH DEAL

KELD JENSEN

WILEY

Library of Congress Cataloging-in-Publication Data:

Names: Jensen, Keld, author. | John Wiley & Sons, publisher.
Title: The elements of negotiation : 103 tactics for everyone to win in each deal / Keld Jensen.
Description: Hoboken, New Jersey : Wiley, [2024] | Includes index.
Identifiers: LCCN 2024014712 (print) | LCCN 2024014713 (ebook) | ISBN 9781394248285 (cloth) | ISBN 9781394248315 (adobe pdf) | ISBN 9781394248308 (epub)
Subjects: LCSH: Negotiation in business. | Negotiation. | Interpersonal relations
Classification: LCC BF637.N4 J46 2024 (print) | LCC BF637.N4 (ebook) | DDC 658.4/052—dc23/eng/20240501
LC record available at https://lccn.loc.gov/2024014712
LC ebook record available at https://lccn.loc.gov/2024014713

Cover Design: Wiley
Cover Image: © Keld Jensen
Author Photo: Courtesy of Justin Segura

This book is dedicated to my late mother, Laura.
She meant so much to all of us.

Contents

Chapter 4   Tactics   147

Chapter 5   Emotions   167

Chapter 6   Things to Consider   201

Chapter 7   Ultimate Level   237

Chapter 8   The Foundation   257

The Great Negotiator's 103 Steps™

Nonverbal · Knowledge · Tools · Tactics · Emotions · Things to consider · Ultimate

Legend: **Number / Symbol / Skill, implement, tool**

Foundation

www.KeldJensen.com

Introduction

In the pursuit of mastering the art of negotiation, the journey began in the year 1976. It was an era marked by a burgeoning interest in understanding the complexities of human interaction, particularly in the realms of business and diplomacy. Recognizing the profound impact that effective negotiation tactics could have on outcomes, my partner Iwar Unt embarked on an ambitious project to dissect and analyze the very fabric of negotiation processes.

Over the course of several decades, Iwar and I meticulously observed and evaluated more than 35,000 negotiations, spanning various industries, cultures, and contexts. This extensive research initiative was not merely quantitative in its approach but deeply qualitative, involving the participation of seasoned negotiators. Together, we sought to uncover the underlying principles that govern negotiation dynamics.

By studying a large group of negotiators to see whether there are significant differences between those who are successful and those who are not, we formed a clear picture of some of the factors that influence the negotiation result in a positive or negative direction. This also gave us an understanding of why problems occur and how they could be avoided or handled. At the same time, we realized that this did not provide a simple explanation for success or failure. Sometimes the fundamental prerequisites were so unfavorable that no negotiation technique could create any further success. Conversely, sometimes the prerequisites were so favorable that failure was nearly impossible. Some negotiators are lucky, while others simply run into bad luck.

Our methodology was rigorous and multidimensional. We employed a combination of observational studies, controlled experiments, and extensive fieldwork. Each negotiation was recorded, annotated, and examined through various lenses, ranging from nonverbal communication patterns to the strategic deployment of information. We analyzed successes and failures alike, learning as much from the stumbles as from the triumphs.

Through this expansive research, we gradually began to identify recurring patterns and strategies that consistently yielded favorable results. These patterns were not happenstance; they were the product of deliberate and skillful execution of specific negotiation elements. We categorized these elements into several domains, including nonverbal communication, knowledge acquisition, strategic tool utilization, emotional intelligence, and overarching strategy.

Each element was then subjected to further scrutiny. We sought to understand not only how and when it was used but also why it was effective. To this end, we integrated insights from behavioral science, economics, and even game theory. Our aim was to construct a robust framework that encapsulated the multifaceted nature of negotiation.

In addition, over the last 20 years, I have researched and studied thousands of companies of many different kinds. As you might expect, I found some were more successful than others. As part of my investigations, I looked into their history of collaborations to see how much of their success (or lack thereof) could be attributed to this variable. I found the companies that were doing better in cooperative situations—whether buying, selling, and project management or otherwise—tended to succeed in proportion to their relative mastery of four fundamental factors:

- Having a defined negotiation strategy (discussed in Element 16)
- Closely monitoring the financial consequences of Tru$tCurrency (discussed in Element 16)
- Articulating the rules of the game before entering into any bargaining situation (discussed in Element 17)
- Practicing NegoEconomics (discussed in Element 17)

The culmination of this research effort is what I now present as the *103 Elements of Negotiation*. These elements are not mere tactics; they are the distilled essence of what we learned from our comprehensive study of negotiation. They represent the science of human interaction, the psychology of persuasion, and the strategy of decision-making.

Keep in mind that as you integrate these elements into your negotiation practice, you are not merely applying techniques; you are embodying a legacy of research and knowledge that has transformed the landscape of negotiation.

How Much Do Mistakes Cost?

Studies show that only two-thirds of all negotiators land a deal, and then even one where they lose, on average, approximately 40 percent of the overall negotiation potential. This potential consists of unrealized yet realizable added value (*NegoEconomics*) that would have enabled the parties to get more out of the transaction without the opponent feeling like the loser. In this potential, we will certainly find part of the added value that negotiators in boardrooms picture when they calculate great merger gains—an added value that will never be realized now, and that contributes to the failure of the majority of all major mergers.

The question of how much all the mistakes cost is impossible to answer by looking at one single instance of negotiation. However, we will try to find out what the consequences are when negotiators fail in finding the most economical solution to the problem under negotiation.

In a negotiated agreement where the price is $1,000,000, the supplier has a gain of 25 percent, which most people would consider a very nice gain. But when we look at all the data that is available to the parties, we can see that an added value (NegoEconomics) of $200,000 in total could have been created. This added value can be realized if they design the agreement differently than originally planned in the offer; for example, by suggesting alternative payment conditions, another delivery time, a changed technical requirement specification, and improved servicing.

During the negotiations, they arrive at some of the changes that will provide the added value (NegoEconomics), but if they negotiate as the average negotiator in our study did, as much as 40 percent of the realizable added value of $200,000, ($80,000) will remain unutilized. If it was the seller, for example, who had found this $80,000 and they alone would benefit, their profit would have grown from $250,000 to $330,000, that is, by as much as 32 percent.

To this can be added that a little more than a third of the negotiators who participated in the test failed completely and never managed to enter into an agreement. The gain they lose is even greater. The overall cost of all the mistakes committed at the negotiation table will most likely amount to very large figures. Added to this are the very negative effects in the shape of superfluous environmental destruction, a poor working environment, unnecessary technical and economic risks, and the time and energy the negotiators invest in fighting.

Even though the mistakes are very costly, we should not let the result depress us. Instead of focusing on the failures, we ought to look at the great potential available. For the skilled negotiator, there is a lot to gain. The negotiation skill can and must be developed. Many of our companies are not so good at protecting and benefiting from the intellectual capital. The money and resources spent on developing the employees' negotiation skills are far too few compared to the enormous potential available.

The Ketchup Effect

The study shows that during the 120 minutes that the negotiators have at their disposal, only about 10 percent can finish without feeling any pressure of time. Fifty-five percent do not reach an agreement until the moment when they feel that time is running out. Under stress and pressed for time, they force a conclusion through. This can also be experienced in real life. When time is almost up, the negotiators are forced to reach an agreement, often in the shape of a compromise where the parties meet halfway, that is, no one must lose more than the other. Since there is no time to reconsider, they cannot be sure that all the significant points have been discussed and studied.

To study whether time had been lacking and whether this had influenced the result, the group of negotiators who had not reached an agreement after 2 hours was given another chance by having the negotiation period prolonged by another

30 to 60 minutes. In the group which had been given more time, only 6 percent managed to reach an agreement. The others could not break their destructive pattern. A skilled observer of negotiations would have realized at an early stage that these negotiators would have a hard time.

Time seems to have been of minor importance. Despite the extra time, 33 percent of the negotiators failed at reaching an agreement. Nothing came of the planned partnership about which they were supposed to reach an agreement.

The study shows that the small group of 10 percent that managed to reach an agreement at their own leisure without getting stressed as a result of lack of time also entered into better agreements than the others. They utilized up to 20 percent more of the available negotiation potential. They spent their time in another way than those who found themselves pressed for time.

It is not lack of time that makes the negotiation fail. What causes the failure is the negotiation methods—a fact that many have difficulty accepting.

During the exercise, we furthermore tried to step in and help the negotiators who got stuck in meaningless arguments and those who reached a dead end, having come up with solutions that were unacceptable for various reasons. Such help they would never get in real life.

In approximately 10 percent of the negotiations that led to a conclusion, one of the parties declared: "If this had been a real negotiation situation, we would have stopped a long time ago and thrown the opponents out. We would never have accepted their behavior. But since this is an exercise, we wanted to give them a chance."

The significance of this is that there is a considerable risk that the negotiators would have been even less successful in real negotiations. It is at the negotiation table that your company can win or lose great sums of money in a short time.

Mastering Negotiation: The Rockefeller Method

In the annals of business history, few moments capture the art of negotiation quite like the iconic encounter between two titans of industry: John D. Rockefeller and J.P. Morgan. This story offers invaluable lessons for professionals, especially those keen on mastering the art of negotiation.

Rockefeller, a legendary figure in the corporate world, owned an enterprise that caught the eye of financier J.P. Morgan. Morgan, known for his keen business acumen, approached Rockefeller with an interest in purchasing his company. However, Rockefeller, unaware of Morgan's intentions and the potential value his enterprise held for Morgan, found himself at a crossroads.

Their meeting, initially veiled in casual conversation about the weather and current business trends, soon took a pivotal turn. Morgan, growing impatient, directly addressed the purpose of their meeting, urging Rockefeller to set his terms for the sale. Yet, Rockefeller, a master of negotiation strategy, responded with a statement that shifted the entire dynamic: "I think you've misunderstood the situation. I'm not here to sell, you're here to buy."

This response wasn't just a clever retort; it was a strategic move that placed Rockefeller in a position of strength. By refraining from presenting any terms and maintaining silence, Rockefeller effectively turned the tables, compelling Morgan, the eager buyer, to reveal his hand first.

This encounter teaches us a crucial lesson in negotiation: the power of information and positioning. Rockefeller recognized that to negotiate effectively, you must understand the other party's motivations and value propositions. His decision not to present terms immediately was a deliberate tactic to gain more information, thereby enhancing his negotiation position.

In your career, whether you're negotiating a business deal, a salary, or a partnership, adopting a similar approach can be incredibly effective. It reminds you to gather as much information as possible and understand the dynamics at play before laying your cards on the table. This approach not only strengthens your position but also helps you make more informed and strategic decisions.

Rockefeller's method underscores the essence of successful negotiation—it's not just about what you are willing to offer or accept, but also about understanding the value you hold in the eyes of the other party and leveraging that to your advantage.

As professionals navigating the complex world of business, incorporating this mindset can transform your negotiation strategies, leading you toward more favorable outcomes and success.

Remember, in negotiations, sometimes silence speaks louder than words, and knowledge truly is power.

Welcome to the Journey

Welcome to a journey through the intricate and exhilarating world of negotiation, where every interaction, every gesture, and every word can tip the scales of success. *The Elements of Negotiation* is not just a book; it's a comprehensive map to mastering the art and science of negotiation. My name is Keld Jensen, and I am your guide through this exploration of strategic partnership which I call *SMARTnership negotiation*.

This book is designed as a modular guide, allowing both novices and seasoned professionals to navigate through the complex landscape of negotiation with ease and confidence. Each element, represented here as a unique piece of the larger puzzle, is a building block toward becoming a great negotiator.

At the heart of this book lies the understanding that negotiation is a complex blend of skills and attributes, ranging from nonverbal communication and emotional intelligence to strategic planning and adaptability. Each of the 103 elements is designed to enhance specific facets of your negotiation ability, ensuring a comprehensive development of your skills.

I start Chapter 1 with the nonverbal—the unspoken yet powerful messages we send through our body language, eye contact, and gestures. These foundational elements set the stage for credibility and influence before a single word is uttered.

In Chapter 2, I delve into the knowledge necessary for any negotiator: under-standing numerical data, grasping the nuances of different languages, and the importance of subject matter expertise. These tools are not just accessories but essential instruments in your negotiation toolkit.

The heart of the book lies in the Tools chapter. In Chapter 3, you learn to select the right approach, utilize visual aids effectively, employ checklists, and find addi-tional value in your negotiation. These tools are your strategies in action—the methods by which you'll navigate through the negotiation process.

In Chapter 4, I discuss the five different tactics—combative, stalling, conces-sion, compromising, and collaborative. This includes how and why they tick the way they do, and how to deal with this behavior.

As you progress, the role of emotions in negotiation (Chapter 5) becomes clear. The chemistry of interactions, the dance of building trust, and the power of lik-ability can turn the tide in any discussion. These steps focus on the human element, which is often the most unpredictable yet rewarding part of any negotiation.

The book does not stop at the mere mechanics of negotiation. In Chapter 6, I consider the things that make a negotiation truly successful – reflection, adapt-ability, and the importance of habits that foster a negotiator's mindset.

Then you'll ascend to the ultimate level of negotiation. In Chapter 7, I intro-duce concepts that transform good negotiators into great ones. It's about reaching beyond the deal for something more profound – the initiative, the strategic silence, the human engineering that create not just agreements, but partnerships that last.

Finally, in Chapter 8, I touch on the foundation for everything – what is needed to master before calling yourself a great negotiator.

In crafting your journey through this book, keep in mind that it's designed for flexibility and personalized exploration. There's no need to adhere to a sequential path from Element 1 through to 103. Feel free to begin at any point, such as Element 45, and navigate in any order that suits your needs and curiosity. Alternatively, you can utilize this book as a reference guide, turning to specific sections as a resource for guidance on your next steps. This approach allows you to tailor your learning experience to your unique situation and objectives in negotiation.

You might consider starting by reading the entire book, as this approach pro-vides a comprehensive understanding and guidance for later revisiting specific topics or content. However, the way you choose to consume the content ultimately depends on your personal preference.

The Elements of Negotiation is both your atlas and compass in the world of negotiation. Whether you're making your first deal or your thousandth, this book is designed to enhance your negotiation skills and enrich your understanding of this complex art.

Prepare to embark on a transformative journey that will not only enhance your negotiation skills but also enrich your professional and personal interactions. Welcome to the world of "The Great Negotiator."

Negotiation skills are essential for everyone. By acquiring and applying these skills, we grow as individuals and contribute to a more harmonious and effective society.

—Keld Jensen
—Award-winning expert in negotiation and SMARTnerships

CHAPTER 1

Nonverbal

Introduction: Orchestrating the Elements of Nonverbal Communication in Negotiation

Negotiation transcends spoken words, entering a realm where silence speaks volumes. This chapter is an exploration of the various elements of nonverbal communication, each integral to the nuanced art of negotiation. I dissect these elements into separate elements, exploring how they harmonize to create impactful, unspoken dialogue in the negotiating space.

- **Element 1: Body language.** The first element delves into body language, examining how our physical expressions and posture communicate messages, setting the tone for negotiations without uttering a single word.
- **Element 2: Eye contact.** This element focuses on the power of eye contact, exploring how it can establish a connection, convey sincerity, or assert authority in the subtle interplay of negotiation.
- **Element 3: Gesticulations.** In this element, I explore the role of hand movements and gestures, which can reinforce or contradict spoken words, significantly influencing the perception and outcome of a negotiation.
- **Element 4: The role of voice.** This element covers the nuances of voice modulation, including tone, pitch, and volume, and their subtle yet powerful impact on negotiation dynamics.

- **Element 5: Use humor.** This element introduces humor as a pivotal nonverbal tool, highlighting how it can diffuse tension, build rapport, and create a more conducive environment for negotiation.

- **Element 6: Use your feet.** Often overlooked, feet can communicate intentions and emotions. This element sheds light on how foot positioning and movement can inadvertently reveal underlying attitudes or reactions in negotiation settings.

- **Element 7: Image.** The final element discusses the importance of appearance and attire, emphasizing how a well-crafted image can influence perceptions and set the stage for successful negotiations.

Each element in this chapter is a keynote in the symphony of nonverbal communication, playing a vital role in the overall performance of a negotiation. From the silent yet expressive language of our bodies to the strategic use of humor, these elements collectively enhance our ability to negotiate effectively, empowering us to communicate beyond words and navigate the complexities of human interaction.

ELEMENT 1

Body Language

This element will assist you in engaging your audience through mastering the nonverbal communication in negotiation.

In negotiations, the ability to captivate your counterpart is not just beneficial; it's essential. Whether you're delivering news or persuading a team, the impact of your message hinges on your presentation skills. Consider the ease of conveying positive developments, like announcing a significant pay raise or additional holidays. Such messages naturally resonate with the audience. However, the challenge lies in presentations that demand more nuance and persuasion.

The Power of Delivery in Negotiation

When engaging in negotiation, your aim is not just to inform but to influence and motivate. To achieve this, you must utilize a range of communicative techniques, including:

- Varying your gaze to maintain engagement
- Employing gestures to emphasize points
- Injecting humor to lighten the mood
- Gesticulating to convey passion
- Using your feet to command presence
- Modulating your voice for impact
- Cultivating a professional image

These elements are fundamental, regardless of the setting – be it a large conference, a sales pitch, an idea presentation, or a one-on-one discussion.

Presentation Skills: Beyond Mere Conversation

Excelling in negotiation requires more than just being a good conversationalist. You must master effective presentation skills to communicate your objectives professionally and persuasively. This mastery begins with understanding the use of your voice and gestures.

The Power of Verbal Communication

Verbal communication, inherently more flexible than written text, is a potent tool in negotiation. The English language offers a vast array of words, yet the average person uses only a fraction of this lexicon daily. To connect with your audience, use familiar words and phrases, avoiding condescension or overly complex language. Short, concise words often carry the most weight.

Aligning with Your Audience's Perspective

In negotiation, you are not just speaking to be heard; you aim to convince, entertain, sell, or persuade. Always consider your audience's viewpoint:

- What benefits will they gain?
- How can you make them feel valued?
- How will you instill confidence?
- Is your message relevant to them?

Show genuine interest in their needs. Remember, we live in an era where attention spans are short. People are accustomed to rapid, concise information. This reality makes your audience more demanding but also more receptive to effective communication.

The Impact of Multisensory Engagement

Research indicates that people remember:

- 10 percent of what they read
- 10 percent of what they hear
- 30 percent of what they see
- 50 percent of what they see and hear

In negotiation, relying solely on a prepared script is insufficient. Your tone of voice and body language are pivotal in reinforcing your message. These tools should be used strategically to enhance your negotiation tactics.

In summary, the science of negotiation extends far beyond the mere exchange of words. It encompasses a comprehensive understanding of how to effectively engage and persuade your audience. By mastering these skills, you position yourself not just as a speaker, but as a powerful negotiator capable of shaping outcomes to your advantage.

Start with Facial Expressions

Children are born with the ability to read other people. They know when to ask their mother or their father about something, and they know when not to ask.

They know when to leave the room and when there is conflict or when their parents are having a row. They "read" people on a different wavelength than adults.

Most people can read ordinary facial expressions – happiness, sorrow, anger, disappointment – but what about all the other nuances? Try to train yourself to interpret different expressions.

Place yourself in front of a mirror and concentrate on a really sad experience, a very happy experience, and a very surprising experience. Look at your eyes. When your eyes smile, your face lights up – when your eyes are sad, your whole face looks sad.

You can also try this out with your television set. Turn on your television set and turn the sound off. Sit down for half an hour and look at the presenter's facial expression. Can you "read" what is going on? A good rule of thumb: If you find the host's facial language and body language so interesting that you want to turn the sound up, it indicates that this person is skillful and has a high ability to inspire others.

An interesting piece of research has classified human beings into three groups.

- Those with closed, almost angry-looking faces
- Those with neutral, almost indifferent facial expressions
- Those with open, cheerful facial expressions

Take a long look around you! People look angry, neutral, or optimistic, not necessarily because their emotional expressions reflect their inner feelings, but quite simply because we are all born with different faces and for this reason exude different expressions.

With me, I know that when I am really concentrating on something I come across as withdrawn or angry. Because of this, I do not naturally come across as showing very much interest or openness toward other people.

Our 80 facial muscles enable us to create approximately 7,000 different facial expressions!

In itself, this provides a number of options for combining expressions. When you introduce a speech or a presentation at a meeting, try to relax, as a person's facial muscles particularly tend to stiffen up when they are nervous. Bear this in mind before you open your speech, and concentrate on your eyebrows, your mouth, and your eyes.

ELEMENT 2

Eye Contact

In any negotiation, capturing the attention of your counterparts is crucial. Eye contact plays a pivotal role in this. Avoid gazing at the ceiling, the ground, or out the window during negotiations. Instead, engage your counterparts with direct eye contact. This nonverbal communication conveys confidence and interest in the discussion.

When negotiating, it's important not to fixate your gaze on a single individual. This can create discomfort, regardless of their apparent receptiveness. Distribute your gaze evenly across the room, making each participant feel personally addressed. This technique is effective whether you're seated at a negotiating table or presenting in a standing position.

In smaller, more intimate negotiation settings, maintain eye contact with each participant for about five seconds. This duration aligns with the average time it takes for a person to process a thought and helps reinforce the points you're making. By making eye contact with various individuals, you create a sense of personal connection without making anyone feel intimidated. Move your gaze smoothly across the room, avoiding sudden head movements or restless shuffling.

Remember, your counterparts in negotiation are keen for your attention and validation, similar to a child's plea for attention. Using eye contact effectively establishes a rhythm and rapport in negotiations.

Begin your negotiation by calmly walking to your designated spot, surveying all participants with a composed and serene demeanor. This initial eye contact asserts your assertiveness and openness. Without this, participants may remain engaged in their own thoughts, unsure of the negotiation's commencement.

Negotiators who avoid eye contact may be perceived as uncertain or insincere. Questions like, "Why aren't they looking at us? Do they lack confidence in their stance?" can arise, undermining your position.

During larger negotiations, when addressed with a question, start by looking directly at the inquirer. Then, gradually shift your gaze around the room to include others in your response. This approach prevents other participants from feeling excluded. Conclude your response by reestablishing eye contact with the questioner, seeking their acknowledgment of your answer.

Finally, as you conclude the negotiation, replicate the initial pattern of eye contact. This reinforces the connection established at the beginning and leaves a lasting impression of your engagement and assertiveness.

ELEMENT 3

Gesticulations

In the intricate dance of negotiation, the use of hands and arms plays a pivotal role in emphasizing and underlining key facts and arguments. Whether seated at a bargaining table or standing in a boardroom, the way you position and move your limbs can significantly impact your negotiation success.

The Do's and Don'ts of Body Posture

A negotiator must be acutely aware of posture. Slouching, hands in pockets, or arms folded across the chest are all signs of disengagement or defensiveness, which can hinder the flow of constructive dialogue. Similarly, avoid displaying nervous habits like clicking knuckles or pens. Initially, keep your hands calmly in front, perhaps resting on a table, before using them to reinforce your points.

Gesticulation: A Personalized Approach

Gesticulation, which is the use of hands, varies from person to person. Reflect on how you naturally use your hands during relaxed conversations. While it's important to be authentic, avoid closed-off postures like folded arms, which can create a barrier between you and your negotiating partner. Remember, your hand movements are a language of their own, speaking volumes about your confidence and intent.

Avoiding Distracting Habits

Distractions, such as fiddling with objects, shuffling notes, or excessive movement, can detract from your message. Be mindful of these habits, as they can shift focus away from the substance of your negotiation.

Illustrating Your Points

Use your hands to visually articulate your points. For example, demonstrating how to fill a lawn mower with gasoline using hand movements can make your explanation more vivid and memorable. This use of body language to depict action enhances the clarity and engagement of your communication.

Conveying Confidence and Respect

Your arm movements can signal self-assuredness and authority. However, be cautious about how you direct attention. For instance, summoning someone with an index finger can seem aggressive; an open hand gesture is more welcoming and respectful. This gesture dates back to the Middle Ages as a symbol of peaceful intentions.

Your stance is just as important as your hand gestures. Avoid rocking or twisting movements, which can reflect nervousness. Instead, adopt a balanced, forward-facing posture. Use your feet to subtly enhance your presentation, moving to mark transitions or to emphasize points. When inviting questions or engaging with a group, adjust your position to reflect openness and engagement. See Element 6 for more about positioning your feet properly.

The art of gesticulation is a vital component of effective negotiation. It's not just what you say, but how you say it – your body language, including the use of hands, arms, and feet, plays a crucial role in how your message is received and perceived. Mastering this art can significantly elevate your negotiating prowess, helping you communicate with greater impact and influence.

ELEMENT 4

The Role of Voice

The importance of using your voice properly during negotiations cannot be understated. Proper use of the voice involves volume, tone, and speed, as well as ensuring that your breathing is controlled and continuous.

Volume

Most people talk too softly. Speak louder than you would if you were having a conversation with a person sitting right next to you. Speak loudly to give the impression of authority and enthusiasm. Emphasize points by considerably increasing volume, or by decreasing volume to get your audience to listen carefully to what you are saying. If you are one of those people who tends to speak too loudly, you should make a special effort to decrease your volume. Speaking too loudly is unpleasant for your audience, as it wears them out, and in order to protect their ears, they will stop listening to what you have to say. Using the volume of your voice correctly gives your presentation vigor.

Tone

A bad speaker will come across as boring and monotonous. By varying your tone, you put life into your presentation.

Speed

The majority of us have a tendency to speak too fast, especially in stressful situations, such as giving presentations. Speak slower than you would in a normal, everyday situation. This will give your audience sufficient time to think about the message you're communicating. By doing this, you have the advantage of having more time to think as well – it will make you feel more confident. This is beneficial to you and to your audience. Pauses are one of the most effective tools you have at your disposal. You should make short pauses to dramatize or to emphasize the point you just made, or the one that you are about to make. A reasonable pause ought to last a little longer than you feel is necessary.

Breathing

Many people who have tried to give a presentation without having prepared properly know the problem of lack of air, especially during the introduction or when the situation is stressful.

Give yourself a few days to learn this simple breathing technique. Say to yourself 1, 2, 3, 4, 5, and inhale. Repeat 1, 2, 3, 4, 5, and inhale. Continue this exercise about five times, three times a day, for about one week and then you will begin to have your breathing under control.

ELEMENT 5

Humor

A few years ago, I attended a wedding with over a hundred guests, all in high spirits and elegantly dressed. The bride and groom were exceptionally charming and stunning. The weather was perfect, the kind that graces us in May, and the ceremony was seamless.

As we sat at the elegantly set table for the meal, we listened to various speeches, some more engaging than others. Then came Erik, known for his humor. The room quieted in anticipation. Erik, understanding humor as a great ice-breaker, started his speech with a joke about a man who stuttered.

Usually, the start of a joke prompts laughter, but not this time. There was only an awkward silence, no smiles. Erik, realizing this, became visibly nervous, fumbling with his tie and speeding through the joke. Eventually, he laughed nervously and sat down, unable to complete his speech. The issue? The bride's father had a stutter, turning a potentially funny joke into something offensive.

This story shows that humor can be as dangerous as it is effective. In times of nervousness, like before a meeting or presentation, consider its long-term significance. Will it be remembered in a hundred years? Probably not.

Leveraging Humor in the Negotiation

In the intricate dance of negotiation, humor emerges not just as a mere social nicety, but as a pivotal tool in the negotiator's arsenal. The strategic application of humor can transform negotiations from a battleground of egos into a collaborative journey. As an expert in both communication and humor, I advocate for a mindful approach to humor, one that enhances connections while cautiously navigating the sensitivities of the negotiating table.

The Dynamics of Humor in Negotiation

- **Icebreakers and atmosphere shifters:** Humor, when aptly employed, serves as a powerful icebreaker. It can diffuse tension, humanizing the negotiators and paving the way for a more congenial dialogue.

- **Cementing rapport:** Laughter is a universal language that builds bridges. A shared joke or a light, humorous remark can quickly establish a common ground, essential for trust and understanding in negotiations.
- **Navigating cultural landscapes:** Humor is culturally contextual. In the global negotiation arena, what's humorous in one culture may be inappropriate in another. The key is cultural intelligence – understanding and respecting these nuances.

A Chinese saying posits, "There are three mirrors that form a person's reflection: how you see yourself, how others see you, and how you really are." Humor demands respect. If mastered, it can create rapport and ease tensions. To be entertaining, one must read widely, beyond job-related literature.

For instance, a technical engineer discussing bridges won't amuse an audience with technical jargon. If humor isn't your usual approach, start by analyzing what makes you laugh in movies or TV shows.

Remember, humor should be relevant and avoid sensitive topics like religion, sexual orientation, job, race, or disabilities, to not offend anyone.

An illustrative example of humor effectively used in international negotiations is the story of former Norwegian Prime Minister Jens Stoltenberg and his humorous approach during a negotiation with Russia over the Barents Sea border.

For many years, Norway and Russia had a longstanding disagreement over maritime boundaries in the Barents Sea, a matter with significant implications for oil and gas exploration. The negotiations were complex and had been ongoing without resolution for decades.

Jens Stoltenberg, during his tenure as prime minister, played a crucial role in these negotiations. Known for his diplomatic skills and affable personality, Stoltenberg used humor as a tool to break down barriers and ease the tension inherent in such high-stakes negotiations.

In one of the meetings, Stoltenberg lightened the mood by joking about the cold weather in Norway and Russia, making a witty remark about how the chilly climate should make it easier for both parties to agree on a "cool-headed" solution. This remark brought laughter to the negotiation table, a rare occurrence in such serious discussions.

The use of humor in this context was not trivial. It served to remind both parties of their shared experiences and challenges, creating a sense of camaraderie. This moment of levity helped to humanize the negotiation process, fostering a more relaxed and cooperative atmosphere.

Ultimately, in 2010, Norway and Russia successfully reached an agreement, ending the 40-year dispute over the maritime border in the Barents Sea. Stoltenberg's approach, including his strategic use of humor, was widely credited as a contributing factor to the successful resolution of the negotiations.

This example underscores the power of humor in diplomacy and negotiations. When used appropriately by skilled leaders like Stoltenberg, humor can be a potent tool to build rapport, ease tensions, and pave the way for more productive and collaborative discussions, even in the context of complex international disputes.

A good source of harmless humor is self-deprecating irony. On a course about questioning techniques, a joke like this might be funny: A young man asks an old man in a bar if his dog bites. After being assured it doesn't, he reaches out, only to be bitten. The old man's response? "It's not my dog." This illustrates the importance of asking the right questions.

Humor is essential. People who take themselves too seriously often talk excessively about themselves. Balancing ego with genuine emotion is crucial in communication and negotiations. Emotions evoke sympathy, enthusiasm, and a sense of participation. There are two types of emotional behavior: rational, guided by the head, and irrational, guided by the heart. When discussing budgets and taxes, we think rationally; when discussing personal matters like illness or child welfare, we are guided by emotions.

Should humor be used in negotiations? Well, instead you could ask why humor should *not* be used in negotiations. Humor is a great tool to defuse a tense situation, especially when emotions are high and everyone is balancing on the edge of leaving the negotiation.

Practical Humor Strategies in Negotiations

- **The charm of self-deprecation:** Humor that targets oneself, in moderation, can be disarming and relatable, demonstrating humility and approachability without crossing lines.
- **Observational wit:** A comment on the neutral aspects of the surroundings or situation can safely introduce humor, easing into negotiations with a light touch.
- **Steering clear of sensitive areas:** Humor must never venture into the realms of politics, religion, ethnicity, gender, or personal beliefs. In the professional sphere of negotiation, this is not just a matter of etiquette but of strategic prudence.
- **Timing and contextual awareness:** The effectiveness of humor hinges on timing and appropriateness. You must gauge the mood and the phase of negotiation to introduce humor without derailing the serious undertones of the discussion.

The Pitfalls of Humor Missteps

- **Risk of misinterpretation:** In the high-stress environment of negotiations, humor can be easily misconstrued, potentially complicating matters.
- **Distracting from core issues:** Excessive or ill-timed humor can divert focus from critical negotiation points, hindering progress.
- **Offending and alienating:** Inappropriate humor can fracture relationships and erode trust, causing long-term damage to the negotiation process.

In the realm of negotiation, humor is not just a frivolity but a strategic element that, when used wisely, can significantly enhance communication and rapport. Its power lies in its ability to soften the rigid formalities of negotiation, fostering a more open and cooperative atmosphere. However, it demands a keen understanding of the audience, cultural subtleties, and the context. As in any skill, its effectiveness is honed through thoughtful practice and mindful application, ensuring that it serves as a bridge to successful negotiation outcomes, not a barrier.

The bottom line: don't take yourself too seriously.

ELEMENT 6

Use of Feet

When you want to deliver a message while standing up (something I always prefer), it is essential to have an air of composure when using your legs and feet and always to have them under control.

It is no good when men rock backward and forward (they often tend to do this, I do not know why) or when women twist their legs round into some odd shape. It reflects nervousness and insecurity, making you immobile at the same time. Point your feet forward, neither inward nor outward. When you stand, are you upright and determined or are you slouched and unsure of yourself?

At the introduction, your position should be balanced, with your legs slightly spread out and loose at the knees. After a few minutes you may start moving. As with mannerisms, you can use your feet to support your presentation. Every time you move on to a new section of your speech, you can mark this by making a movement.

When you want to emphasize a point, consciously move toward your audience without confronting them head-on, but respecting their need for personal space. This grabs their attention.

When you invite questions, you may move slightly backward. If you are talking at a gathering seated in a semi-circle, you should attempt to ease yourself into the center. For some people, this can be really difficult the first time, but it comes quite naturally the third or fourth time. This signifies self-confidence, involvement, and interest.

You may question the relevance of this advice in a seated negotiation scenario. The key is not to remain seated throughout. Seek opportunities to rise – whether it's to utilize the flipchart, grab a coffee, or gaze out the window. Utilize these moments on your feet to effectively communicate your points. Standing up noticeably amplifies your presence and impact in the negotiation.

ELEMENT 7

Image

Before drawing up a plan, I give a great deal of thought to dress, its significance, and what it tells us about other people. I decided to carry out an experiment.

I got one of my good friends to stand inside a very busy train station in downtown Copenhagen and ask passers-by for money. The first day, he stood there dressed as a successful businessman in a smart suit, a newly pressed shirt with an elegant silk tie, wearing well-polished shoes, carrying a fashionable and expensive attaché case. He asked for money, telling people that he had accidentally left his wallet at the office and needed some money to get home. Several business people and office workers stopped to give him money, quite considerable amounts. Several people suggested that he should take a taxi. At the end of the day my friend had collected over $200.

The next day my friend stood at the same spot with the same purpose in mind. This time he was wearing ordinary jeans and an ordinary light windbreaker. Just the same as the one the previous day, he asked for money, saying that he had accidentally left his wallet at work. The reaction was different on that day. Passers-by were not as generous as the day before. They suspected him of having some sort of ulterior motive. At the end of the day, he had collected $50.

On the third day, my friend stood there dressed as a tramp. His clothes were really shabby and dirty and he looked scruffy. He had not combed his hair or shaved. Just as he had done on the previous days, he asked for money. Very few people stopped on that day and the money he received was far less than the other two days.

The lesson: Image is sometimes misunderstood. Your image is not how you see yourself but how others see you!

If you do arrive at a meeting or at a presentation one morning and you tear your jacket on the way there, you should start by telling people at the gathering what happened. The alternative is that people will find out anyway, as the participants will sit there and wonder why you are dressed so badly and why you don't want to show them any respect.

Your image should correspond to the message you want to convey, and it should be commensurate with the intended target group. Appropriate behavior is everything. If I needed to address my clients directly in a hut on a building site, I would probably not come dressed in a suit. If I am to meet the managing director of the construction company, I will at least make sure that I am dressed to the appropriate standard.

A good bit of advice is this: It is best to be slightly better dressed than normal. This is an expression of respect for the person to whom you're speaking.

Not very long ago, I was at a presentation. The lecturer was eloquent and entertaining and knew his subject well, but the whole time he kept fiddling with his clothes, straightening up his collar, adjusting his tie, hitching up his trousers, and patting his jacket. This continued throughout the whole presentation, one and a half hours it was. Just like everyone else in the audience, I became really distracted by this, so much so that I did not take in much of what he had to say.

Look at yourself in the mirror. Think of a presentation you gave recently to the board of directors, to investors, or to staff. Try to put yourself back into that situation. Resume the posture you believe you had when you put forward your proposals. Take a look at your shoulders. Are they tense or are they relaxed?

Good Advice

- **Always point your feet forward.** This reduces the risk of talking at the flipchart after you have written something on it. Remember to turn round.
- **Don't have an aggressive stance.** Rest your hands calmly down your sides, keeping your legs a reasonable distance apart.
- **Don't use your body in an uncontrolled manner.** Keep your movements under control.
- **Given that your audience tends to imitate your body language, make sure that your movements are calm and balanced.**

Through conscious body language, you may produce situations that are perceived as very stressful and frustrating. Silence and physical encroachment – that is, sitting or standing too close to someone – can disrupt their equilibrium. By establishing eye contact, raising or lowering your voice, and appropriately touching the person you're speaking with, you can build their trust and make them more attentive.

How closely do you hold your arms to your upper body? Do you tend to place your arms on your hips (this can express superiority, called "head teacher syndrome")? Also look at yourself sideways on. Are your shoulders raised or are they slouched?

In a negotiation team, unconscious gestures can mark acceptance, support, distance, and tension. People who convey these signals are not aware that they are revealing themselves in this way. Speakers sometimes unconsciously turn their back on a member who they do not like in their own delegation. They position themselves farther away, and they do not give the person the same support through eye contact and short nods as they do with other participants. They may shake their head when that person speaks.

Once I participated in a discussion where a woman in the other delegation was an observer and took down precise notes. When we commented on the requirements that had been specified, I found that she gave a satisfied nod each time our suggestions seemed acceptable and shook her head whenever they seemed superfluous. Her co-representatives commented on all the points by saying: It is not enough, we must have more! When this discussion was over, I asked her if she had intentionally tried to manipulate us by nodding and shaking her head. She was really taken aback by this and said that she did not send out any signals.

It is not easy to decipher another person's body language. A single gesture may not mean anything. There are countless stress signals, but all these are confined to the individual, and people use them in different ways. Not until you get to know the speaker and their usual pattern of communication can you benefit from being aware of their body language. People have different ways of communicating their attitudes:

- **Openness:** Open hands, unbuttoned jacket.
- **Defensive posture:** Arms folded over the chest, crossed legs, gestures with clenched fists, gestures with index finger, karate chop.
- **Concentration:** Hands are placed on face, head is turned from one side, a hand on the bridge of the nose.
- **Suspicion:** People look away, fold their arms, increase the distance from the speaker, and button up their jackets.
- **Cooperation:** Open hands, sitting forward on their chair, and reducing physical distance.
- **Stress/nervousness:** Coughing, puffing noises like "puh," holding a hand in front of the mouth when they talk, sweating, not looking at the person they are speaking to.
- **Frustration:** Letting out short puffs, tightly clenched fists, massaging the neck, aimlessly kicking with the feet.

This is not an exhaustive list. In many situations, all these signals may be empty gestures or express completely different attitudes. As a communicator and a negotiator, you should develop insight into this area.

CHAPTER 2

Knowledge

Introduction: Understanding Negotiation as an Art and a Science

This chapter presents a comprehensive exploration of the multifaceted nature of negotiation, delving into its linguistic, mathematical, educational, and technological dimensions. It deals with the complexities of negotiating in a foreign language, emphasizing cultural understanding and communication styles. Mathematical acumen in negotiations is then highlighted, stressing the importance of financial knowledge and cost-benefit analysis.

The learning process's stages and the value of human engineering in negotiation skills are explored, contrasting formal education with interpersonal abilities. The significance of structured negotiation training is underscored, offering a framework for developing negotiation strategies. The concept of creating additional value through cooperative negotiation strategies is introduced, advocating for constructive dialogue.

Finally, the potential of artificial intelligence in enhancing negotiation skills is examined, showcasing its diverse applications from strategy formulation to real-time assistance and emotional analysis. Each element in this chapter collectively contributes to a deeper understanding of negotiation as an art and science, weaving together diverse perspectives and methodologies:

- **Element 8: The crucial role of mathematics.** Highlights the fundamental role of mathematics in negotiations, particularly in the context of commercial transactions. It emphasizes the importance of precise financial knowledge, including understanding both costs and benefits, as well as the value of concessions. The element illustrates this with examples, such as the impact of delivery time reductions and the significant costs associated with seemingly minor concessions in large-scale deals. It underscores the necessity of being fully aware of the numerical implications of each negotiation element to achieve mutual benefits and avoid costly oversights.

- **Element 9: Negotiating in a foreign language.** Discusses the complexities and challenges of negotiating in a language that is not native to one or both parties. It emphasizes the importance of understanding not just the language but also the cultural nuances and body language associated with it. The document highlights how gestures and expressions can have different meanings in different cultures, which can lead to misunderstandings. It also delves into the dynamics of individual versus group communication styles, the significance of status and titles in negotiations, and the potential pitfalls in discussing religion and politics. The document advises on adapting to cultural differences, the importance of local legal advice, and being aware of differing business practices and technical standards across cultures.

- **Element 10: The journey of learning.** Explores the concept of learning as a gradual process through four stages of competence. It uses the metaphor of a child, Kruise, learning to pour milk to illustrate these stages. The first stage is unconscious incompetence, where one is unaware of their lack of skill. The second stage, conscious incompetence, is marked by an awareness of one's limitations. The third stage is conscious competence, where one can perform a skill but with considerable effort. Finally, the fourth stage is unconscious competence, where a skill becomes second nature and can be performed effortlessly. This metaphor serves as a framework for understanding the learning process in various contexts, emphasizing the progression from unawareness to proficiency.

- **Element 11: Education.** Contrasts two individuals, Maria and Martin, who have different educational backgrounds and personal attributes. Maria, academically brilliant but lacking in interpersonal skills, is juxtaposed with Martin, who possesses strong social intelligence and negotiation skills. The document questions the traditional emphasis on formal education and technical knowledge, suggesting that success might hinge more on human engineering—likeability, communication, and negotiation skills. Citing a Carnegie Institute of Technology study, it notes that a significant portion of success relies on understanding human behavior and effective communication, highlighting the importance of these skills in negotiation and professional success.

- **Element 12: Negotiation training.** Emphasizes the importance of formal negotiation training for professionals, highlighting its vital role beyond on-the-job learning. It explains that structured negotiation training provides a framework and proven techniques, an understanding of the psychological aspects of negotiation, exposure to diverse scenarios and perspectives, and skill enhancement and refinement. The training also helps in building confidence, reducing anxiety, offering feedback for improvement, and facilitating networking and learning from peers. The document argues that structured training is essential for developing a deep and broad understanding of negotiation strategies and their psychological underpinnings, preparing professionals to handle a variety of scenarios confidently.

- **Element 13: Asymmetric value.** Discusses the concept of NegoEconomics and the SMARTnership model in business negotiations, which contrasts with the traditional win-lose or zero-sum transactional model. It emphasizes the potential for creating additional economic value by adopting cooperative deal-making strategies. The element uses a detailed example to illustrate how both parties in a negotiation can benefit by understanding and leveraging differences in costs, such as cost of capital. It argues for the significance of identifying and dividing this additional value, stressing the importance of creative and constructive dialogue in negotiations.

- **Element 14: Subject matter.** Discusses the role of negotiation expertise in various industries and its growing recognition in the corporate world. The document references the Apple TV show *Ted Lasso* to illustrate how skills in human interaction and coaching can transcend specific industry knowledge, exemplified in a scenario where a football coach leads a soccer team successfully. It also touches on the concept of a chief negotiating officer (CNO) and the formation of specialized negotiation teams within organizations, emphasizing that the key competency in negotiations is often the art and skill of negotiation itself, rather than in-depth subject knowledge.

- **Element 15: Leveraging AI to enhance your negotiation skills.** Explores how artificial intelligence (AI) can enhance negotiation skills. It emphasizes that while AI won't replace human negotiators, those using AI will have a significant advantage over those who don't. The document outlines various ways AI can be utilized in negotiations, including pre-negotiation preparation, strategy formulation, real-time assistance, analyzing emotional cues, simulating negotiation scenarios, crafting alternatives, streamlining communication, and assessing agreements. Each area is elaborated with example prompts to illustrate how AI can be integrated into negotiation practices.

ELEMENT 8

The Crucial Role of Mathematics

It may come as a surprise, or perhaps a disappointment to some, that commercial negotiations fundamentally revolve around the creation and distribution of value, which inherently involves mathematics. My appreciation for numbers in these negotiations stems from their ability to convey unambiguous facts, devoid of emotions or subjective interpretations.

In negotiations, it is essential to have a precise understanding of your financial inputs and outputs. It's not just about knowing your expenses and revenues; it's also crucial to comprehend the value of your concessions to the other party. Sometimes, you can offer concessions that are cost-neutral to you but carry significant value to the other party.

For instance, if reducing your delivery time doesn't incur additional costs for you, it could still offer immense value to your client. Imagine a scenario where a $10 million investment's delivery time reduction, costing you nothing, accelerates the client's production start, potentially adding a value of $200,000 to $300,000 per month for them. This is an example of leveraging *NegoEconomics* for mutual benefit. (See Element 20 for a description of NegoEconomics.)

EXAMPLE | Know Your Numbers

Consider a real-life situation: A customer was negotiating to lease 120 cars for three years. In the final moments of the third round of negotiations, the customer insisted that the leasing company provide winter tires for the cars, free of charge, upon request. This request, the customer argued, is minor, costing only $85 per tire. The seller, without much thought, agreed.

However, the seller failed to calculate the total cost of this concession. If all 120 car users requested winter tires, at $85 per month over a 36-month lease, the cost would be a staggering $367,200 (120 cars × $85 × 36 months).

The lesson here is clear: Know your numbers. More importantly, understand the implications of any changes in terms. Being fully aware of the costs and benefits associated with each negotiable variable is crucial in commercial negotiations.

ELEMENT 9

Negotiating in a Foreign Language

Sharing a language is very often a prerequisite for socializing. It's possible, but difficult, to communicate through an interpreter.

You should learn one or more foreign languages. Sometimes your negotiation language is a foreign language to the other party. In that case, the risk of communication problems will increase.

It isn't enough to speak a foreign language. You should also have insight into the body language of the other party. Understand the uniqueness of the culture, as body language isn't universal.

A survey of typical gestures shows that they occur normally in a majority of all countries, but that their meanings differ greatly. Gestures that, in the West, have a positive content, may for instance be an insult with sexual connotations in other countries. Gestures meaning yes in one country may mean no in another and vice versa. A gesture by which the other party wishes to indicate that you've gained his trust can be interpreted as a sexual invitation. This entails a major risk of confrontation.

To what extent should you learn some phrases in the other party's language? Should you insist that the other party speak a foreign language so that you're both linguistically handicapped? For instance, should you speak English with German and French speakers even though you could manage perfectly well in both of these languages?

Language and culture are so much more than just language and culture.

Individual versus Group

When should you be speaking in the first person singular (saying I) and when in the first person plural (saying we)? Emphasizing oneself, one's own experience, knowledge, and skill is unheard of in certain cultures. In many places, knowledge and responsibility are vested in the group. Individuals can neither make their own decisions nor table their own viewpoints. Everything is done collectively and in a group.

Status, Titles, Mode of Address, and More

Sometimes negotiations are high-level, and they begin at a socially elevated plane. If the first impressions is positive, the subsequent negotiations will start at an appropriate level. In that case, it's not good enough to send engineers to handle the opening phase. It will be seen as an insult. A negotiator who is inexperienced can't be made any older, but their status may be improved by means of titles and the presence of one or more inferiors.

Dependent on the closeness of the relationship, there are strict rules concerning the use of titles, first names, or all of the names when addressing someone. High social position acquired through inheritance or education means that a great deal of respect will be shown in many countries. In many parts of the Western world, it sounds unnatural to address somebody by all their titles and names.

Religion and Politics

Religion and politics are obvious minefields – especially if the religious and political systems are very different. Remember that you are not in the country to offer your personal assessments of the society you meet. You're there to do business.

Should You Blot Out Yourself?

When socializing, important choices constantly have to be made. How far should you go when you want to provide your visitors with insight into the way you live, and to what extent should you try to protect them against cultural shocks? You should never go so far as to blot out everything that's strange and exotic to visitors by offering them a sterile international environment. It's certain that visitors want to get to know something about your country. People who've been traveling like to have something to talk about when they return home. You'll have to find out how much they can handle, what can be misinterpreted, and where the limit of losing face is.

Questions that are often asked in this connection are: Why should we be the ones who must always adjust? Shouldn't the other party adjust to the culture they encounter? Aren't their businesspeople traveling abroad updated about the situation, like we are when we go abroad?

You might find the following attitudes behind these questions:

- Since I'm the buyer, the other party must adjust.
- This is very demanding on me. To give up preconceived ideas and values and gather new impressions is something that can be done only by individuals who are fundamentally sure of themselves and who know their own value.

- Foreigners should learn to behave properly when coming to my country.
- The insistence of equal value and justice should be universal.

If you know how to be open, positive, and receptive, to take the first step and show respect for and interest in others, you will get a positive response. You need to be a civilized, pleasant person in whom people have confidence and with whom they'll do business.

It's sometimes easier to avoid falling into traps in a foreign country than at home. When we are visitors, we leave it to the host to show the way. Openness, interest, and a positive attitude toward new impressions and values are helpful factors. On the home turf, we often hide ourselves. Maybe we even take it for granted that the other party is familiar with our customs.

Pay more attention to the other party than you normally do. It's not just a question of common civility but also of acting in your own best interest. You should convince the other party that cooperation entails advantages. Taking account of their norms will make them more open and willing to cooperate. You must use all of your persuasive powers if you are to be successful, and that includes being more responsive to cultural differences and being more flexible in your behavior.

Behavior

Legislation and business practices of different countries may include rules that are completely topsy-turvy compared to your notions of proper business procedures and may entail expenses that are not normally included in your calculations. For example:

- Interest and commission may be banned.
- Refunding money in connection with complaints may be banned.
- A certain percentage of the payment you receive must be in goods/services.
- All contracts must be approved by the authorities, which will demand a certain percentage of the contract amount as stamp duty.
- Local staff are required to do part of the work. The costs involved in this may be considerable.
- The Central Bank must approve all payments.
- If a cooperation venture turns out not to work, the other party will question the written agreement and its validity.

Sometimes a handshake and a short written statement of the guidelines agreed will suffice for a lengthy collaboration to work. At other times, an extensive and detailed contract is required. The extent to which you trust the other party in the course of the negotiations will depend on their willingness to the more or less formal contract practice that is stipulated in your culture.

You should always consult local legal experts before venturing into unknown markets. Lawyers can give you valuable advice before and during the negotiations. Once you sign a document, there isn't much they can do to help you. Never forget that your possibilities to negotiate are best before you have signed.

Make sure that any dispute concerning the interpretation of contract provisions will be settled under Western law. Make sure that arbitration will ensure quick decisions. An arbitration tribunal can take many years in some countries and may be very costly. For financial reasons, you may be forced to accept an unsatisfactory settlement because you can't wait for an arbitration proceeding.

Make sure that what you have agreed is written in a language you master. Don't accept a translation from the original text into English if it's the original version that will constitute the basis of interpretation.

You should familiarize yourself with the standard contracts that foreign organizations, authorities, and companies use well in advance. You can turn to companies who've been in a similar situation before. This way, you'll avoid some unpleasant surprises, and you'll get a better understanding of what can be negotiated, what you should be on your guard against, and so on.

Formal Contact Paths

Examine how the decision-making process looks, and what decisions, authorizations, and personal contacts you should have. If you're doing business with a public authority in a foreign country, you shouldn't expect that they'll automatically inform you of everything. If, for instance, you need a working permit to carry out installation work under your own auspices, this may turn out to be very costly. You have to negotiate with a completely different authority, one whose primary interest may be to fleece you. Familiarize yourself with their decision-making process. Who are the stakeholders of the enterprise, and what sort of power do they have?

Technical Competence

Sometimes you may need to train the staff of the other party, provide operation warranties for the machines, or use workers who are not your own for installation jobs. From the word go, you have to rely on the skills of the staff in the other country. Despite guarantees issued by the other party that they are technically skilled, they know English, can read a blueprint, and have many years of experience, you may be in for serious problems.

For example, foreign staff have arrived to get special training in operating busses and trucks, and upon arrival it was revealed that they had no driving license for busses or trucks. They proved unable to learn in English, German, French, Spanish, or any other major language. Nevertheless, the customer claimed that they were trained drivers who speak English, that they were used to driving a horse and carriage, and they know a few sentences in English will, according to the buyer, suffice to meet the contract provisions "years of driving experience, and knowledge of English."

It's not easy to get an idea of the work level and pace of foreign staff. People from different nations are often very proud. If you ask them if they can read a blueprint or if they know how to operate a given piece of equipment, they might say yes, despite the fact that they can't see what's up and down in the blueprint and they don't know what the equipment even does. Nor is it always enough to use knowledge tests.

For example, a group of officers came to Denmark to participate in a military training course, but first they had to undergo a test in mathematics so that the Danish supplier could check if they had the necessary qualifications. All but one passed the test. He was very offended. Unfortunately, he was the one with the highest rank in the group. On the following day, he left for home, taking the whole group with him. It would have been a better solution first to have held a meeting with the group. An experienced instructor or supervisor can form an impression of the level of competence, work pace, and any communication problems. It's important to be discreet and avoid stating that the purpose is to evaluate the competence level of the staff, as this may be a very touchy subject considering the feelings of pride inherent to many cultures.

Staff members who have been trained will automatically move up a step on the status ladder in many countries. In everybody's eyes, they now belong to a higher class, that of the educated. It may seem completely unthinkable to them that they are to carry out work within the production for which they received training. Instead, they demand completely different job assignments. The training opens up completely new prospects in society. In this way, you'll never manage to get personnel who are able and willing to do the work.

Evaluation Norms for Technical Standards

The norms on which people base themselves when they compare offers and proposed solutions vary a great deal from one culture to another. For example, in the Nordic countries, people assume that others are rational and look at efficiency, quality, and productivity, and they assume that people will always make the correct choice. Nordic products are of consistently high quality. In connection with negotiations with countries in the third world, problems may easily arise. The Nordic workers think that they're better able to judge what they need. Somewhat oversimplified, they assume that the highest quality is the appropriate quality.

Choice of Strategy

In many cultures, often totalitarian ones, cooperation is an alien concept. It's perceived as a sign of weakness. You may encourage cooperation, but find that your endeavors are simply exploited. Many cultures only respect tough negotiators who protect their own interests.

Time Factor

Discrepancies in the decision-making process often serve to explain why negotiations seem to drag out interminably. In some Western cultures, decision-making is often delegated. The salesperson who is on an assignment abroad has wide discretionary powers when it comes to making decisions. A certain observation mightn't come amiss: Many of these salespeople often find the negotiations with customers easier than the negotiation that awaits them when they come home and have to "sell" the deal they've made.

Let's compare this with the Japanese system. In Japan, a complete consultation is required in advance with all the individuals who will be affected by the decision. Not taking account of this is considered a very serious matter, and the Japanese prefer spending time ensuring that everyone understands what's at stake. Every executive affected must seek confirmation and advice from their employees. The counterproposal you receive will be the result of the executive group's efforts. The result is that negotiation can take a long time. Trying to force an early decision won't work.

Special Economic Features

Among these are the ability to pay, access to foreign exchange, interpretation of conditions of payment, and authorization from the Central Bank or another authority before payment can be effected. Always consult the available expertise, and do so before signing the agreement.

The following examples from China demonstrate how conditions of payment can be interpreted. In connection with purchases in China, the buyer must open a confirmed, irrevocable transfer and divisible letter of credit approved by the Bank of China. What does it mean?

- Confirmed: The bank of the importer guarantees payment provided the documentation meets the contract provisions.
- Irrevocable: This prevents the buyer from holding back on payment for any reason.
- Transfer and divisible: The Bank of China can use it directly, in part or in full, to pay for other transactions.

Letters of credit must be opened 30 days before the Chinese agent ships the goods to the buyer, which means when the goods leave the factory. If the shipment is delayed en route, that's the buyer's headache.

Rules like these have been introduced solely for the benefit of one country. So in connection with exports to China, completely different rules apply.

Corruption

In certain cultures, bribes are the rule rather than the exception. Under European and US law, any kind of bribe is illegal. European law applies in other countries for European subjects. It's a different matter that the authorities are capable of evincing a great deal of understanding for the fact that bribes actually exist, and expenses for these are tax-deductible for the enterprise, provided the expense can be documented. You can't simply apply your own values to condemn bribes abroad; conditions in other countries may be completely different from yours.

Bribes constitute a difficult problem, both in moral and practical respects. There have been many corruption scandals in which Western countries have been involved.

ELEMENT 10

The Journey of Learning

L earning is an intricate process, often misunderstood or underestimated. We traverse through distinct stages of competence without even realizing it. Let's explore these stages through a simple yet profound narrative, illustrating the journey from ignorance to mastery.

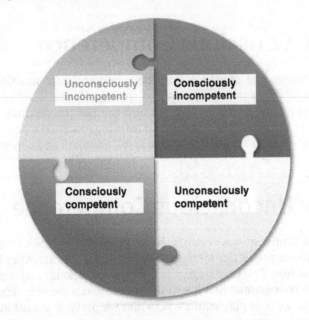

Stage 1: Unconscious Incompetence

Picture a two-year-old boy named Kruise. His self-confidence is immense, yet his actual skill is minimal. Kruise sees a milk carton on the breakfast table and decides he wants to pour the milk himself. He's observed his parents do it effortlessly. However, Kruise doesn't yet understand his limitations. His initial attempts are clumsy and are quickly intercepted by his parents to prevent a messy catastrophe. This stage mirrors our own when we first encounter a new skill. Like Kruise with the milk, we are blissfully unaware of our incompetence.

Stage 2: Conscious Incompetence

Kruise, ever persistent, finds an opportunity. With his father away and his mother momentarily distracted, he attempts to pour the milk again. The result is a flood of milk. At this moment, Kruise transitions to the second stage: he becomes painfully aware of his inability to perform the task. This realization is akin to watching a recording of ourselves in a new endeavor, like public speaking, where we can recognize our errors and areas needing improvement.

Stage 3: Conscious Competence

With determination and guidance from his parents, Kruise practices diligently. Eventually, he learns to pour milk without spilling. He has reached the stage of conscious competence, where he can perform the task successfully but requires significant focus and effort. This stage in our learning process is where we can apply a new skill effectively, yet it still demands our full attention and concentration.

Stage 4: Unconscious Competence

As time passes, Kruise grows. Now six, he effortlessly pours milk every day, along with mastering other skills like biking and swimming. These activities have become second nature to him. This final stage of learning, unconscious competence, is where a skill becomes so ingrained that it requires no conscious thought. It's comparable to how we drive a car or play tennis – activities we perform almost automatically. This stage is the epitome of learning, where practice and experience transform conscious effort into unconscious proficiency.

Our learning journey is a transition from unawareness of our incompetence to a stage where our skills become an intuitive part of who we are. Each stage is crucial, and understanding this process can profoundly impact how we approach learning and personal development.

ELEMENT 11

Education

Envision Maria, an exceptionally bright and driven woman, immersed in studying international tax laws at a top-tier university in the United States. She's being mentored by outstanding professors and consistently ranks at the top of her class. Naturally, she graduates as valedictorian and swiftly lands a position at a leading global tax advisory firm.

Now, consider Martin. Like Maria, he's pursuing international tax law, but at a less renowned university known for its lower rankings, subpar teaching staff, and lackluster faculty. Furthermore, Martin lacks the drive typically seen in top students and is nowhere near valedictorian status.

Nevertheless, Martin completes his studies and secures a job at an international tax advisory company.

The question arises: who is more likely to succeed, Maria or Martin? Intuitively, many would suggest Maria.

However, the narrative shifts when considering their interpersonal skills. Maria, despite her brilliance, isn't well-received by her peers and clients. They perceive her as arrogant, overly confident, and humorless—a classic "tax nerd" with limited social finesse.

In contrast, Martin is universally liked. His social intelligence, negotiation skills, and ability to connect with people make him a favorite among clients and colleagues alike.

So, who's more likely to achieve greater success? I'd argue for Martin. His knowledge may be less than Maria's, but he compensates with his ability to learn and adapt.

Here's a provocative thought: What if success in life is less about education, experience, and knowledge, and more about human engineering—likeability, communication, and negotiation skills?

This idea often meets resistance from professionals who believe firmly in the value of education. But the data might suggest otherwise.

The Carnegie Institute of Technology's study reveals a compelling insight: while professional and technical knowledge accounts for only 15 percent of your success, a staggering 85 percent hinges on your understanding of human behavior, including skills in negotiation. This emphasizes the profound role of effective communication and negotiation in achieving success.

Effective communication is inherently two-way. It involves active listening, engaging in dialogue, asking and answering questions, and considering alternatives. This approach fosters respect and understanding, moving away from confrontational stances on demands and proposals. Successful communication in negotiation involves understanding and respecting the other party's viewpoints.

However, when communication falters from the start, finding common ground becomes challenging, often leading to each party withholding information and becoming entrenched in their positions. This scenario typically results in a deadlock, not necessarily due to conflicting interests or solutions, but because the parties fail to comprehend each other's perspectives.

The essence of effective communication, particularly in negotiation, is the exchange of credible information. The credibility of this information is judged by the receiver. A common misconception is blaming the receiver for not understanding, but it is the responsibility of the sender to convey the message effectively.

One-way communication, which is often riddled with misunderstandings, obstructs mutual comprehension. To understand the stark contrast between one-way and two-way communication, you can conduct simple experiments and observe their effects. Ask a question and evaluate the feedback. Do you get an actual answer to your question or an explanation and a counter question? This exploration highlights the importance of two-way communication as a pivotal element in successful negotiation and interpersonal interactions.

ELEMENT 12

Negotiation Training

Negotiation training is vital to professionals beyond on-the-job learning. Negotiation stands as a pivotal skill, crucial for success across various industries. I don't need to explain that to you since you already bought a book that gives you additional knowledge on how to improve your negotiations. However, a shocking amount of professionals have either never received any formal training in negotiations or they last received a training course 18 years ago.

While on-the-job experience and practical exposure are valuable, they are often insufficient in isolation for mastering the art of negotiation. Here's why structured negotiation training is indispensable for professionals.

Structured Framework and Techniques

Negotiation training provides a structured framework and proven techniques that are often not instinctive. These frameworks – such as the Harvard Principled Negotiation, the SMARTnership strategy, or the Fisher and Ury model – offer a systematic approach to negotiation, ensuring that professionals are not merely relying on intuition or ad hoc methods. This structured approach is essential in complex negotiations where stakes are high and outcomes significantly impact businesses or careers.

Understanding Psychological Aspects

Negotiations are deeply rooted in psychology. Training helps in understanding the psychological dynamics that play out in negotiations, such as cognitive biases, emotional intelligence, and persuasion tactics. On-the-job learning might expose professionals to these aspects, but formal training provides the theoretical underpinning and strategies to effectively navigate and leverage these psychological components.

Diverse Scenarios and Perspective

Professional experience often limits individuals to a specific industry or a certain type of negotiation. Training, on the other hand, exposes individuals to a wide range of scenarios, including cross-cultural negotiations, high-stakes deals, and conflict resolution. This diversity is crucial for developing a well-rounded skill set that is adaptable to various situations.

Skill Enhancement and Refinement

Like any other skill, negotiation requires continuous refinement and updating. Training programs provide the latest insights, trends, and strategies in negotiation, something that on-the-job learning might not keep pace with. This ongoing learning is crucial in a rapidly changing business environment.

Building Confidence and Reducing Anxiety

Negotiations can be high-pressure situations filled with anxiety. Training in negotiation builds not only skills but also confidence. It prepares professionals for a variety of situations, reducing anxiety and enabling them to perform under pressure. This aspect of training is hard to replicate through experience alone, as unguided experiences can sometimes reinforce fears or misconceptions.

Feedback and Improvement

One of the key benefits of formal training is the opportunity for feedback from experts and peers. This feedback is vital for identifying areas of strength and weakness, something that might not be as clearly evident in real-world scenarios. The opportunity to simulate negotiations in a training environment provides a safe space for experimentation and learning from mistakes, leading to continuous improvement.

Networking and Learning from Peers

Negotiation training programs often bring together professionals from different industries and backgrounds. This diversity offers a rich learning experience and the opportunity to network. The insights gained from peers can provide new perspectives and strategies that are not typically encountered in one's immediate professional environment.

While on-the-job learning is valuable, it is not a comprehensive approach to mastering negotiation. Structured negotiation training is essential for developing a deep and broad understanding of negotiation strategies, techniques, and their psychological underpinnings. It prepares professionals to handle a variety of scenarios with confidence, ensuring they are not just experienced but also expert negotiators.

ELEMENT 13

Asymmetric Value

Billions of dollars are left untouched in business dealings across the planet because the current culture of business negotiations measures success through a win-lose or zero-sum transactional model. If this model is abandoned in favor of the SMARTnership/NegoEconomic model, billions of dollars of NegoEconomics will be infused into the global economy. (Element 20 defines NegoEconomics.)

The formation of a SMARTnership enables negotiating parties to expand the potential that lies within a commercial transaction and broaden the vision of what is possible for the business relationship.

My estimate is that $3,250 billion would flow into the U.S. economy if the lost 42 percent of commercial transactions could suddenly manifest. How did I get that number? I looked at the total revenue from the 1,000 biggest corporations in the United States and identified the portion related to negotiations – whether it is the result of procurement or sales – and calculated 42 percent of that amount. $3,250,000,000,000 is an enormous amount of money.

Are you shocked or don't believe in this calculation? Let's assume, for the sake of argument, that the researchers working on this project were not the brightest in the world and the real number is only $2,500,000,000,000. Wouldn't this number still be large enough for you to want to explore the potential?

Let's pretend that the researchers were drinking when they were doing their calculations and that the real number is only $1,500,000,000,000. Are you suggesting you would not be interested if you were the CEO of one of the top 1,000 largest corporations in the United States? This number would represent at least an additional $1.5 billion per company in profit annually.

How Does NegoEconomics (Asymmetric Value) Work? A Bigger Pie Means More to Share

Think of the total value of a commercial transaction as a pie. A freshly baked, right out of the oven, cherry pie. You feast your eyes on its perfectly golden brown crust and smell the sweetness of the cherries. You are hungry and you want the biggest piece, perhaps even the entire pie, for yourself. The value of the deal is like this cherry pie. Everyone wants the biggest slice possible for themselves – or, if you are really greedy, the whole thing. What most negotiators fail to realize is that there is a way for each of the delegates to get more pie.

Two parties can divide a small pie equally or they might agree to some other ratio, say one-third/two-thirds. But if both parties mutually pursue the additional value in the deal, then the pie becomes larger and both can net more than the value of their original half. NegoEconomics is the active pursuit of that additional value through cooperative deal-making; in other words, a mutual effort to increase the size of the pie and expand the room for negotiation.

The added – or *asymmetric* – value that results from NegoEconomics can come in a variety of forms. It may come in the form of money, reduced competition, increased inventory, intellectual capital, or brand awareness. Once the asymmetric value has been located, all that remains to negotiate is how to divide it. The objective of NegoEconomics is to establish a creative and constructive dialogue that will improve the conditions for finding a distribution that is acceptable to both parties.

EXAMPLE | Nathan and the Blossom Company

Nathan is a supplier running a small company with very little cash on hand. He is sign-ing a $10 million contract with a manufacturing company called Blossom. Blossom is a very successful company with loads of cash. Blossom's negotiators want to pay him only at the time of delivery, which is six months in the future.

This puts Nathan in a difficult situation. His sub-suppliers, on whom he depends to be able to fulfill the order to Blossom, are demanding an upfront payment from him in order to deliver the parts he needs to build the components Blossom is buying from him. The sub-suppliers all require 30 percent up front on the total order value, which adds up to $3 million. This is money Nathan doesn't have.

Nathan has two options:

- He can go to his bank and ask for a loan for $3 million.
- He can ask Blossom if it will pay $3 million up front.

He opts for the second choice. Blossom's lead negotiator tells Nathan that the upfront payment is out of the question and adds that if he requires it, the negotiator will cancel the contract and search for an alternative supplier.

Nathan's only remaining alternative is to approach his bank and ask for a loan. The bank approves the loan but charges him interest in the amount of $150,000. This, of course, reduces his profit on the deal by $150,000.

Blossom's cost of paying Nathan the $3 million up front is $60,000.

The reason? Blossom's cost of capital is lower than Nathan's.

Blossom's negotiator believes he won a strategic victory by not paying Nathan anything up front. Nathan knows he did not handle this negotiation well, but in reality, both parties have lost. Both parties lost the potential of creating NegoEconomic value by leveraging the terms of payment variable.

What NegoEconomic potential was lost in this transaction? The difference between Nathan's cost and Blossom's gains:

$150,000

− $60,000

$90,000   was lost between the two parties

What should Nathan and Blossom have done instead? By figuring out the difference between their respective costs of capital, they would easily have discovered that by utilizing this difference they created $90,000 of NegoEconomics to divide between them. Imagine if Nathan reduced his price by $120,000 – Blossom would make an additional $60,000 and Nathan would save $30,000. A win for everybody (with the exception of the bank, who is not part of the deal).

Who Has the Lowest Cost of Ownership?

NegoEconomics distributes tasks to the party who can perform the function at the lowest cost. If one side's costs are higher than the other side's, the task is allocated to the party who has the lowest cost ownership.

NegoEconomic value shows itself when a supplier who offers to shorten its delivery times bears lower costs than the net gain accrued to the buyer. By making an extra effort, the supplier can increase the quality of its services or products. If the benefit accruing to the buyer exceeds the costs incurred by the supplier, NegoEconomic value is created for both parties.

Money costs money. Actually, money is a commodity just like this book you are reading, a computer, a car, a table, or a house. We can put value on money, on people, and on organizations. Look at your credit card statement. Are you paying 15 or 19 percent interest on your balances, or more than that? That percentage quantifies the value to you of using the bank's financial leverage.

When I present this very simplified example of NegoEconomics to executives, some will tell me they do not have the time to focus on $150,000 when they are working on a $10 million deal. Then I ask them if they personally make more than $150,000 an hour. Most people I meet tell me they don't. Then I respond that in a negotiation that has a total value of $10 million, they will easily find 200–300 variables each having the potential to deliver $150,000 in NegoEconomic value.

In the last few years, I have noticed a trend stemming from corporate management who have directed their procurement departments to generate positive cash flow by expanding the credit from suppliers. Prior to these new directives, the typical credit term might have been 30 days. Under the new directives, the terms are expanded to 60–90 days.

Who do you think typically has the lower cost of capital – a major publicly traded company or a local supplier with 50 employees?

It always costs the smaller company more to obtain financing. A large corporation generally has the lower cost of capital. With these new directives coming from the procurement department, the small supplier with the higher costs is picking up the bill for the huge company with the lower cost of capital. This makes very little sense by anyone's standards.

ELEMENT 14

Subject Matter

Negotiation expertise is an invaluable asset across various industries, a fact that is increasingly recognized in the corporate world. This principle is vividly illustrated in the Apple TV show *Ted Lasso*, where an American football coach, despite lacking soccer knowledge, successfully leads a British soccer team. His success is attributed more to his human and coaching skills than to his familiarity with soccer.

In my role as a negotiation advisor, I frequently enter scenarios where my understanding of the specific subject matter – whether it's in construction, technology, or services – is limited. However, I've found that not being entrenched in the specifics of the industry can actually be beneficial, allowing for more creative and effective negotiation strategies.

This approach to negotiation is gaining traction in the corporate world. A recent study by McKinsey & Co revealed that a majority of CEOs from Fortune 500 companies support the creation of a new executive role: the chief negotiating officer (CNO). According to the study, implementing a CNO could boost an organization's earnings by at least 5 percent. This significant finding underscores the value of specialized negotiation expertise at the highest levels of corporate strategy.

The concept also bolsters the argument for forming specialized negotiation teams within organizations. Such teams, consisting of individuals whose primary expertise is negotiation, can provide invaluable support across various departments. My encounters with organizations that have adopted this strategy – developing elite negotiation units for diverse negotiations – have demonstrated the effectiveness of this approach. It highlights that, often, the key competency in negotiations is not in-depth subject knowledge but rather the art and skill of negotiation itself.

ELEMENT 15

Leveraging AI to Enhance Your Negotiation Skills

AI can be instrumental in several stages. Humans started negotiating thousands of years ago, but in the most recent years, technology has arrived to support our effort to achieve better deals. Right now, the question is not whether AI will replace humans at the negotiation table but how much negotiators using AI will replace negotiators not using AI. And that's a fact.

If you haven't already started to embrace AI, the time is now. You'll need to acquaint yourself with the world of technology in negotiation. Where and how are you able to utilize AI? Let's take a look at a few areas. I have created prompt examples to make it easier for you to get started:

- **Prepare for pre-negotiations:** Analyze historical data of similar negotiations to identify common patterns and successful strategies.

  Example AI prompt: Analyze historical data on tech industry negotiations over the past five years, identifying key success factors and common pitfalls.
- **Formulate a strategy:** Help to create a tailored negotiation strategy by evaluating strengths and weaknesses and considering market trends.

  Example AI prompt: Evaluate my company's position in an upcoming contract negotiation with a supplier, considering market trends, and suggest strategic approaches.
- **Get real-time assistance during negotiations:** Provide real-time data analysis and feedback during the negotiation.

  Example AI prompt: Monitor the ongoing discussion with our business partner and provide real-time feedback on the progression and tactical advice based on their responses.
- **Accurately respond to emotional cues:** Analyze tone, facial expressions, and body language to provide insights into emotional states.

Example AI prompt: Analyze the tone, facial expressions, and body language of the participants in this video of a negotiation session and provide insights into their emotional states.

- **Simulate potential negotiation scenarios:** Create virtual scenarios to practice different negotiation strategies and see potential outcomes.

Example AI prompt: Create simulation scenarios for a salary negotiation with different strategies, including aggressive, moderate, and conciliatory approaches, and predict potential outcomes.

- **Craft your next best alternative (NBA):** Develop a strong NBA by analyzing market data, resources, and constraints.

Example AI prompt: Based on current market data and our company's resources, suggest viable alternatives for our primary goal in the upcoming property acquisition negotiation.

- **Streamline communication:** Assist in organizing and prioritizing communication during the negotiation process.

Example AI prompt: Organize the main points of discussion from these negotiation transcripts and prioritize them in order of relevance and importance to our objectives.

- **Critically assess the finalized agreement:** Review the agreement post-negotiation to ensure alignment with goals and expectations.

Example AI prompt: Review this draft agreement from our recent negotiation and compare it against our predefined objectives and benchmarks to ensure alignment with our goals.

It's crucial to note that the way you communicate with the AI, or your prompting technique, plays a pivotal role in the quality of feedback you receive.

Example AI prompt: Given my objective to secure a better pricing structure in a vendor negotiation, what specific prompts should I use to generate the most effective strategies and analysis from an AI tool?

CHAPTER 3

Tools

Introduction: Tools for Negotiation

N egotiation is a skill. As with most skills, negotiation skills are something you can train and improve if you are willing to invest in developing that skill.

No great surgeon, architect, or athlete has ever succeeded without practicing, studying, and improving themselves repeatedly, spending hundreds and even thousands of hours bettering themselves.

Being a great surgeon, architect, or athlete requires a toolbox with the right tools. Tools that are carefully picked. Tools that are tried out and improved over years. Based on experience and knowledge.

You can develop these tools yourself or choose to short cut your way to greater success by learning from someone who has already traveled the road of trial and error and save yourself the headache.

This chapter consists of 36 sharp tools especially selected for you, as they represent solutions to most of the situations you'll find yourself in—not only in negotiation but in life. The 36 different tools are created for you to use immediately in various negotiations.

If you have experienced one negotiation, you have experienced one negotiation is a saying. This is very true, as one negotiation often is very different from the next. Use the tools carefully and adjust them to the actual situation. Some of the tools are more compatible with a zero-sum negotiation and others are well suited for a collaborative negotiation.

You are not able to remember all the tools in every situation where you need them. This is why Element 44 discusses one of my favorites-the checklist. I am a strong believer in using checklists prior to, during, and after negotiations. Actually,

I would go as far as saying you should never embark on a negotiation without having checked your checklist.

This chapter is like most of the other chapters-not meant necessarily for you to read sequentially, from Elements 16 to 51. Instead, dive into the tool you think is appropriate for the situation at hand.

Good luck and enjoy the reading.

ELEMENT 16

Negotiation Strategy

More and more professional negotiators have discovered that collaboration produces superior results and more durable relationships. More and more organizations understand that having a negotiation strategy is just as vital as having a sales, communication, R&D, or market strategy. Negotiation is truly a management strategy.

Choice of Strategy

Your choice of strategy and tactics is one of the most important points for you when preparing to negotiate. If you haven't identified your strategy and tactics, you leave the initiative to the other party and will be forced to negotiate on their terms and conditions.

The *strategy* is the philosophy according to which you work, and it impacts your behavior during negotiation. Tactics are those moves, ploys, and stratagems you use in the negotiation.

Most negotiators have never really planned any strategy. They adjust their behavior to the moment, and they change their strategy in a poorly planned manner in the course of the negotiations.

Your choice of strategy permeates the negotiation and determines the negotiation climate. It influences your relations with the other party. Your choice of strategy also influences the signals you receive from the other party, your perception and interpretation of the negotiation, and your personality. It's in itself a result of your upbringing and your heredity. The behavior you demonstrate in a business negotiation is often very much in keeping with your behavior vis-à-vis your family members, your neighbors, and your colleagues.

Your choice of strategy is often affected by your expectations regarding a negotiation. If you believe that the other party will be quite aggressive and spoiling for a fight, you will favor a fight without first examining whether another strategy would be better suited to the purpose, or if a fight will, in fact, take you to your goal.

If the other party appears to be willing to cooperate, you will tend to be cooperative. If you register aggressive signals from the other party, you will be more inclined to respond aggressively. In negotiations, as well as in physics, there is a law of nature stating that pressure engenders counterpressure.

The organization's policy and general view of the surrounding world will affect your choice of strategy. The negotiator will adjust their behavior to what they think the organization and its managers expect.

There are negotiators who are aware of the importance of their choice of strategy. They very consciously plan a strategy and how to implement it. They always take into account the topical negotiation situation and have learned how to vary their strategy and how to switch between different existing strategies. They see the negotiation in two steps: to create and to divide NegoEconomics (see Element 20).

Their behavior at the negotiating table is governed by goal-oriented planning and by a feeling of how their own behavior and reactions to the other party's moves bring them closer to their objective. They have developed their register of emotions and are sensitive to human interaction. They avoid all types of verbal combat, provocation, locks, and prestige-oriented conflicts that aren't part and parcel of a conscious set-up for the negotiation.

Flexible Tactics

There is no such thing as a general tactic that will work no matter what the circumstances. Tactics will always have to be adjusted and adapted to your objectives, the strategy of your choice, your own resources, your knowledge and the objectives, strategy, resources, and knowledge of the other party.

Some tactics are constructive and lead to greater openness and better understanding. They create trust. Using them will make it easier for you to find the paths that can lead you to the NegoEconomics. However, much of the tactical play aims at manipulating the other party, at making them insecure, and at exerting pressure that may become overwhelming and make them give in. These stressful moves may be efficient in the short term; however, they tend to ruin relationships, trust, and openness. There are negotiation situations in which cooperation between the parties work well so that all tactical, clever moves are superfluous and do more harm than good.

Sometimes it's difficult to determine in advance whether one tactic is superior to another, or whether clever gambits and moves do more harm than good. Only when negotiations have been completed will you know the outcome. But you never know what the outcome would have been if instead you had chosen another strategy.

A good principle in your choice of tactics is to begin with gambits that don't lock the negotiations by limiting the possibility of choosing different routes at a later stage. Try to design the negotiations with a view to cooperation from the outset. If you're uncertain about the intentions of the other party, you should take it easy and wait until you think you can read them. Be wary of using any gambits yourself that the other party might interpret as combative. Such gambits may easily lead to negotiations being deadlocked and preempting future cooperation.

Tactical moves must be made with good sense and caution. Clever tactics tend to be double-edged swords. If the other party sees through your intentions, a clever countermove may still put them where you want them. Negotiations are reminiscent of chess. Just like the chess player, the skillful negotiator is always some moves ahead of their opponent.

Never use a tactic without making clear to yourself what reactions and countermoves this might provoke on the part of the other party, and how you intend to handle these responses. Put yourself in their shoes. Consider how you would have reacted to your gambits, and what your own countermoves would have been. In this way you can see whether you're about to ruin relations and openness before it's too late. This is similar to what I said earlier. Think before you speak.

Keep in mind that my assessment of behavior at the negotiating table and choice of strategy and tactics isn't shared by everybody. I'm a staunch believer in cooperation. Cooperation is based on trust and open and honest communication between the parties together with a willingness to listen and understand each other's needs and judgments. Cooperation in no way means shirking the issues or relinquishing your own needs and judgments. The purpose is to make the stake as large as possible, to the benefit of both parties.

ELEMENT 17

Rules of the Game

I magine you are about to compete in a tennis match. You have your racquet and are looking forward to a good match. You are tremendously surprised when you arrive at the court and your counterpart has set up two chairs and a table on the side. On the table is a chess board, stocked with knights, rooks, and pawns. They look expectantly at you and ask, "Are you ready to play?"

This scenario plays out every day in millions of cases worldwide. Not with a tennis racquet and a chessboard, but in a negotiation. One side comes to the table with an understanding of the rules of play and their opponent arrives with a completely different set of assumptions. Many of my clients over the years have been amazed when I open with the question: Shall we talk about how we are going to negotiate? You have to define the Rules of the Game before you can begin.

The Rules of the Game dictate how parties are going to negotiate. They must be articulated and agreed to before any conversation takes places regarding the merits of the matter to be decided or the deal to be made. Who are the teams? What are the rules of play and the conditions for termination? This process can be time consuming—in fact, it can sometimes take more time than the actual negotiation. But establishing the ground rules prior to commencing the bargaining saves a lot of time down the road, avoids misunderstandings, and enhances the prospects for cooperation.

Earlier in my career, I remember receiving a call from one of my most important customers. He wanted to check a number of details concerning the forecast for the following year. The customer was the head of production, so I had expected the conversation to be about technical details. This typically occurred every year around the same time, yet this time was different. It turned out he wanted to discuss terms, delivery, and financing. He also had other executive team members on the call. I wasn't prepared and ended up entering into an uncomfortable agreement.

I was angry. I was ambushed! There was no way I could have known that the production manager wanted to discuss terms, delivery, and financing with me. He normally did not do that until the end of the year.

What I later came to realize is that I should have started the discussion by asking, "What are we going to talk about, and who will be at the meeting?" If I had done this, I would have been prepared. If I was not ready to negotiate, I could have asked for more time. Time is negotiable—we could have scheduled a follow-up call for the next day after I had time to review the facts.

This was a priceless lesson for me; one that I've shared in countless seminars.

In some negotiations, establishing common rules may be as simple as asking the question in the prior example. For more complex situations, it goes further to include an agreed upon agenda, select a negotiation strategy, and agree on the Code of Conduct. Questions to be addressed include:

- Who will open first for the exchange of information?
- How do you establish trust? Cooperation?
- How do you present all variables? Who lists them?
- Who will take care of the whiteboard and visual aids?
- Must breaks be agreed to and when should they be?
- Do all delegates have the authority to conclude? And if so, what is their mandate?

According to studies by Copenhagen Business School, and myself, negotiators are forfeiting as much as 42 percent of the value of a transaction due to failure to bargain for hidden variables. Due to lack of trust, information, and cooperation, discussions are often limited to just price and quantity and both parties miss opportunities to create value. There is no framework for these developing these components! By defining the Rules of the Game, you create a better playing field for discussions to take place and optimize your chances of a winning result.

ELEMENT 18

Questions

I was once at a negotiation in Berlin when the counterpart asked, "Are there any questions?" One participant raised his hand and said, "I have doubts about the actual contents of your presentation." The speaker immediately answered, "This question is about the gentleman's wish to discuss the validity of my facts."

The answer the negotiator gave was incredibly humiliating, and what was otherwise a successful presentation developed into a real conflict situation between two losers. How should the negotiator have answered the question?

"The question is about the source of my data, which is . . ."

The problem in that situation was that the speaker felt personally criticized by the man asking the question. He felt he was being attacked in the situation, and his response was aggressive. Every day, conferences, seminars, negotiations, meetings, and training courses take place by the thousands, and included in these events there is usually a round of questions. Very often, the conclusion is the most informative part, as it provides participants with an opportunity to explore the content from their own standpoint.

The technique of asking questions, and preferably plenty of them, is one of the most important techniques in negotiations. When we ask relevant questions, we do it primarily to uncover areas that are not clear to us. However, we also ask questions to show that we are interested in what our conversation partner is talking about.

Without questions, communication would become nonexistent. As I pointed out in the element on presentation, questions are crucial in presentations so that the speaker can clarify points and make sure that everyone has understood what they were speaking about. But how do you ask the right questions? Well, good questions are related to the ability to listen and to listen properly.

Types of Questions

This section looks at four different techniques for asking questions: open, closed, leading, and follow-up.

Open Questions

Open questions lead to more information. An example of an open question might be: "How are manuals used in teaching?" This forces the other person to say something other than yes or no. Furthermore, open questions give you the opportunity to receive other information, which can be used as a basis for evaluation. Don't ask questions such as, "It is important to use body language as a channel of communication. What do you think?" In your introduction, you have already given the "correct" answer, which prevents the other person from contributing their own opinion. Possibly, this person may answer, "That is what I thought as well." This does not give you much information. You do not know whether it was said to accommodate your wishes; you don't know whether the person has understood the concept of body language and how they understand it. Instead, the question should be: "What do you think are important channels of communication?" On the basis of the study carried out concerning people's tendency to lie, asking an applicant a question such as: "Are you willing to work overtime?" would be wrong. Instead, you should ask, "What is your attitude toward overtime?"

Closed Questions

Closed questions lead to yes or no answers and should be used for decisions or for finalizing situations. Use questions such as: "Are you fetching the manuals from the cellar?" or "Can you sign the contract today?" A closed question does not open up the possibility for the other person to launch into long explanations and it limits possible answers to a bare minimum. Closed questions can be rightfully used after a series of open questions or leading questions as a technique for finishing off.

Leading Questions

Examples of leading questions include: "Can you imagine yourself not having well-trained staff?" or "What time will you fetch the manuals?" instead of "Are you going to fetch the manuals?" Leading questions can sometimes be used in a similar way to closed questions, that is, to explain or to conclude. Here we are sending the other person in the direction we ourselves would like to go. Instead of asking, "Are you going shopping today?" we ask, "What time are you going shopping?"

Follow-up Questions

When people are talking or discussing something, it often happens that someone asks a question that remains unanswered for a number of reasons. I have noticed that on these occasions the person who has asked the question does not follow this up but lets the whole thing lie. When they watch a video recording of this conversation afterward, it becomes clear to them that some very relevant and important questions remained unanswered.

A politician on television news has some questions put to them. The journalist asks the question, "People say that the unofficial unemployment figures are much higher than the published figures, since they do not take certain categories of people into account. Is this correct?" The politician tilts their head sideways, clears their throat, and says, "Christian, we should all join forces and do as much as we can for the job market and in this way . . ." Three minutes later, the journalist has still not received an answer to their question about the employment figures. On rare occasions, the journalist repeats the question. Politicians have an ingenious way of sidestepping when it comes to questions that they cannot answer!

One good rule is to follow up the minute you realize that your original question is not being answered. You should do this immediately and in order to follow up you must be good at listening. The best thing is to assume full responsibility for the communication. It is possible that your question was unclear. You should also give the other person a chance in case you are the one at fault. Ask, "I may have mentioned this before, but how was it with . . .?"

If the other person still does not provide an answer to your question, you can use a technique whereby you go back to the last proper direct answer you received and begin from there. If the person does not respond to any of these approaches, you can either wait or go back to the question or you can confront them by saying directly, "What are the unemployment figures?"

Questions for Your Audience

If you want to put a question to your counterpart, it is sometimes preferable to address the group as a whole. Wait a couple of seconds before you choose someone to answer your question. When choosing someone, you should be gentle and have an air of humility, as people can feel frightened or provoked in these situations. It is possible that the person who has been asked the question may feel embarrassed and that is something they will not thank you for. Do not demand an answer—try and invite an answer to your question. When you select someone to answer your question, other members of the group will switch off, so it is a good idea to repeat the question so that you update everyone on what is being said and make a point of retaining their concentration.

Questions from Your Counterpart

Start your round of questions by inviting questions from your audience in a friendly way and step toward askers. This approach makes you appear more amenable and encourages people to ask questions. We often fear questions because we anticipate objections. Remember, you rely on questions for feedback and to gauge whether the audience has understood your message. Consider these guidelines:

- When announcing it's time for questions, raise your hand. This gesture indicates that everyone is welcome to do the same.
- Open the session with total communicative behavior, and remember to pace yourself. Instead of saying, "I don't know whether there are going to be any questions" say, "Now, I would like to hear what questions you have. Let's start with the front row."
- Make direct eye contact with the person asking the question.
- It's also beneficial to thank them for asking. Tell them it was a good question (but avoid exaggerating).
- Repeat or rephrase the question, possibly using different words to show that you have understood and to ensure everyone else has heard it.
- Pause briefly to allow the audience to absorb what has been said.
- Direct your answer to the entire group, not just to the individual asking.
- Check if the person is satisfied with the answer and thank them again for asking.

If there are no questions, speakers often feel awkward. In such cases, it's not a bad idea to pose the first question yourself, such as, "I have often wondered why . . .?" Invite questions by asking something like, "What do you think your division will make of it?"

Dealing with Questions You're Not Able to Answer

If you can't answer a question, admit it or ask someone else in the group to answer it. Most people respect those who acknowledge not having an immediate answer. However, it's crucial to say that you will find out and return with an answer later. Avoid making a hasty response with a confident tone if you lack sufficient expertise. Your audience will likely see through this, casting you in a negative light. It's acceptable to say that you believe your response is correct, provided you clarify that you are not entirely certain about its validity.

If you know someone in the audience is knowledgeable on the subject, possibly more so than you, involve them and seek their assistance. Such individuals are a resource, and everyone will respect you for utilizing their expertise. People often find it flattering to be asked for help.

Be Specific in Your Questions

Be clear about what you want to know: how much, where, how, why, who, in what way? Avoid playing "emotional hide-and-seek." Make the person you're asking feel special. Information is powerful; don't expect to receive an answer simply because you asked a question. Create an incentive for the person to respond to your query. For example, if you have a great business idea and need funding, don't just ask for money. Explain how the investment will be used and what can be achieved for both you and the investor. The value you create might be just a hope or a dream, but it can often be enough. If you merely say, "I could do with a million pounds," the likely response will be, "There are many others like you!"

Ensure your question is focused, appropriate, and honest. Displaying uncertainty is a sure way to fail. If you're unclear about what you're asking, nobody else will know either. Show confidence in your query. Your body language and verbal behavior should convey your expectation of a response.

Precision with Language

Much of our communication is based on nothing—on generalizations and assumptions. This kind of conversation, known as superficially structured, can be detrimental. For instance, if a client complains about a salesperson, saying, "All your salespeople are completely useless! They never give proper advice," it's an overgeneralization. Perhaps that one salesperson is ineffective, but it doesn't mean all are. When you encounter such generalizations, challenge them. Ask, "All?" to prompt a more accurate response.

Many people habitually say, "I can't!" When someone expresses this, it sends a definite signal to the brain that they are incapable of a certain task. However, asking, "What would it be like if you could do it?" opens up possibilities and encourages them to consider the pros and cons. Apply this technique to yourself too. Next time you think, "I can't," ask yourself, "What would happen if I could?" This approach can reveal new opportunities and expand your horizons. Then ask, "What is stopping me from doing it now?"

Our language and communicative behavior are often filled with empty words and generalizations. For example, if someone says, "I am depressed," they're merely describing a condition without providing actionable information. Ask them to specify what makes them depressed to gain a clearer understanding. Similarly, when people make statements like "They don't understand me!" or "I don't have a chance against them," challenge these vague assertions to identify specific individuals or situations. This helps move the conversation from generalizations to facts.

How to Hold a Conversation

Pay attention to the way people speak. Try to identify the superficial (surface structure) and the deeper meaning (underlying structure) of their words. When you hear statements like "It's a bad idea," respond with questions like "According to whom?" or "How do you know that?" Choose "how" questions over "why" questions, as they tend to yield more concrete reasons and explanations rather than excuses.

ELEMENT 19

Openness

I f you want to locate better solutions than those already at hand, or if you want to obtain extra information about the counterparts interest and values, you should use a different negotiation method—the one I refer to as SMARTnership/partnership. It's characterized by constructive dialogue. The foundation for such cooperation is trust and openness.

Lack of openness means that when the negotiators are deciding on the terms they will ask for, or they are willing to accept, they will only look at the consequences to themselves. They do not have, nor have they attempted to obtain, information about the consequences of the terms and conditions to the other party. The decision leads to sub-optimization. The existing possibilities for rationalization and optimal distribution of costs aren't taken advantage of.

In a SMARTnership negotiation, the emphasis is on mutual gain and transparency, rather than the traditional zero-sum game where one party's gain is another's loss. Let's consider an example scenario where two negotiators are discussing the terms of payment, particularly focusing on the cost of capital.

EXAMPLE | Using Openness to Everyone's Advantage

Negotiator A represents a company seeking to purchase a large quantity of goods. Negotiator B represents the supplier of these goods. Negotiator A is concerned about the cost of capital—essentially, the cost of financing the purchase.
Negotiation example:

- Negotiator A: "We're interested in your products, but we need to discuss the payment terms. Our main concern is the cost of capital. Could you provide some flexibility in the payment schedule to mitigate this?"

- Negotiator B: "We understand your concern. However, we also have to manage our cash flow effectively. Could you share more about your cost of capital constraints?"

- Negotiator A: "Certainly. Our current cost of capital is 8 percent, which affects our ability to make large upfront payments without incurring significant financial strain."
- Negotiator B: "I see. Our cost of capital is 4 percent. Would a staggered payment plan work for you, where payments are spread over a period, aligning with your cash flow, thereby reducing the financial burden?"
- Negotiator A: "That could be a workable solution. What terms are you considering?"
- Negotiator B: "We propose a down payment of X percent followed by monthly installments. This way, we can cover our initial production costs while providing you with a manageable payment structure."

SMARTnership Approach

In a SMARTnership negotiation, both parties openly share their financial constraints and needs. This transparency is crucial in finding a mutually beneficial solution. Instead of pushing for maximum immediate gain, both parties look for a solution that balances their needs, leading to a sustainable business relationship. By discussing openly, both parties can brainstorm innovative solutions like staggered payments that might not have been considered in a more adversarial negotiation. This approach fosters trust and lays the groundwork for a long-term partnership, rather than a one-off transaction. Both parties show willingness to adapt their initial positions in response to the other's needs.

In a situation where one negotiator is asking about the cost of capital, the key is to approach the conversation with an aim to understand and accommodate, within reason, each other's financial limitations and requirements. This might involve sharing more detailed financial information than usual, but doing so can lead to more effective, tailored solutions that benefit both parties.

ELEMENT 20

The Hidden Value: NegoEconomics

When individuals in an organization are driven by motivation, open-mindedness, and the freedom to explore new avenues, the potential for significant NegoEconomics emerges. *NegoEconomics* is the asymmetric value that is generated between your cost and my value. This is contingent upon negotiators knowing where to direct their focus. NegoEconomics effectively broadens the scope of negotiation, enlarging the "pie" that can be divided among parties.

Room for Negotiation

Traditionally, the room for negotiation is defined as the difference between the highest price a buyer is willing to pay and the lowest price a seller is prepared to accept. For a successful deal, this room for negotiation must be positive, meaning the buyer's offer exceeds the seller's minimum threshold.

For instance, if the highest price a buyer can pay is $12,500 and the lowest a seller can accept is $11,900, the $600 difference represents the room for negotiation, within which a deal is feasible.

However, the actual room for negotiation typically extends beyond this. It comprises not only the traditional room but also the additional value derived from NegoEconomics. This expanded view allows agreements to be reached even when the buyer's maximum price falls below the seller's minimum.

A Simple Model to Identify NegoEconomics

In searching for NegoEconomics, thorough preparation is crucial. Negotiators often prepare by considering the following in the offer:

- How will you submit and explain your offer?
- What questions and objections might the other party raise?

- What initial terms, conditions, and price should you propose?
- Where is your threshold of pain?

If your opening price is $118,000 and your pain threshold is $103,000, then your negotiation room is $15,000.

Defining the aim of negotiation as simply clinching the deal while conceding as little as possible of the $15,000 can be overly restrictive. This narrow view risks entrapment in a zero-sum game. As a seller, reducing your price by $5,000 not only decreases your profits by the same amount, but also improves the other party's deal by an equivalent $5,000, creating a direct 1:1 effect.

Instead, it's advisable to adopt a broader perspective during preparation, setting the stage for more effective bargaining.

The Four-Step Model

1. The offer: With a negotiation margin of $15,000, consider how to use this amount beyond just lowering the price.
2. Beyond monetary value: What additional services or products can you offer?
3. Reduce the package scope:
   a. Identify which services or products can be removed.
   b. What elements can the other party handle themselves?
   c. Is a simpler solution viable?
4. The last resort:
   a. If the other party is uninterested in added value, aim for a compromise.
   b. Negotiate toward a counteroffer. If your offer is $118,000 and the customer proposes $88,000, consider splitting the difference to reach a middle ground.
   c. Avoid starting with one-sided concessions, as this can lead to continual reductions, possibly leading to your lowest acceptable price.

Offering additional services or products can be cost-effective, as the associated expenses might be considerably lower than their perceived value to the other party, thus providing leverage. This could even justify a price increase.

EXAMPLE | Computer Package Negotiation

Imagine negotiating a deal for 10 computers with included software installation and delivery, priced at $118,000. The buyer, having an alternative offer, demands a price reduction to just under $100,000, while your pain threshold is $103,000.

Rather than accommodating the buyer's demand with a unilateral price cut, consider what additional services or products could be added to the package. For example, offering training for staff on software included in the package could add significant value without incurring substantial costs.

Identifying NegoEconomics in Projects

In any project, multiple areas exist where NegoEconomics can be explored:

- Follow the entire process from inception to the end-user phase.
- Examine financial variables, quality and performance, technical specifications, economies of scale, timing, purchasing patterns, and rights.

Remember the "From Ear of Corn to Loaf of Bread" analogy. Just like the film that traced the process from farming to the finished bread product, follow each step in your project and question every aspect:

- Why are things done this way?
- What happens when the need for a product or service ends?
- How does each element impact costs, risks, and profits?
- What alternatives exist, and what are their potential impacts?

From Public Authority to Commercial Enterprise

As an example, reflect on the evolution from a single, impractical telephone point per household to the current flexibility in telecommunications. The transformation from a public authority to a commercial enterprise illustrates the importance of adapting to customer needs and market demands.

In summary, understanding and applying NegoEconomics can lead to more successful and mutually beneficial negotiations. It requires a shift from traditional negotiation tactics to a more comprehensive, value-oriented approach that considers both the tangible and intangible elements of a deal.

ELEMENT 21

Tru$tCurrency

Negotiations carried out in a spirit of cooperation and trust are more efficient and achieve better results for the parties. Unnecessary conflict can be avoided by creating a positive negotiation climate built on a foundation of open, honest communication. This is best achieved if the negotiators make an investment in the interpersonal dynamic before getting down to business. When the personal chemistry clicks, delegates often make decisions based on their feelings rather than logic and rationality. Their perception of the situation becomes so positive that their decision-making may become skewed in favor of the opponent's solutions.

Trust is vital in the pursuit of creating a *SMARTnership*, the advanced collaborative approach, and generating NegoEconomics (see Element 20). Negotiations can be concluded without trust, and they do every day, but the negotiators are leaving considerable value on the table.

The Water Bottle Experiment

I have tested the importance of trust in a simple experiment with more than 3,000 people globally. They are confronted with a very simple choice. They must buy plastic water bottles for their operations. Here's the scenario.

For the last five years, you have purchased the water from supplier A for a total of $4 million. You really like supplier A. The relationship is great. You got the same humor, communicated well, and trust is present.

A new supplier enters the market, and they are able to deliver exactly the same product. A completely identical bottle of water. There is absolutely NO difference in content, packaging, or quality.

The only difference is that the new supplier is 2 percent lower priced. The challenge is that you don't really trust or like the new supplier. You can't really put your finger on what is wrong, but there is no personal chemistry. You do not communicate fluently and have difficulty understanding each other. Who will you buy your water from going forward?

With a price difference of 2 percent, 97 percent of the respondents continue to buy from supplier A. Then I slowly increase the difference in price in 1 percent increments and ask the respondents who they prefer to do business with.

What do you think the price difference must be before the respondent chooses supplier B?

Supplier B, who they don't really trust or like!

My research shows that for most people, the pain threshold 10–20 percent. I meet test objects who go all the way to 30 percent price difference before they choose a new supplier. This means that the majority of the 3,000 people agrees to pay 10 percent more for an identical product solely based on increased confidence and higher likeability.

Furthermore, it is my conclusion that the higher the complexity of a service or product is, the greater the importance of likeability and trust.

ELEMENT 22

Strategy Access Matrix (SAM) Model

First, you'll learn about the importance of selecting the right strategy and tactics. Going into a negotiation without a clear plan is akin to surrendering control. It forces you to operate on the other party's terms, impacting your attitude, decisions, and behavior throughout the process. Tactics are the individual moves you make during a negotiation, but they must be underpinned by a solid strategy.

Now, consider the Strategy Access Matrix (SAM) model, a tool I developed to help you identify the most appropriate negotiation strategy based on the mutual importance of the parties involved.

Take a look at the model in the figure: the vertical line represents your importance to your counterpart. The more crucial you are to them, the higher you'll be placed on this line. The horizontal line represents how significant the counterpart is to you. The more important they are, the farther to the right you'll place them.

In a scenario where both parties find each other equally important, you'll land in the top right box of the matrix. What's the best strategy here? If you're thinking SMARTnership, you're spot on. This is where both parties can derive significant mutual benefit from a cooperative, transparent approach.

Conversely, if you find yourself in the bottom left box, where neither party is particularly important to the other, a zero-sum approach is more fitting. In these situations, investing time and resources in a SMARTnership doesn't make sense, as there's little value in the relationship.

But what about unbalanced negotiations? These are represented by either the top left or bottom right corners of the matrix. Here, one party holds more importance than the other. In such cases, a partnership strategy is most effective, balancing the dynamics and ensuring a fair negotiation process.

Through the SAM model, negotiators can strategically assess their position and choose the most appropriate approach, be it zero-sum, partnership, or SMARTnership. This assessment is a cornerstone of successful negotiation, ensuring that you enter any negotiation not only prepared but also with a strategy that aligns with the unique dynamics of each situation.

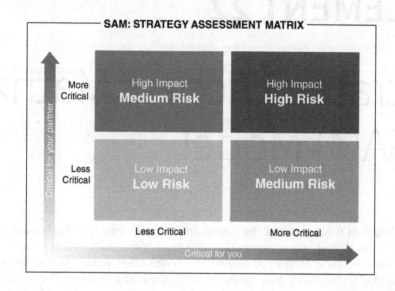

ELEMENT 23

Threats

Years ago, when my daughter was about five years old, we entered a major toy store in downtown Copenhagen. Our purpose was to buy a birthday gift for a boy named Sillas.

He had his heart set on something specific, which I was trying to find. While I was preoccupied, my daughter wandered off. I wasn't immediately concerned; during our visits to toy stores, she was invariably drawn to the Barbies, much like a moth to a flame.

Unfortunately, the toy Sillas wanted was sold out. It was time to locate my daughter and leave. I couldn't spot her behind the shelves due to her height, so I headed toward the Barbie section. Sure enough, she was there, clutching a large Barbie doll. "Daddy, I want this Barbie doll!" she declared, leaving no room for negotiation. It was a demand, and I don't respond well to demands. So, I replied firmly, "No, please put the Barbie back. You just had a birthday and received plenty of toys. Put it down; we need to leave."

To my surprise, she stood her ground, reiterating her demand for the Barbie doll.

Taking a deep breath, I resorted to a threat that had always worked before: "Either you put down the Barbie and come with me, or you'll stay here by yourself in this huge toy store because I'm leaving now!"

This threat had always been effective, but this time, my daughter, not showing the best judgment, defiantly stated she wasn't moving and insisted on the Barbie. I turned and started walking away, expecting her usual response—running after me, pleading to wait. Instead, her voice rang out, loud and clear: "Dad, Mom is going to be really angry if you leave me alone in the city!"

I was stunned. I hadn't expected her to call my bluff. I turned back and walked toward her, realizing she had seen through my threat, turning it into a mere bluff.

Lesson learned: Never use a threat you are not prepared to follow through on. Carefully evaluate whether to use a threat and consider the potential consequences.

ELEMENT 24

Activating
Several Senses

When you transmit on several channels at the same time, you occupy a greater share of the other party's attention and reduce the risk of competing signals distorting the message. This primarily means using a combination of words and images. Humans are better at remembering visual impressions. An extensive and complex message will be more easily received if words and images are combined. By means of pictures you can draw several models that will facilitate understanding and illustrate the connection.

How often do you use images in your negotiations? If there is no blackboard, PowerPoint presentation, or flipchart, you can always use paper and pen. Virtually everything can be expressed and summarized in images: columns of figures, timetables, keywords, arguments, and so on. You can even use little stories, examples, and references to create an image that the other party can see in their mind's eye. In this manner, you activate information and experience stored deep down in the long-term memory.

Your message should be linked to well-known situations, create aha experiences, reduce uncertainty, and create trust. Remember, "The ball will roll into the right whole."

Physical or Intellectual Demonstrations

If you demonstrate your message, you activate several of the other party's senses. A product is demonstrated by having the other party try it out. That's a physical demonstration. But how do you demonstrate an idea? In an intellectual demonstration, you describe the principle by means of down-to-Earth, simple example. When the other party listens to you, they must be able to see the chain of events before them.

When you have presented the proposal and have made the audience understand the principles, you ask questions of the following type: What happens if you switch to …? You force the other party to grasp your proposal and think about it. You get feedback as to whether they caught the message, and a reaction concerning their assessment of it. You'll know if the message was received as you intended it to be.

Visual Aids

An old proverb says, "A picture is worth ten thousand words." We could change this around a bit and say that PowerPoint will not replace a 20-minute speech, but it can add improvements to a presentation and make it more effective.

Visual aids enhance communication because human beings tend not to think in chronological order, but in pictures. The fact is that we absorb graphics faster than words, so verbal presentations can be reduced. It has been found that we have seven times more brain cells available for pictures than we have for sounds and touch!

Your audience will be more attentive when you animate your ideas and your presentations—that is because they are being given both color and perspective. It will also give you a more realistic overview of your presentation, and consequently people will perceive you as being well prepared and professional.

The Professional Picture

Use pictures and symbols to highlight the following:

- Ideas
- Emotions
- Attitudes and values
- Facts
- Events

Be consistent. Each slide or page needs to have an identical layout and pattern. Don't vary the background and color. Choose a format and stick to it.

Use as few words as possible. The maximum should be six lines with four to seven words per line. More than that confuses people and means that your audience will start reading from the page. Make the transparencies horizontal.

Use only key words, preferably with color, and keep a lot of empty space on the page so as not to confuse the message. When there are two messages on the same page, make them distinct by using two different colors. If the first message is written in blue, the next one can be written in red. An exception is when using a data projector. PowerPoint, for instance, has multimedia features that give you several additional options for presenting your material besides color.

Typical mistakes include these:

- Adding too many ideas to one page
- Taking too long on one transparency
- Producing a transparency of a written page
- Having too much content on one page

Limit yourself—only one idea for each page. Do not overload it with information. It is better to have several pages with just a few points made on each page.

Remember: One page for every two minutes of talking.

Use bullet points to emphasize text. Avoid numbering bullet points, as this may confuse people.

Use just one type face, for instance Times New Roman or Ariel. Be careful with CAPITAL LETTERS, as it takes longer to read them than it does to read ordinary print. They are also perceived as shouting in some cultures. Use capitals only with headings.

When you are using bold-faced type, don't use more than two different typeface sizes on the same transparency sheet. The size should be between 26–32 point. When you insert a logo or another illustration, you should make sure that it is reasonably small and that it is in the same position on each slide or transparency sheet.

When graphic elements are centered, they should be in proportion to one another, which means that they should look symmetrical. The graphic elements are all the objects on the page, such as letters, lines, shapes, colors, pictures, and empty areas. A graphic element can look "heavy" or "light."

Use Colors Effectively

Research has demonstrated the importance of color. Seven thousand presentations were analyzed and evaluated as follows:

People's attention was considerably increased when colors were used rather than black and white. When people were shown a black and white page, their attention was held for 8 seconds. When the same people were shown an identical page with colors, their attention was held for 11 seconds. When pictures or photos were placed on the page as background, their attention span increased by 16 seconds per page.

In addition, it has been noted that people memorize faster and are more efficient at remembering the contents of a page when colors are used, in which case attention span increases by 55 to 78 percent and audience participation increases by 80 percent.

It is important, however, to limit the use of color and have a maximum of three to four colors per page.

Warm, bright colors hold people's attention for longer than cold and dark colors. Use different color variations to designate areas or indicate different sections. Cold colors are blue, brown, dark green, light green and black. Warm colors are red and orange. Use yellow, orange, or light brown to highlight.

Pacing

It is not advisable to talk for more than 10 to 20 minutes without using a visual aid of one kind or another. Visual aids should be used with discretion; do not overuse them.

Swamping your audience with transparencies will not improve your presentation. The aim is for visual aids to supplement what you say, not repeat what you have said.

When you use a board, be careful not to talk into it but to your audience. Produce your visual aids when you need to refer to something on them and keep them covered up until you are ready to use them.

Erase the information or cover it up until you have finished. If you need to distribute material, you should wait until it is time to refer to it or after you have referred to it.

PowerPoint

There are hundreds of millions of PowerPoint users in the world and the number is growing rapidly. As a consequence, we also see a growing number of presentations. Even though PowerPoint presentations are produced at a rate not previously seen, the standard of quality and professionalism hasn't changed much. It is actually quite bad when only 4 percent of all presentations have professional touches and content that conforms with guidelines from leading communication experts.

The situation becomes even more terrifying when you calculate the time spent preparing these presentations, and perhaps more importantly, the time spent in their delivery—which means presenter time plus audience time. As illustrated earlier, time wasted on presentations means large sums of wasted money every year.

This is why there is such great value in improving your PowerPoint presentations, both in preparation and in delivery.

If we compare the two most widely used means of communication, email and PowerPoint, we do find some major differences. The recipient of an email can choose to ignore or even delete it, if it appears to be irrelevant or a waste of time. When attending a PowerPoint presentation, however, you are likely to be stuck in your seat until the end, hoping you'll eventually leave the room with something useful in tow.

Compared to other common forms of communication, a PowerPoint presentation is different in many ways. For instance, books and bulky reports take many hours, weeks, or even months to make ready for distribution. A PowerPoint presentation usually takes less than 24 hours to prepare, often considerably less. Delivery usually takes about 60 minutes, including set-up and take-down.

Similar to a book or report, a PowerPoint presentation very often ends up being a one-way form of communication, with little or no interaction between presenter and audience. It is far more effective, though, when the audience can get involved and become an active part of the presentation.

Audience involvement can be brought about by using open questions, playing games, or through other activities. But beware, unless the content and its delivery are interesting and engaging all on their own, you're not likely to get much willing involvement, no matter what questions you ask or games you offer.

A PowerPoint presentation should be regarded as the storyboard and screenplay of a great movie in which you are the narrator, the director, and the lead character. A great deal of a movie's success also hinges on another vital element: the supporting characters. This is why you need to get your audience involved—they are essentially the supporting characters in the "movie" you are producing. When you achieve this, your audience will leave with the feeling they have learned something and been part of the presentation. Hopefully they'll feel they gained much more than they expected. Only then will you leave a lasting impact and be remembered!

Your Personality Is 80 Percent of Your Presentation

In the end, it's not so much about whether your graphic presentation is good or bad—that is simply a part of the path to success. The largest factor in deciding whether your presentation is a success or not is you—not your PowerPoint, not the participants, not even the words you say. It depends primarily on your "PowerPoint personality."

To be clearer, it is not necessarily your usual personality that is the deciding factor, but rather how you perform. And everyone can learn to perform well, even though it takes practice. A good speaker has practiced their presentation—both how to present it and what it contains. When you have made it absolutely clear in your own mind what you want to share with your audience and how to go about sharing it, it will be easier to do it right, and you'll make a greater impact!

Therefore, by allocating a large part of the total time you spend on your presentation to the preparation stage, and providing you're effective in how you go about preparing, you will be able to give your presentation in a confident, professional, and natural manner.

ELEMENT 25

Using an Agenda

An agenda is used to achieve a number of advantages in the negotiation. This tactic isn't used as much in connection with commercial negotiations, as is the case in other types of negotiations. Use an agenda; make sure that the other party gets it in advance so that they can prepare and so that decisions can be made with reference to the agenda.

Taking the Initiative

The other party takes you by surprise by having an agenda when the negotiation begins. You haven't seen it before and want to take a break to study it in peace and quiet. If you accept proceeding with it without any changes, you may be exposed to the following unpleasantness:

- You lose the initiative and find yourself on a completely different negotiation platform than you had originally envisaged. You are lured into a discussion and a decision phase that you haven't prepared for.
- The other party determines the sequence of points on the agenda. They build up their negotiating strength by listening and summarizing. They obtain new information without having to provide information.
- Questions, which the other party wants to avoid, are not on the agenda at all or only way down on it. You never manage to reach those points.
- Under the unspecified heading "Any Other Business" the other party may have hidden unpleasant surprises. Here they might place issues that they previously "forgot."

Controlling the Other Party

Be sure that the agenda is sent to you in advance. Study it in peace and quiet. The following can still occur:

- It influences your expectations for the upcoming negotiation. You lower or raise your level of ambition.
- It determines your preparations concerning documentation and background.

- It affects the composition of the negotiating delegation.
- You bring all the information and authority required for you to meet the objectives set out by the other party in the agenda.

Demand a Set Agenda Before You Meet

This gives you a picture of the other party's intentions, who they might bring along, and a stable point of agreement during the proceedings.

Prepare Better

You can discuss an agenda internally. It helps you keep the negotiation in order so that you don't skip around between the various questions. The team members stick to their roles at the negotiating table, and you can avoid the frustration of everyone doing their own thing, which ill-prepared negotiations can so easily come to resemble if there's an unclear distribution of roles.

Know What the Other Party Wants

If you demand that the other party send you an agenda ahead of time, you can avoid a number of unpleasant surprises when you sit down at the negotiating table. You can bring along the information needed to be well prepared.

When an Agenda Is Unsuitable

Note that some negotiators will become overly thoughtful if you present them with an agenda. It can have a negative effect on the other party, and make them feel manipulated. In other situations it becomes an obstacle to the very creativity that is required to move the negotiation forward.

Sometimes an agenda will constitute no advantages at all. That has to do with the fact that the individual who has prepared it, presented it, and obtained approval for it never follows it.

ELEMENT 26

Planned Target

Before entering any negotiation, it's crucial to establish three key parameters: your starting point position, your threshold of pain, and your target. Entering a negotiation without clarity on these aspects is akin to embarking on a journey without knowing your starting point, destination, or estimated arrival time.

As a supplier preparing for negotiation, it's essential to define these three benchmarks. For instance, if your initial proposal to a buyer is $40,000, this becomes your starting point. Your goal might be to close the deal at $38,000, while your threshold of pain, or the lowest price you're willing to accept, could be around $36,000.

Conversely, if you're the buyer in the same negotiation, your perspectives on these parameters will differ. Your starting point would be the supplier's quoted price of $40,000. Your tolerance limit could be influenced by a competing supplier's offer, say $38,000, with your target set at a more favorable $37,000.

Understanding your starting point is vital throughout the negotiation process. This is one of the reasons that team-based negotiation is advantageous. In a team setup, you can designate a member as the "calculator," responsible for tracking and updating the financial aspects in real-time. This role is especially critical for the negotiation team leader, who must manage multiple facets like strategy, questioning, listening, and more, making it challenging to stay updated on every financial detail.

ELEMENT 27

Walking Away

*T*ake it or leave it should be used only after you have tried to reach a conclusion by other means. It can be difficult to determine how to use this tactic in a convincing manner. Due to its harsh nature, you can essentially only use it once throughout the entire negotiation process and still be taken seriously. The method is fraught with risk. If you use this approach, the dynamic of the negotiation will change and from that moment forward will be governed by the bargaining equity of the parties.

If you play this card, your counterpart will be provoked. Instead of surrendering and entering into the agreement you have offered, they may turn it down to see how much you can handle. They want to show you that they have stronger bargaining equity. Before you use the *take it or leave it* tactic, mentally prepare yourself for the best *and* worst possible outcomes. You should use this tactic only if you are ready to carry out the threat, which is to walk away from the table and break off negotiations.

Always be ready to walk away, having your next best alternative (NBA) ready. Negotiating without knowing your NBA is dangerous, as you suddenly are negotiating with a monopolist.

EXAMPLE | Take It or Leave It

The offer we are presenting has been structured to meet all the requirements you have stated, and this is as far as we can go on this transaction. If you delay the negotiation further, we will not make you a better offer. Because we have other orders coming in, there is a possibility that we can't guarantee these delivery dates and pricing if we do not firm this up immediately.

ELEMENT 28

Team Dynamics

You might be surprised about what I am about to tell you. You cannot negotiate on your own!

You might be thinking that can't be true. You are probably also thinking that you have successfully conducted hundreds if not thousands of negotiations on your own.

Since 1998, I have studied negotiators in simulations and real-live negotiations, and without any doubt, the negotiators performing the best are negotiating as a team. Believe me, I know.

Obviously, if you are negotiating a better price on a suit or a box of wine, you're not required to arrive with a small army, but in any negotiation of any importance, you are required to involve a team.

A team should be carefully put together and compensate for each other's strong and weak traits. As part of the preparation, discuss the function and responsibilities of each member of the team. I talk more about the individual roles in Element 29.

The idea of a lone, charismatic negotiator skillfully navigating complex deals is an attractive but often unrealistic image. Successful negotiations, especially those of significant magnitude, demand a variety of skills, perspectives, and expertise that one person alone cannot provide. That's where the power of a team comes into play.

A well-constructed negotiation team is not just a group of individuals working together. It's a carefully selected unit where each member's strengths complement the weaknesses of others. For example, one member's analytical skills can provide critical insights into the quantitative aspects of the negotiation, while another's emotional intelligence can be crucial in building rapport and understanding nonverbal cues.

The team's composition should be deliberate, with clear roles and responsibilities for each member. This clarity ensures that everyone knows their function in the negotiation, leading to a more streamlined and effective process. One team member might lead the discussions, another could be responsible for tracking agreements and taking notes, and a third might focus on observing and interpreting the reactions of the opposing party.

This team approach extends to preparation and strategizing as well. Team members can collectively challenge assumptions, refine strategies, and anticipate challenges. Such collaborative preparation ensures a well-rounded and robust approach to the negotiation table.

In the subsequent elements, I explore the specific roles within a negotiation team and how each contributes to the team's success. Drawing from both simulated and real-life examples, I demonstrate why a team approach is not just beneficial but is essential for effective negotiations in any significant context.

ELEMENT 29

Division of Roles on the Team

A successful negotiation team spends more time preparing and works with an agenda. They are used to always summing up before they move from one discussion point to the next and they take joint notes on the board. There should be many breaks with the purpose of establishing within the group whether they are on the right track and agreeing on a joint attitude internally in the negotiation delegations.

This way of cooperating can seem stiff and formal to many people, but you need such discipline before you can let go and improvise without entirely losing control of the negotiation.

The traditional division of roles with the manager as the negotiation leader and the different experts in charge of each their part functions poorly. For example, consider when a customer asks the supplier: "Is it possible to equip the data system with more functions that make day-and-night work possible?" Before the negotiation leader on the seller's side has had time to formulate the necessary questions about the customer's new needs, the systems specialist takes over: "We have already done that for another customer and their system works very well. We do not need to make new changes in order to equip your system with similar functions." The sales manager saw an opportunity to sell and once again receive payment for the expertise built up, but in their eagerness to demonstrate how clever they are, the systems specialist has given it all away for free.

In order not to fall into this trap, the team should have done as follows. Until the group is properly welded together and a natural and well-functioning role division has set in, the negotiators should maintain a strict discipline and divide the roles in a different way.

- **A negotiation leader:** Choose the person who is best with words and not automatically the person who has the highest status, formally speaking. In principle, the negotiation leader is the only one who talks. The negotiation leader does not have to be the boss.

- **A listener and an observer:** Choose a negotiator who has sufficient experience to follow and understand the negotiation game. This person can, if possible, sit somewhat away from the negotiation table and take continuous notes. During each break, it is the observer's job to provide the others with a picture of how the negotiations are progressing, what signals the opponent is sending out, and how the opponent has reacted to the negotiation leader's own propositions. The negotiation leader must be able to use the observer for summaries during the negotiations.

- **Someone who manages "the economy":** What have you given away? What have you got in return? What do the opponent's demands entail? How large a scope is left? Where are you now in the negotiations in relation to your goals?

- **The possible experts who address different issues:** The group must decide how they want to communicate internally during the negotiations. Should they pass messages? Can they whisper, or do they need to take breaks?

The group must agree that, before anyone else other than the negotiation leader speaks, they must be given a signal from this person.

If the leader strays onto thin ice, becomes too aggressive, or finds themself in a situation where they have no answer, the others should intervene to suggest a break.

The group must agree to have a break prior to all important decisions, whereby everybody can speak.

ELEMENT 30

The Trial Balloon and Highball/Lowball Techniques

In the nuanced world of negotiation, certain tactics stand out for their strategic impact. Among these, the *trial balloon* and *highball/lowball* techniques are particularly noteworthy for their psychological and strategic influence. This element delves into these tactics, offering insights into their effective application and potential pitfalls.

The Trial Balloon: Testing the Waters

The trial balloon is a subtle yet powerful tactic used to gauge the other party's reaction to a proposal without committing to it fully. It involves floating an idea or suggestion indirectly to observe how it is received. This tactic allows the negotiator to gather valuable information about the other party's preferences, limits, and flexibility without revealing their actual position or intention.

Here are the key elements of the trial balloon technique:

- **Subtlety:** The proposal should be presented in a manner that doesn't commit you to the position.
- **Observation:** Pay close attention to verbal and nonverbal cues from the counterpart to gauge their reaction.
- **Flexibility:** Be prepared to retract or adjust the proposal based on the feedback received.
- **Strategic use:** Employ this tactic to explore possibilities in complex negotiations where direct proposals might be risky or premature.

The Highball/Lowball Technique: Setting the Negotiation Range

The highball (for sellers) and lowball (for buyers) tactics involve making a deliberately extreme initial offer, knowing it will not be accepted but will shift the negotiation range to your advantage. This technique establishes a starting point from which you can make concessions while still aiming for a favorable outcome.

Effective application of highball/lowball tactics:

- **Initial offer:** Set your initial offer far enough from your target to allow room for concessions but close enough to be taken seriously.
- **Anchoring effect:** This initial extreme position can anchor the subsequent negotiation discussions and influence the final agreement.
- **Concession strategy:** Plan a series of concessions in advance to gradually move the negotiation toward your desired outcome.
- **Credibility:** Ensure that your initial offer, while aggressive, is still within the realms of reason to maintain credibility.

Ethical Considerations and Risks

While these tactics can be effective, they must be used ethically and with consideration of the potential risks. Overuse or misuse can lead to a breakdown in negotiations, damage relationships, move the negotiation into zero-sum, harm your reputation, or harm any trust built in the relationship. It's crucial to balance these tactics with a genuine intention to find mutually beneficial solutions. I generally do not suggest using either of these tools in a collaborative negotiation environment.

The trial balloon and highball/lowball tactics are nuanced tools in the negotiator's arsenal. Used judiciously, they can significantly influence the direction and outcome of negotiations. However, the key to their success lies not only in their strategic implementation but also in the negotiator's ability to maintain ethical standards, build trust, and foster long-term relationships. By mastering these tactics, negotiators can enhance their strategic effectiveness while upholding the principles of smart partnership and ethical negotiation.

ELEMENT 31

Starting Point, Threshold of Pain, and Target

Understanding your starting point, threshold of pain, and target is crucial before entering any negotiation. Not knowing these three elements is akin to embarking on a journey without knowing your point of departure, destination, or the time you will arrive.

If you are a supplier, it's imperative to determine these three positions before commencing negotiations. Consider this scenario: You propose a price of $40,000 to a buyer. This figure represents your starting point. Your target might be to secure $38,000, while your threshold of pain—the minimum price you're willing to accept—could be, say, $36,000.

Conversely, if you're the buyer in the same negotiation, your starting point, threshold of pain, and target will likely differ significantly. Your starting point would be the supplier's quoted price of $40,000. Your threshold of pain could be based on an alternative supplier's price, possibly $38,000, and your target might be to negotiate down to $37,000.

During the negotiation, maintaining a clear understanding of your financial status is essential. This is one of the reasons I advocate for team-based negotiations. Within a team, you can designate a *calculator*—someone responsible for handling the calculations and continually updating the team on the real-time financial situation. Leading the negotiation team can be challenging, as it requires balancing an understanding of various variables while strategizing, asking questions, listening, and so forth.

By being aware of these aspects, you can navigate negotiations more effectively, increasing your chances of reaching a desirable outcome.

ELEMENT 32

Variables

The concept of NegoEconomics, the asymmetric value, arises, as is known, through asymmetric values or costs (for a full description of NegoEconomics, see Element 20). One party has higher costs than the other, which is why the task is placed with the owner of the lowest cost.

A majority of, if not all, negotiations are negotiated on too few variables. "The usual suspects," as I call them. By limiting ourselves to a few variables, we make an agreement harder to achieve and certainly leave value on the table.

The nonprofit organization World Commerce & Contracting conducts a yearly global survey identifying the most negotiated variables. Every year the top 10 are almost identical:

- Limitation of liability
- Price/charge/price changes
- Indemnities
- Liquidated damages
- Termination
- Scope and goals/specification
- Payment/payment options
- Warranty
- Cybersecurity/data privacy
- Intellectual property and responsibilities of the parties

The scary part is that only two to three of these variables generate NegoEconomics—scope and goals, specification, payment, and warranty.

I often conduct brainstorming tasks where the client's purpose is to think outside the box and "invent" as many new variables as possible. However, there is often a task before the creativity task, and that is to establish the current variables. Ask yourself right now, what variables does your organization negotiate on?

Is it:

- Price
- Delivery time

- Quality
- Inventory
- Payment terms
- Operational efficiency
- Specification
- Discount

I hope you have more than the aforementioned, but many purchasing or sales organizations I visit look at me in amazement when I challenge them on variables.

How many variables exist in a car purchase? Many would immediately say price! Which of course is a variable. But besides price, what else do we have? I set out to investigate the matter and came up with more than 52 variables—all crucial for a good deal!

How many exist in a commercial negotiation of much greater value and complexity? I have listed a gross list of variables that might be used. It is far from exhaustive, and is only meant as inspiration:

1. Project discounts
2. In store
3. Customer study trips
4. Payment of shelf goods
5. Space management
6. Education (product)
7. Calculation office
8. Product news exclusivity
9. Dealer exclusivity
10. Sales promotion
11. Internet advertising
12. Packaging
13. Code of conduct
14. Green profile
15. Climate policy
16. Recycling policy
17. Kam—assortment strategy
18. Reciprocal sales
19. Company trips
20. Profile clothing
21. Store fixtures
22. Package size
23. Complaint handling
24. Franco delivery
25. Special order conditions
26. Postage
27. Electronic discount
28. Seasonal orders
29. Innovation
30. Capitalization of shared costs
31. Behavior bonus
32. Marketing plan
33. Ergonomics
34. Safety
35. Sustainable production
36. Primary choice as private label
37. TV advertising
38. Loyalty program
39. Trade fairs
40. Consignment stock

41. Data sharing
42. Joint visits
43. Warehouse location
44. Online trading
45. Labels
46. Price/cost price
47. Price increase
48. Terms for price increase (deferred price increase)
49. Base price
50. Technical specifications
51. Volume
52. Discount rate
53. Goods discount
54. Central warehouse discount
55. Bonus
56. Annual bonus
57. Volume bonus
58. Bonus payment (monthly on account, annually)
59. Alternative product (in relation to what the specification prescribes)
60. Quality
61. Penalty/sanctions (e.g., if not delivered and stock runs out)
62. Complaint
63. Lectures (e.g., for user groups)
64. Education and training
65. Delivery terms

66. 24-hour delivery to departments
67. Express delivery
68. Delivered free
69. Stocking
70. Supplier vs. region
71. Central vs. decentralized
72. Electronic invoicing
73. Payment terms
74. Discount for cash payment
75. Advance
76. Service
77. Documentation
78. Transport
79. Free transport
80. Warranty
81. Delivery date
82. Delivery size (pcs., package size, whole pallets, etc.)
83. Instruments for co-delivery
84. Return policy
85. Frequency of purchases
86. Ongoing meetings with the supplier
87. Contract length
88. Extension period
89. Payment of offers in connection with tenders
90. Liability
91. Insurance
92. Options

Your assignment is to develop more variables in your negotiation.

ELEMENT 33

The Art of Managing Non-Negotiables

In the intricate world of negotiation, a key to success lies not only in identifying and leveraging your variables for optimal NegoEconomics but also in adeptly handling non-negotiable variables. These are elements that, due to constraints like company policies or legal regulations, remain inflexible and require a different strategic approach. For example, your management doesn't allow you to change delivery terms, or you are legally prevented from asking for a longer line of credit from the supplier.

Non-negotiables, by their nature, may seem to limit the negotiation space. However, with strategic transparency and understanding, they can be managed effectively. When engaging in collaborative negotiations, especially within partnerships or SMARTnerships, it's crucial to declare non-negotiable variables early on. This approach fosters trust and sets clear boundaries for the negotiation process. Moreover, explaining the rationale behind these non-negotiables can maintain, and even elevate, the level of trust, ensuring a smoother negotiation flow.

However, the way these non-negotiables are communicated is key. Simply stating that certain variables are off-limits, without offering explanations, can lead to a breakdown in communication and potentially shut down the negotiation entirely. It's important to be empathetic and consider the perspective of the other party, understanding their potential non-negotiables as well. This mutual respect can foster a more collaborative environment and lead to mutually beneficial outcomes.

In contrast, in a positional or zero-sum negotiation approach, there might be a temptation to conceal non-negotiable elements, using them as tactical leverage. Remember, though, that such tactics often impede the emergence of NegoEconomics, as they focus on dividing a fixed pie rather than expanding it.

To navigate non-negotiables successfully, consider leveraging them to redirect negotiations toward more productive avenues. For example, a budget limit might lead to creative solutions or alternative offerings. Flexibility in addressing and working around non-negotiables can often lead to innovative solutions that satisfy both parties' core interests.

Furthermore, handling non-negotiables with respect and understanding can build long-term relationships. Demonstrating a willingness to work within constraints shows reliability and can build trust, invaluable in long-term business relationships. Sometimes, educating your counterpart about the reasons behind your non-negotiables serves not only to explain your position but also to increase mutual understanding.

In mastering the art of negotiation, recognizing and adeptly managing non-negotiable variables is not just a strategy but a necessity for excelling in smart partnership negotiations. This element emphasizes not just the challenges but also the opportunities presented by non-negotiables, offering a comprehensive and nuanced view of their role in successful NegoEconomics.

ELEMENT 34

Cross-Cultural Negotiations

In today's global business landscape, the traditional concept of an "international assignment" is evolving rapidly. The days when an individual, possibly with family, was sent overseas for two or three years are still here, but now, the permutations of international business activities are far more varied and complex.

Businesspeople today might find themselves on short-term assignments, ranging from a month to half a year in a different country. Others are frequent travelers, continuously visiting subsidiaries and clients across the globe. Some manage long-distance teams, collaborating on new products for markets in other countries. These varied scenarios have a significant impact on how we understand and engage in cross-cultural interactions, especially in negotiations.

Negotiations involving parties from different cultures carry an increased risk of misunderstandings, insults, and mutual distrust. Navigating these cultural differences requires heightened awareness and skill. Even seasoned politicians and business leaders occasionally falter, creating conflicts over value norms and exacerbating tensions. This begs the question: What challenges might arise when employees with less experience in these arenas enter the fray?

My experience, drawn from thousands of negotiations, has shown that personal chemistry is a critical factor in successful international business relationships. If there's a lack of rapport between negotiators and potential partners, establishing a long-term cooperative agreement becomes exceedingly difficult. In such scenarios, energies are often diverted to conflict, with each party seeking success at the other's expense.

We've all experienced meetings where rapport was immediate, as well as those where we were on guard or even dismissive from the outset. This "personal chemistry" is a complex interplay of our sensory perceptions—what we see, smell, and hear—and is shaped within seconds. Our reactions, influenced by past experiences, knowledge, and preconceptions, not only reveal much about ourselves but also significantly influence the outcome of negotiations. The challenge lies in discerning whether to trust these initial perceptions or to give others a chance, resisting the sway of preconceptions and happenstance.

It's important to remember that cross-cultural issues aren't confined to international travel. Culture clashes can occur within the same country or even within the same company, as every department in an organization represents a unique "culture." Consider the distinct cultures of the C-suite, sales, production, logistics, legal, and finance departments, to name a few.

For successful international negotiations, awareness of cultural nuances is crucial. The next section contains a checklist to consider for navigating these complexities effectively.

Checklist for International Negotiations

- ☐ **Interpersonal dynamics:** Recognize that negotiations can fail if relationships between the parties are strained.
- ☐ **Attire:** Understand appropriate dress codes.
- ☐ **Physical space and contact:** Be aware of personal space norms and physical gestures.
- ☐ **Gender dynamics:** Acknowledge and respect differences in men-women relations.
- ☐ **Dining etiquette:** Be familiar with mealtime customs.
- ☐ **Gift-giving:** Know the cultural significance and appropriateness of gifts.
- ☐ **Time perception:** Respect different attitudes toward time.
- ☐ **Small talk:** Learn the value of casual conversation, like discussing the weather. (See Element 59.)
- ☐ **Language barriers:** Be mindful of challenges when negotiating in a foreign language.
- ☐ **Individual vs. group orientations:** Understand the emphasis on individualism versus collectivism.
- ☐ **Formalities:** Pay attention to forms of address, names, titles, and considerations around age.
- ☐ **Sensitive topics:** Be cautious about discussing religion and politics.
- ☐ **Building trust:** Recognize the varying ways trust is established and maintained.

By paying close attention to these areas, negotiators can navigate the intricate landscape of cross-cultural negotiations with greater skill and sensitivity, leading to more successful outcomes.

ELEMENT 35

Emotions, Stress, and Personal Chemistry

In negotiations, we often think of ourselves as rational beings, engaging in predictable behaviors. However, the reality is that negotiations are a psychological game where rational and predictable behaviors are mixed with unknown and irrational behaviors. You can change your behavior, but you cannot change your counterpart. By understanding yourself better, you understand your counterpart better, and you get a chance to adapt to the situation.

Negotiations aim to satisfy different types of needs—both material and psychological. Material needs are often synonymous with a company's needs, measured and expressed in monetary terms, market shares, product features, and delivery reliability. At a superficial glance, negotiations revolve around these material needs. However, psychological needs are equally important and significantly impact individual negotiators, often more than most of us would admit. These are the negotiators' own needs, including:

- **Self-actualization:** Achieving budget goals, conquering new markets, trying new technology, and the freedom to follow your own path.
- **Social needs:** Gaining respect, appreciation, and being liked by others. This can be achieved by meeting material goals, appearing as a winner (which may mean the counterpart loses), reaching an agreement with two winners, showing competence, making friends at the negotiation table, or not losing face.
- **Security:** Avoiding technical and commercial risks in negotiations. New technology and new suppliers are perceived as dangerous. Settling for meeting the budget instead of aiming for maximum profit. Avoiding unknown people and environments.
- **Need for revenge:** The desire to retaliate.
- **Need for self-assertion:** Showing yourself to be more competent, bigger, and stronger than others. Wanting to control and manipulate others.

For more on how people are driven by their needs, you can look up Maslow's theories and his hierarchy of needs.

Personal Chemistry Is More Important Than Technique

Negotiations are largely about emotions. Whether an agreement is reached often depends on how the parties function socially. If they enjoy each other's company and feel a sense of belonging and respect, this facilitates an agreement. What makes personal chemistry work between two people can have the opposite effect on others. Success in negotiations doesn't require you to violate your personality and adopt a contrived and rehearsed behavior. This feels false and often has the opposite effect in many relationships.

Emotions spread rapidly. Negative or positive signals put the recipient in a negative or positive mood in fractions of a second. Long before our conscious mind perceives the signal, we react to it. We are affected whether we want to be or not.

You must become aware of what makes things sometimes work and sometimes not in your relationships with partners. Be aware of the type of signals that others may be sensitive to. Use this knowledge constructively.

The Importance of Communication and Awareness

Negotiations involve constantly sending out various signals. You want to influence, inform, impress, manipulate, and demonstrate. Some signals are conscious and well-formulated, while others you may be more or less unaware of. The interplay between two people is based on emotional reactions that bounce back and forth between them. To get on the same wavelength and achieve good communication, the traffic needs to be fast and smooth. If one person has an expressionless face, they are a poor sender. If the other reacts slowly to incoming signals, they are a poor receiver, and communication between them is poor.

Negotiators can be swept away and manipulated when chemistry works. They stop making rational decisions. In the hands of a less scrupulous counterpart, you can become naive.

Rational Decision-Making: A Myth

Negotiators are irrational. Negotiation is a psychological game where people try to satisfy their needs. The thoroughly rational decision-maker does not exist. In 1978, Herbert Simon received the Nobel Prize in economics for helping us out of the delusion of the decision-maker as a superhuman.

That you would rather do business with people you like, trust, and feel a kinship with, rather than chase after what best meets your technical and economic needs, may seem irrational. But it shows that your psychological needs are more important than your material needs, and your decision, in your eyes, is highly rational.

For your decisions to be perceived as rational, your values and experiences must align with those of your counterpart. You must have an identical perception of the reality you are negotiating about. There is no objective truth; your view is no more true than your counterpart's, and your values are not more correct than theirs. There are different perceptions of what has been and how what is to come should be described and valued. Negotiators always work from different maps.

Choosing Between Alternatives

To choose and justify your choice, different alternatives must be evaluated and compared. The evaluation is facilitated if everything that distinguishes the alternatives is translated into the same currency (e.g., money). You zero out the alternatives and choose the one that gives you the best value.

It is easy to calculate what shorter delivery time, longer life span, better warranties, faster service, higher quality, lower operating costs, and better payment terms are worth. The differences are calculated based on the added values and additional costs that arise. Comparisons are made with LCC calculations, where one tries to calculate the cost of a system's entire life span. But whether these calculations can be fair is another matter. The accelerating rate of change can overturn the assumptions for the calculation even before the system is delivered. Decision-makers easily overlook benefits, costs, or risks that affect someone else's account. The subjective valuations increase when evaluating differences due to proximity, when you belong to the same culture and speak the same language, when you have previous experience with each other, when you have risks with new solutions, and when you feel security with proven constructions.

It becomes even more difficult when you mix in emotions. For example, consider two seemingly equivalent houses that are priced at 2.2 million and 2.8 million USD. They were built the same year, have equally large spaces, and are of the same quality. When the husband and wife have to make their choice, the wife says:

WIFE   Let's take the one that costs 2.8 million.
HUSBAND   Why? It's 600,000 more and doesn't seem to be in better condition.
WIFE   I like that house; it had a lovely atmosphere. A happy family lived in it.
HUSBAND   But what was wrong with the other house? It can't cost that much to repaint some of the rooms if the colors were wrong.
WIFE   I don't like the other house. It didn't feel good; it had bad vibes.
HUSBAND   What are you talking about?
WIFE   Didn't you notice that it was a divorce house?

The husband faces a difficult situation. He does not think that the house his wife wants has an added value of 600,000. He does not feel any vibrations, positive or negative. Should he accept her assessment and realize that the feeling for her is worth 600,000, or should he start to argue, then she might be right that it will become a divorce house. Should he give up his position? Is there a compromise solution, a third house? He can also ask himself, isn't his wife worth these 600,000? Shouldn't he consider it a good investment in future love and happiness?

Can and should all values be measured by a material yardstick? No! There are countless examples of how so-called soft variables have a greater impact than technical performance. In many industries, we must take into account emotions and imagination. When Apple's founder Steve Jobs was asked why the new operating system was so good, he answered: "The buttons on the screen are so attractively designed that you want to lick them." To attract some customers, intense experiences are required. For example, Mercedes Benz tried to attract female buyers in the United States with a commercial where a woman enjoys driving the car so much that she has an orgasm after 20 seconds.

Irrational or Rational?

Decisions made by the counterpart often seem irrational. What is rational for you does not have to be rational for others. You may want to sell the latest model of a product, the one that shows your technical superiority. You feel pride in your construction and that you are leading the technical development. To your great surprise, the buyer wants to buy the model you launched five years ago. You believe you have very strong arguments for why they should take the latest model instead. It has superior performance and you can show with a simple calculation that it will be more economical. Yet the buyer insists on buying the old model. This is incomprehensible to you.

You consider them ignorant and stupid; they don't recognize their own best interest. You argue and try to open their eyes. In the buyer's eyes, you come across as a persistent and unusually dense seller who does not respect their choice. The buyer's choice, the five-year-old model, seen against the backdrop of their needs and valuations, may be a correct choice. They do not need the new technology, lack trained personnel for it, and may not be able to utilize its features. What you consider to be strong technical arguments are worthless from their point of view.

You can assume that your counterpart, unconsciously, weighs the wallet, the heart, and the ethics when making decisions and that they probably place a different weight on these three factors than you do. This does not make their choice better or worse than yours, just different. The more knowledge you have about your counterpart, the greater the likelihood that you will hit the mark with your sales pitch.

Constructive Negotiations Require a Balance between Feeling and Reason

Your judgment is influenced by your feelings. If you find yourself in a situation where you feel anger, insecurity, or if you are threatened and stressed, your rational thought process is short-circuited and you respond with an emotional reaction, fight or flight.

Say you are waiting for a calculation from a colleague. They have forgotten their promise to you and when you remind them, they answer: Sorry I forgot you. I can get the documents to you by the middle of next week. You get angry and answer: *I can do it without your help.*

You make a hasty decision rather than waiting, even though you have time. If your decision later turns out to be incorrect and costly, who is to blame for this if not your colleague?

In another context, you feel enthusiasm and exuberance at the first meeting with a counterpart. Thoughts and ideas coincide. Together you decide to start a collaboration, but it does not take long before you realize that you have overlooked important facts and made a hasty decision. The judgment has been influenced by positive feelings, but the decision was as incorrect as when you felt negative feelings in the previous case.

For example, say you have been looking for a house for a couple of years. Finally, you find the house you are looking for. The seller has several speculators and sells the house at auction. The bidding is approaching ever higher levels. You are one of four interested parties. Everyone gets to submit written final bids and you go significantly higher than you originally thought. The seller contacts you again and says: You are the second highest; if you want the house you have to go up another 50,000. On the spot, you raise your bid. It is difficult to negotiate with reason when it comes to your own coveted needs. Intense feelings dominate over reason.

In a discussion about a collaboration, your prospective partner starts to hesitate and says: "We can't afford to go in on these terms, the risk is too great." Coldly you answer: "You do as you want, but I don't think you've calculated properly on the project."

Communication risks suffering if you do not try to show some emotion and understanding for your counterpart. If you do not understand what the counterpart feels when they talk about the risks that are too great, it becomes difficult for you to convince them. You mark a clear emotional coldness with the words: *You do as you want.* You cannot understand what the counterpart feels because you do not even ask them to expound on their thoughts.

The counterpart presents their proposal for a solution and you answer: "Now you are thinking wrong. You understand that the environmental emissions will increase if we go for your proposal." The counterpart locks up; they perceive the criticism as personal. If you had instead answered: "I wonder how this affects the environmentally hazardous emissions?" the likelihood would have increased that you could enter into a constructive dialogue.

When Emotions Take Over

- **Take a break:** Leave the negotiation room, make coffee, go to the bathroom. If you stay, the pressure that triggered your strong emotions continues. Former Prime Minister Thorbjörn Fälldin explains how he got out of many difficult and emotionally charged political negotiations by sitting quietly and sucking on his pipe. Sooner or later, the others calmed down and then it was possible to talk to them again.
- **Count to 10:** Before you get to 10, rational thinking may start.
- **Consult with someone else:** If your arguments no longer hold when you present the situation to others, something is missing.
- **Talk about the feelings:** Tell what you feel: "I get angry and feel exploited every time you try to take . . ."
- **Be mentally prepared for strong emotions to arise during the negotiation:** Take a break when it gets hot.
- **Create a positive climate:** Talk about the weather, offer coffee, and avoid surprising the counterpart. Don't put them in situations where they can't answer and where they lose face.

When Decisions Are Based on Incomplete Information

You do not have a clear and complete overview of your own goals, values, available alternatives, decision variables, and previous events. You rarely even take into account a few alternatives but often choose one that in the best possible way ties in with previous solutions. You are not guided by material needs. You have a limited ability to only weigh in facts when making decisions. You are influenced by your own psychological needs, which you usually unaware of. You have a need for power, security, approval. You do not want to lose face; you want to perform good material results or you want to take revenge on a counterpart.

Humans are not machines or mere complements to them. The corporate economic image of humans as rational decision-makers is based on an outdated perception of the company, human beings, and machinery as a technical and material system. Therefore, you cannot influence your counterpart solely with a massive technical or economic argumentation backed by test protocols, calculations, and all sorts of documentation. Often, more factual information is used in negotiations than what the counterpart can assimilate. This creates confusion, uncertainty, and suspicion. It's easy to talk a deal to death but hard to kill it with silence.

You must learn to approach the counterpart also on an emotional level. It's important to get the "personal chemistry" to work. Use your common sense to create a positive atmosphere, where understanding for each other and respect for each other's needs and values result in cooperation.

Unfortunately, I see that many negotiators, especially in technically advanced companies, are completely locked into their machines, nuts, and bolts. They assume they can only achieve results at the negotiation table using "factual" methods and technical reasoning. These negotiators are strong and rational as long as the negotiation revolves around technology and performance. When the technical negotiation is over and the haggling begins, they become uncertain. They feel uncomfortable with the bargaining. Their negotiation goals are set low, just to stay within the frame they have. Instead of negotiating toward an optimal solution, they settle as soon as they reach their lower limit. The confidence they exude as long as they can stick to the old well-known technical reasoning disappears.

It is dangerous to build all success in business solely by having a strong position, based on technical advantages or monopolies. The time is past when industries can base their successes on technical superiority or an undervalued currency. A technical advantage can be eradicated within a month. In many industries, competitors monitor and copy each other so effectively that the actual differences between their products are negligible. Instead, they differentiate themselves by building strong brands. This involves communicating emotions, success, safety, audacity, boundary-crossing, moderation, and sex.

When the power position based on a technical advantage disappears, other methods are required at the negotiation table. Many companies and organizations can testify to this.

Identifying Your Counterpart's Needs

Before you can present a proposal and start arguing for it, you must understand your counterpart's needs. This is a truism that is often violated in negotiations. Do not assume that the counterpart has specified all their needs in the request. The request often contains many technical and economic demands and wishes, but the background as to why these demands are made is missing. Therefore, you do not know which needs the buyer wants to satisfy. The personal, psychological needs are never apparent from the request. For the solution and the arguments you put forward to be accepted by and influence the counterpart, they must feel relevant (i.e., they must correspond to their needs).

For example, a manufacturer was about to sell his company. Together with the board and the bank, it was valued. An acceptable bid was supposed to be between 5 and 10 million USD. Therefore, joy was great when they received three bids, all exceeding 10 million.

Bidder A offered 14 million, B offered 16 million, and C offered 21 million. The manufacturer wanted to accept C's bid right away. This bid was so much higher than the other two that further negotiations with them were considered uninteresting.

Many negotiators would have reacted in the same way as the manufacturer. But after consulting with me, he did not take C's bid. He did not know enough about why A, B, and C wanted to buy his company, that is, what needs they wanted to meet with the purchase. If he did not know the buyers' needs, he also did not know what the company was worth to them, and he could not judge whether their bids were reasonable and negotiable.

All were called to negotiation and asked to explain how they intended to run the company further. A was interested in premises and machinery and planned to run a completely different operation. They had no intention of raising their bid. B was interested in the industrial property. They planned to sell the machines and rent out the property. C was interested in the manufacturing the manufacturer had, his products, and established brand.

The needs of the buyers did not compete with each other and explained the differences between the bids. In the end, C bought the manufacturing and sales rights to the products and decided to move production abroad. C was spared the work of having to sell off the rest of the company himself. B bought the property and leased it to A, who bought the machines.

The manufacturer got over 30 million for his company and felt like a winner. A, B, and C also felt like winners; they all had their needs met but at a lower cost than they initially thought. The involved parties were wise enough to open up at the negotiation table instead of driving a hard line with prepared arguments. It became a collaborative negotiation where significant added value was created.

Negotiations and Stress

Your negotiation ability is impaired if you are forced to negotiate under undue stress. A certain amount of stress can be beneficial. It raises your performance level. Where the threshold lies in which stress goes from being beneficial to harmful varies from person to person. Many events in connection with negotiations easily create stress that lies above this threshold.

The Classic Stress Reaction

When the body perceives stress signals, adrenaline is released. This is a defense mechanism that raises our readiness for physical activity. It's often called fight or flight. Maximum power goes to the muscles, while the brain, normally a major consumer of energy, goes into standby mode. This blocks our intellect; we can no longer think rationally or access previous experiences and knowledge. The brain's creative and critical functions are blocked. The blood's coagulation ability increases.

When we can no longer make rational decisions, we act on instinct. This is a defense mechanism that has remained with us from ancient days. We are designed to survive.

How Our Brain Works

When humans developed, they first gained the ability to deal with their emotional and instinctive feelings. Faced with threatening situations, they learned to take up fight or flee. This helped us survive, but at the same time, it hampered our ability to think logically.

The rational brain developed later and gave us the ability to hold back instinctive reactions while threatening circumstances blocked our rational thought process.

The cerebral cortex is the seat of the higher mental functions, thinking, and consciousness in humans. In the middle of the brain is the reception center for our sensory impressions, sight, and hearing. Sensory impressions are sent from this center, the thalamus, to the cerebral cortex for processing.

The "normal" path for a sensory impression is as follows: The eye perceives, the thalamus receives the signal and sends it on to the cerebral cortex where the processing takes place, and then comes the emotional reaction. We walk on a path. The eye sees a snake. The signal is processed in the cerebral cortex, and we become aware that it is a snake lying in front of us. We feel fear.

We can experience fear without being aware of the real cause. The signal that triggered our fear never passed the cerebral cortex where our thinking and consciousness reside. The nerve pathway for emotional reactions does not go through the cerebral cortex but is evoked outside the control of consciousness and reason.

During our first years of life, large amounts of emotional information, which never reach the level of consciousness, are fed into our brain. This shapes emotional patterns that become permanent and lead to actions that we ourselves may be alien to, such as taking up the fight or fleeing instead of trying to handle our stress in a more balanced way.

Choosing Between Fight or Flight

A highly stressed person is not in their full senses. They are faced with the choice of fight or flight. In a negotiation, we do not physically attack the counterpart, but do so with words. We move from negotiation to verbal combat. This can quickly escalate, and we let out one stupid comment after the other.

We flee from the negotiation table by making unilateral concessions—concessions that we cannot clearly oversee or find alternatives to. Negative aspects of our personality are reinforced. A negotiator who cannot escape the stressful situation created by their counterpart will pressure themselves to seek every available form of relief, usually by making concessions. Stressful moves have therefore become one of the combative negotiator's most important weapons.

The pause is often the best counter-tactic to restore balance. Try to anticipate the stressful moments that may arise and prepare yourself for how to handle them. This raises your stress tolerance, and you will react less intensely and emotionally to the counterpart's moves.

Time Stress

Time stress occurs when you discover that you will not meet an important deadline. You are negotiating in a foreign country. The negotiations drag on, and an agreement seems distant. At the same time, the day you have to fly home is approaching. Your holiday is about to start, and the whole family is booked on a charter trip. A long-planned, long-awaited, and much-needed holiday for all of you is just around the corner. Finally, the day arrives—the day you have to fly home. The agreement is not yet in the harbor. In the choice situation you find yourself in, you may only see three alternatives:

- Skip the holiday with your family and continue the negotiations.
- Force an agreement by lowering your ambition level.
- Realize that you have failed and go home.

Do not accept the deadline set by the counterpart. Negotiate a new time. Never inform them of your deadlines so that they can actively, by delaying the negotiation, put you in a time crunch.

If you are forced to negotiate under time pressure, you should discuss the issues the counterpart wants to bring up but postpone your decisions. Try to gather as much decision-making material as possible and ask to come back. If a deadline is set to try to pressure you, you can try to get out of it in one of the following ways:

- "I don't know how we solve this. We need to schedule a new meeting." You "give up" and interrupt the negotiation to wait out the counterpart. They might be pressured by their own deadline and must therefore try to get the negotiation going.
- Have ice in your stomach and test the counterpart. "If you demand an answer today, it will be no, but give me one more day, and I may be able to give you a positive answer." You entice with a favor to get a time respite.

Stress Caused by Negative Expectations

There are clear pitfalls if you enter the negotiation with negative expectations:

- "It's no use, they will never agree to this."
- "Cooperation is pointless, they are just out for combat and devilry."

The result is as you expect; you ensure that your expectations are fulfilled. Remember that as long as negotiations are ongoing, anything is possible.

Situational Stress

You find yourself in a situation where you risk "losing face" and being exposed to the counterpart's disapproval. You have, for example, forgotten your documents at home, made gross miscalculations, or forgotten to send promised documents to the counterpart. You avoid stress of this kind by being well prepared. If disaster should strike, admit your mistake and apologize. Avoid going into a defensive position; it only worsens your situation.

Confrontation Stress

Confrontation stress is caused by other people. The rules for negotiations that you are used to or expected no longer govern the counterpart's behavior. You may have experienced an unconscious confrontation, a culture shock, or a deliberate provocation where the counterpart uses stress as a weapon. You can avoid this by informing yourself in advance about the cultural peculiarities you may encounter in different markets.

If the provocation is deliberate, take a break in the negotiation. Use the break to relax and get back into balance. Avoid responding to the provocation, do not exaggerate it, and do not lose sight of the goal of the negotiation. Read more about culture shocks in Element 34.

Sometimes it can be good to try to change the place and environment for the negotiations or delay the conflict the counterpart has played up. Spend some time in socializing and relax with the counterpart over food and drink. Avoid any discussion about the negotiations. Meet one of your counterparts informally and solve the situation one-on-one. Or do as the Finns do, and settle it in the sauna.

Examples of Stress Signals

You should learn to recognize the signals your own body sends out when your stress levels increase. When stress comes, take a break to come back into balance:

- Your heart and circulation increase. Your blood pressure increases and your pulse increases and becomes stronger. All color can disappear from your face.
- Your lungs expand. Breathing increases, and blowing sounds from strong breaths can be perceived. Smokers take heavy puffs.
- Your muscles tense. You suffer from headaches because you tense your neck muscles.
- You start to sweat. Your mouth dries out, and you have problems with your voice. You cough and clear your throat.
- You need to go to the toilet to urinate.
- You adopt a defensive position with your crossed arms over your chest.

- You increase the physical distance to your counterpart; you need a larger territory.
- One hand starts involuntarily and unconsciously touching your face.
- Your blinking frequency increases four to five times.
- Blood is drawn away from your fingers, and they become cold.

Note that all these signals are individual and can be confused. A person with crossed arms does not necessarily have to be stressed or need to protect themselves.

Stress-Inducing Behaviors

Examples of moves that combative negotiators engage in:

- Interrupts the counterpart, talks in their mouth, and counters everything. Note, however, that this is not perceived as stressful in all cultures. In France, for example, one expects to be interrupted.
- Shows disinterest, such as by refusing eye contact, sitting, and filling in papers while the counterpart speaks.
- Suppresses their body language.
- Does not answer questions.
- Responds with standard arguments, such as, "We have always done it this way."
- Shows confusion and insecurity.

ELEMENT 36

Prioritizing Variables: The Key to NegoEconomics

The concept of NegoEconomics is pivotal. It is defined by the creation of asymmetric values or costs, where tasks are strategically placed with the party that bears the lowest cost. This chapter aims to guide negotiators in identifying and prioritizing variables that generate significant NegoEconomics, thereby optimizing negotiation outcomes.

The Trap of Limited Variables

Many negotiations fall into the trap of focusing on a limited set of variables—the "usual suspects" like price, scope, and warranty. This limited view often leads to leaving valuable opportunities on the table. The key is to expand your variable horizon, going beyond the traditional to explore more innovative and impactful variables.

Identifying and Expanding Variables

The first step is to establish current negotiation variables, which typically include price, delivery time, quality, and payment terms. However, this is just the starting point. As noted earlier, a car purchase alone can involve more than 52 variables. In more complex commercial negotiations, the number can be even higher. A "gross list" of potential variables is provided, ranging from project discounts to climate policy and ergonomics, serving as an inspiration for negotiators to think creatively.

Prioritization for NegoEconomics

With a comprehensive list of potential variables, the challenge lies in prioritization. The goal is to identify variables that not only align with strategic objectives but also have the potential to create asymmetric value. Variables like scope and goals specification, payment terms, and warranty are noted as key generators of NegoEconomics. Prioritization should be based on the potential economic impact, relevance to the negotiation context, and the ability to create a win-win situation.

Do not start with *zero-sum variables*, which are variables that generate progress for one side at the expense of the counterpart or no value to either side. Zero-sum variables could be price, discount, limitations, and so on.

Your Assignment: Developing More Variables

The element concludes with a practical assignment: develop more variables in your negotiations. This task is designed to encourage creativity and strategic thinking, pushing negotiators to go beyond the conventional and discover new avenues for value creation in their negotiations.

Effective negotiation is about strategically identifying and prioritizing variables that maximize NegoEconomics. By broadening the scope of variables considered and carefully selecting those with the highest potential for asymmetric value creation, negotiators can significantly enhance the outcomes of their negotiations.

ELEMENT 37

Listening Skills

Effective negotiation hinges on two-way communication. This involves not only speaking and presenting your points but, crucially, listening and responding appropriately. By actively listening, asking questions, and considering alternatives, negotiators avoid unnecessary conflicts and instead strive to understand the other party's perspective. Respectful listening is synonymous with respecting the opposing party.

The Vital Role of Two-Way Communication

Being a good listener requires more talent than most people realize. Try and think of a very good friend, one you really like or turn to when you have problems. What are this person's characteristics? It is most likely that this person is a good listener. What are the characteristics of a good listener? Even if you are capable of doing five jobs all at the same time while one of your colleagues is telling you something, it is a good idea to stop everything that you are doing. People find it frustrating if you continue to work while they are trying to tell you something.

Always remember to meet the other person's gaze and maintain good eye contact. Even if you look away for a fraction of a second, there is a risk that the other person will think that you are not concentrating on what they are saying. Raise your eyebrows and tilt your head slightly. If you hold your face with one hand and at the same time let one finger touch your cheek, it conveys a nonverbal message that indicates that you are listening quietly.

Remember to nod appropriately at regular intervals. If you do this too frequently or too fast, it looks as if you are impatient and feel like interrupting. Don't say anything, even when the speaker appears to have finished. A short pause every now and again shows that you are taking in what is being said to you.

Be aware that cultures vary and the descriptions here convey expectations in typically Western cultures.

One of the greatest impediments to communication is interruptions and questions. When adults talk to each other, they tend to interrupt one another in mid-flow and finish off each other's sentences. They do not have sufficient patience to let the other person finish what they are saying, and they seem to assume they know what the other person is going to say. With children it is different, because adults give them more time. This is because they assume that children have more difficulty in expressing themselves and so need more time and attention. People should transfer this listening technique to conversations with adults. Learn and wait until the other person has finished speaking.

Rather than interrupting your speaking partner with a question while they are in mid-flow, you should develop a technique for remembering what you want to ask them. For example, it is a good idea to have a notepad available when you are at meetings.

Show empathy and avoid being judgmental. Have you ever been in a situation when you have admitted that you did not know who the European champions were in football and the person you were talking to says loudly "You are kidding, I thought everyone knew that!" So that people will trust you, you should not judge, argue, or make light of what they are saying. On the contrary, make sure you do not correct, criticize, or make fun of the person you are talking to. Use an assertive questioning technique.

Holding your head with your hand, with one finger on your cheek, and using eye contact all show that you are a good listener.

When asking questions, your body language should be appropriate. Display positive attitudes, nod a little, lean over toward the other person, maintain eye contact, and make a point of smiling. Remain at arm's length. In some cultures, it is acceptable to stand closer to the person who you are talking to. Touch is also acceptable in some cultures. If you know the other person well, it is perfectly all right to touch them lightly—for instance, by tapping them on the arm or the back.

The Pitfalls of Ineffective Communication

When communication is ineffective from the beginning, finding a common denominator becomes a challenge. Lack of clear understanding often leads to withholding information and entrenchment in one's own proposals. This can create a perception of the other party as being rigidly attached to their position, showing little interest in a meaningful dialogue.

The Power of Credible Information Exchange

A negotiation's success is largely determined by the exchange of credible information. The perception of credibility lies in the hands of the listener. If a message is not believed, the fault often lies not with the receiver but with the sender, who may have failed to communicate effectively.

Active Listening: Beyond Hearing Words

True communication in negotiations requires active listening. This means engaging with the conversation by asking questions for clarification, expressing interest, seeking additional information, or testing new ideas. Active listening also involves interpreting and responding to the answers received.

EXAMPLE | Deciphering the Unspoken in Negotiations

Consider this scenario: A negotiator states, "We would like to move the delivery time by three weeks." On the surface, this might seem like a straightforward request. However, effective listening involves understanding the deeper implications or the unsaid motives behind such a statement. It might imply a financial benefit or constraint related to the change in delivery time. Real listening requires interpreting these underlying messages and responding appropriately.

In this example, the negotiator isn't just discussing delivery times; they are indirectly referencing broader operational or financial considerations. To uncover the true intent, you must listen attentively and ask the right questions. This approach enables a deeper understanding of the other party's needs and concerns, paving the way for more effective negotiation outcomes.

Effective listening in negotiations transcends mere auditory processing of words. It requires empathy, active participation, and a nuanced understanding of both spoken and unspoken messages. By mastering these listening skills, negotiators can achieve more meaningful, respectful, and successful negotiations.

ELEMENT 38

Understanding and Navigating Salami Negotiations

A *salami negotiation* is a tactic whereby a party incrementally requests concessions, often beginning with minor issues before progressing to more significant demands. Think about a salami that is being sliced. This approach can gradually erode the other party's position without them realizing the full extent of the concessions being made until it's too late.

The Anatomy of Salami Negotiations

In a typical salami negotiation, the opposing party starts by addressing a seemingly minor issue. For example, they might seek to reduce transport costs, arguing that competitors offer free shipping. They may present this as their only demand, making it appear reasonable and easy for the seller to agree, especially if the cost impact is minimal.

Once this concession is made, the buyer progresses to another term, such as payment conditions. Here, the seller's costs are higher, but again, capitulating may seem the easiest path, particularly when the buyer cites competitive practices as justification. The seller, hoping to secure the deal, may acquiesce.

However, this is rarely the end. The buyer continues to push for more, ultimately demanding significant price reductions. Even if the seller's profits are squeezed to the minimum, the buyer may add yet another request, like a year of free service. By asserting that this will be their final demand, the buyer pressures the seller into yet another concession.

The seller, having made several unreciprocated concessions, finds themselves in a weakened position, their initial willingness to accommodate small demands having inadvertently raised the buyer's expectations. This situation often leaves the seller compromising far more than intended. The smarter approach is to engage in package negotiation, considering all demands collectively rather than individually.

Example of a Salami Negotiation

Consider the following fictional example to illustrate salami tactics in action:

1. Ellen's Electronics is negotiating a large order with TechWorld, a potential new client. TechWorld's negotiator, Mark, begins by asking for a minor concession—a 2 percent reduction in shipping costs, arguing that Ellen's competitors offer free shipping. Ellen, eager to make a good impression, agrees without much resistance.

2. Next, Mark requests extended payment terms, stretching from 30 to 60 days. Ellen, having already made one concession, feels compelled to agree, hoping this will be enough to finalize the deal.

3. However, Mark doesn't stop there. He then requests a 5 percent discount on the total order, citing that Ellen's competitors offer similar discounts for bulk purchases. Ellen, now heavily invested in the negotiation, agrees to this as well.

4. Finally, Mark pushes for a one-year warranty extension at no additional cost, assuring Ellen that this will be his last demand. Ellen, feeling cornered and anxious to close the deal, reluctantly agrees.

5. In the end, Ellen realizes that she has significantly reduced her profit margin and extended more resources than initially planned, all while receiving nothing extra in return from TechWorld.

Strategies to Counter Salami Negotiations

To prevent falling victim to salami tactics, negotiators should:

- **Recognize the pattern:** Be aware of the incremental nature of these negotiations and the potential for escalating demands.
- **Set clear boundaries:** Determine in advance what concessions are acceptable and where the line must be drawn.
- **Seek reciprocity:** For every concession made, request something of equal value in return.

- **Consider the entire package:** Rather than responding to each demand individually, negotiate all terms collectively.
- **Be prepared to walk away:** Sometimes the best negotiation strategy is to be willing to end discussions if they become unreasonably one-sided.

By understanding and effectively responding to salami tactics, negotiators can protect their interests and work toward more balanced and mutually beneficial agreements.

ELEMENT 39

Mastering Package Negotiation: A Holistic Approach

In the realm of negotiation, understanding and effectively utilizing package negotiation is crucial. This element delves into the intricacies of package negotiation, contrasting it with more piecemeal approaches like salami tactics.

The Essence of Package Negotiation

Package negotiation is a comprehensive strategy where multiple components of a deal are considered in tandem, rather than individually. This approach acknowledges the interconnected nature of various negotiation elements such as price, quantity, quality, service, and payment conditions. Unlike salami negotiations, where concessions are made incrementally on single issues, package negotiation requires a holistic view of all demands and requirements.

The Process of Package Negotiation

- **Listening and noting requirements:** The initial step involves actively listening to and writing down the other party's requirements and demands. It's essential not to react or give opinions on these demands individually.

- **Questioning and investigating:** Understand the rationale behind each requirement. Question and probe to uncover the underlying reasons and motivations.

- **Assessing and formulating a proposal:** Once a comprehensive understanding is achieved, assess the situation to determine the alternatives and options available. Then, formulate a new package proposal that addresses these needs collectively.

- **Demanding reciprocity:** Crucially, ensure that your package proposal includes demands from your side as well. This establishes a give-and-take dynamic, steering clear of one-sided concessions.

- **Being prepared to reassess:** If the proposal is not accepted, be ready to reassess the situation. The advantage here is that you haven't lost any ground or made unilateral concessions.

EXAMPLE | Package Negotiation

Imagine a scenario where a tech company, InnoTech, is negotiating a large contract with a supplier, GreenTech. GreenTech starts by demanding a 10 percent price reduction. Instead of responding to this demand directly, InnoTech's negotiator, Sarah, listens and writes down all of GreenTech's requirements, which include extended payment terms and a faster delivery schedule.

Sarah then questions the reasons behind these demands, learning that GreenTech is under pressure to reduce costs due to a tight budget and needs quicker deliveries to meet its project deadlines.

Armed with this information, Sarah proposes a comprehensive package: InnoTech can offer a 5 percent price reduction, but in exchange, GreenTech would need to commit to a longer contract term, ensuring steady business for InnoTech. Additionally, InnoTech can expedite deliveries, provided GreenTech agrees to more flexible payment terms.

This package addresses both parties' needs and concerns, creating a win-win situation. By not responding to GreenTech's initial demand for a 10 percent price reduction and instead proposing a holistic solution, Sarah ensures that InnoTech doesn't make unilateral concessions and that the deal benefits both parties.

Package negotiation requires a strategic approach, focusing on the overall value of the deal rather than individual concessions. It encourages a deeper understanding of the other party's needs and fosters a more collaborative and mutually beneficial negotiation process. By mastering package negotiation, negotiators can achieve more sustainable and rewarding outcomes, moving beyond the limitations of traditional, piecemeal negotiation tactics.

ELEMENT 40

Total Cost of Ownership

In the context of SMARTnership negotiation (a collaborative process above partnership), a deep understanding of the *Total Cost of Ownership* (TCO) is essential. SMARTnership, focusing on creating mutual gains and fostering cooperation, necessitates a thorough appreciation of all costs associated with an agreement or purchase, not just the upfront price. TCO, the sum of all costs associated with an asset or service over its life cycle, becomes a crucial component in such negotiations.

TCO encompasses both direct and indirect costs incurred throughout the life of a product or service, including maintenance, operation, and even disposal. This broad perspective allows negotiators in a SMARTnership to make more informed, long-term beneficial decisions.

For example, consider a company planning to purchase new office printers. A traditional negotiation approach might focus solely on the printers' purchase price. However, in a SMARTnership negotiation, the focus shifts to TCO. Various suppliers offer different terms:

- **Initial purchase price:** Lowest from Supplier A.
- **Maintenance and repairs:** Longer warranty and lower costs from Supplier B.
- **Ink/toner costs:** More efficient usage and long-term savings from Supplier C.
- **Energy efficiency:** Higher upfront cost but lower energy bills from Supplier D.
- **Downtime and efficiency:** Reliable printers with less downtime from Supplier E.

In a SMARTnership approach, the company engages suppliers in a discussion to minimize TCO, considering extended warranties, bulk deals on ink, or energy-saving solutions. This collaborative effort transforms the negotiation from a simple price discussion to a comprehensive value assessment, leading to a mutually beneficial agreement.

Incorporating TCO into SMARTnership negotiations leads to a holistic, transparent approach, fostering trust and collaboration. Parties share information about all costs, allowing for creative, cost-reducing solutions. This approach aligns with SMARTnership's ethos of creating additional value and expanding the negotiation pie, focusing on long-term sustainability and profitability.

The upcoming elements delve into practical examples of TCO in SMARTnership negotiations. This discussion showcases TCO as not just a tool for understanding deal implications but also as a means to build stronger, more cooperative negotiation relationships.

ELEMENT 41

Confirming a Mandate

Here's a crucial, albeit sometimes challenging, guideline: Always ensure you're negotiating with someone who has the authority to finalize the agreement.

Picture this scenario: You've been in discussions with Jeff all day, reaching a mutual verbal agreement. You confidently present the contract for his signature, only to be taken aback when Jeff reveals he's not authorized to sign. Instead, he must refer it to his superior, although he expresses optimism about its approval.

However, the following day brings an unexpected twist. Jeff's boss contacts you, approving only 8 of the 10 negotiated terms and requesting a renegotiation of the remaining 2 items. Suddenly, you're thrust back into a negotiation you believed was settled just a day prior. This could be a strategic move on their part, employing a "salami slicing" tactic to incrementally gain more concessions.

To prevent such scenarios, initiate every negotiation by clarifying if your counterpart possesses the necessary mandate to make binding decisions. Equally, confirm your own authority to represent your side in the discussions.

What If Direct Negotiation with Decision-Makers Isn't Feasible?

In certain situations, like union negotiations, immediate decision-making at the negotiation table isn't always possible. Representatives may need to seek approval from their higher-ups or the "back office." It's essential to understand these procedural nuances—the rules of the game—before diving into negotiations. This awareness helps set realistic expectations and guides your strategy throughout the negotiation process.

ELEMENT 42

The Double-Edged Sword of Ultimatums

An *ultimatum* in negotiation is a final demand or statement of terms, the rejection of which will result in retaliation or a breakdown in relations. While it can be a powerful tool, it's akin to a double-edged sword that must be wielded with utmost caution and strategic foresight.

The Strategic Use of Ultimatums

From my perspective, the key to effectively using an ultimatum is timing and legitimacy. It should come after all other avenues have been explored and when you, as the negotiator, are prepared for either outcome. Ultimatums can be a show of strength, signaling resolve and seriousness. In certain scenarios, such as when negotiations are at a stalemate or when time is of the essence, a well-placed ultimatum can break the impasse and expedite the process.

However, the effectiveness of an ultimatum is largely contingent on its credibility. An ultimatum that is seen as bluster or easily retractable loses its impact and can weaken your position. Therefore, before issuing an ultimatum, it's crucial to ensure that it is realistic and that you are fully prepared to follow through with the consequences.

The Risks of Ultimatums

Despite their potential power, I always caution against the liberal use of ultimatums. The risks involved are significant. Firstly, ultimatums can escalate conflict and create a confrontational atmosphere. They reduce the negotiation to a zero-sum game, often leading to a breakdown in communication and, potentially, the end of the negotiation with no agreement reached.

Moreover, ultimatums can damage relationships. In my experience, negotiations are not just about the immediate deal; they are about building long-term relationships. An ultimatum can leave the other party feeling cornered and resentful, which might harm future interactions or dealings.

Finally, there's the risk of misjudgment. Issuing an ultimatum underestimating the other party's options or resolve can backfire. If the other party calls the bluff or is willing to walk away, it can lead to a worse outcome than if the ultimatum had not been used.

Carefully evaluate when and if you want to use an ultimatum. In general, when negotiating in a collaborative environment like a partnership or SMARTnership, I don't recommend ultimatums unless all roads have been explored.

While ultimatums can be a powerful tactic in negotiations, they must be used sparingly and judiciously. The key is to assess the situation carefully, understand the stakes involved, and be prepared for all possible outcomes. In my advisory role, I advocate for a balanced approach, where negotiation strategies are tailored to foster not just immediate gains but also long-term relationships and goodwill.

ELEMENT 43

Time Out: Embracing Preparation and Patience

When you spearhead negotiations, preparation is your ally. Entering negotiations with a clear plan and understanding of your goals sets a strong foundation. However, you must be cautious not to rush to conclusions, especially when the other party initiates the dialogue. Familiar scenarios may tempt you to quick decisions, but remember, each negotiation is unique and warrants thoughtful consideration.

EXAMPLE | The Memory Module Negotiation

Consider a scenario involving a telephone salesperson offering a customer a special deal on memory modules (RAM) at a reduced price.

Scenario 1: Swift Decision Leads to Immediate Purchase

Salesperson: "We've secured RAM EDO 256Mb at 15% off for orders over 100 units."

Customer: "Interesting, we use that model frequently. I'll check our needs and get back to you momentarily."

After a brief check, the customer orders 300 units, pleased with the quick deal.

Scenario 2: Calculated Response Yields Strategic Advantage

Salesperson: "We've secured RAM EDO 256Mb at 15% off for orders over 100 units."

Customer: "This is intriguing. How many units are available?"

Salesperson: "Between 3000 and 4000 units."

Customer: "And the price for bulk orders?"
Salesperson: "A potential additional discount. How many were you considering?"

Customer: "I'm entering a meeting now. I'll reconnect in 30 minutes. Meanwhile, consider your best offer for 500 units."

The Power of Alternatives

In the second scenario, the customer didn't actually have a meeting but sought time to reflect and explore options. Understanding the market's saturation with RAM, they inquired with other suppliers. Equipped with competitive offers, they returned to the original seller.

Customer: "What's your best price now?"
Salesperson: "An 18% discount for 500 units."
Customer: "I've got a similar offer elsewhere."
Salesperson: "Our RAM surplus is significant, but it might not last."
Customer: "To make a deal, I need a better price."
Salesperson: "How about an extra 1% discount?"
Customer: "19% off sounds good, but I'll only take 300 units."
Salesperson: "Agreed, we have a deal."

This example illustrates the importance of not rushing into decisions, especially when under pressure from the other party. Taking time to evaluate offers, understanding market dynamics, and exploring alternatives can lead to more favorable outcomes in negotiations. Patience, combined with strategic thinking, often turns the tables in your favor.

ELEMENT 44

Checklists

Any successful negotiator embraces the use of checklists. Compare this to a pilot, sitting in the flight deck, going through various checklists to make sure everything is working and nothing is forgotten. As a negotiator, you'll need to go through the same procedure, pre-negotiation, during negotiation, and post-negotiation.

The necessary checklists in most negotiations are the following:

- The dos and don'ts of negotiation
- Pre-negotiation checklist
- Post-negotiation evaluation

The Dos of Negotiation

- Make sure to prepare before a negotiation. Use the negotiation planner and checklists as tools and create an agenda before entering the negotiation room.
- If you work in a team, have a leader, listener/note taker/ and observer.
- Ask questions instead of arguing.
- Listen to what your counterpart is really saying.
- Know your starting point, threshold of pain, and target goal in a negotiation.
- Learn how to identify when a negotiation is occurring.
- Identify your negotiation strategy—zero-sum, partnership, or SMARTnership.
- List and value your variables.
- Try to expand the number of variables, preferably with your counterpart.
- Create and develop trust.
- Be sure to negotiate with a counterpart who has authority to sign a deal.

- Use breaks during negotiations.
- Summarize what you have discussed during negotiation.
- Identify the negotiation style of your counterpart.
- Use visual aids.

The Don'ts of Negotiation

- Negotiate price as the first or only variable.
- Use ultimatums.
- Negotiate on your own without a team, unless it's a simple negotiation.
- Ignore the value in face-to-face negotiations vs. virtual negotiations.
- Give something away without getting something in return.
- Allow your counterpart to dictate the terms or agenda.
- Begin a negotiation without proper preparation.
- Make final decisions without a break.
- Ask closed-ended questions in the beginning of a negotiation.
- Assume you know the culture of your counterpart.
- Assume or guess what your counterparts want.
- Put yourself under time pressure.
- Lie, threat, or bluff in collaborative negotiations.
- Ignore the importance of relationship and likeability.
- Ignore a request from your counterpart, even if the request would cost you more than benefit you.

Checklist for a Successful Negotiation Before and During Negotiations

Checklist for a Successful Negotiation
Before and during negotiations

Are you ready for your negotiation?

Want to make sure that everything goes as well as expected? To negotiate is a major responsibility for the negotiation team. They need to pay attention to detail while planning the negotiation.

Follow this checklist to ensure a smooth and successful negotiation experience.

You can tweak or update this checklist, depending on your organization's unique needs.

A thorough checklist will help you easily manage your negotiation.

the SMARTnership negotiation organization

www.smartnership.org

Strategy	
O	Zero-sum (positional)
O	Partnership (collaboration)
O	SMARTnership (collaboration)
O	Sharing costs and benefits
O	Prepared list of negotiable variables
O	Agenda, developed, own/mutual/order
O	Rules of the game
O	Do you know your target, starting point, and threshold of pain?
Team	
O	Head, notetaker, and calculator
O	Mandate
O	Mandate for counterpart
O	How to utilize and support the team
O	Counterpart's team
Variables	
O	Do you have all variables listed?
O	Do you know all variables costs and benefits?
O	Do you know your counterparts variables?
O	Do you wait to discuss price and legal issues to the end?
O	Do not share without getting something back.
O	Ask open questions.
Process	
O	Minimize argumentation.
O	Generate trust.
O	Did we secure a positive enviroment?
Planning phase	
O	Are new openings made?
O	Do you give too much or too little information?
O	Who got the initiative?

Checklist for a Successful Negotiation
Before and during negotiations

Are you ready for your negotiation?

Want to make sure that everything goes as well as expected? To negotiate is a major responsibility for the negotiation team. They need to pay attention to detail while planning the negotiation.

Follow this checklist to ensure a smooth and successful negotiation experience.

You can tweak or update this checklist, depending on your organization's unique needs.

A thorough checklist will help you easily manage your negotiation.

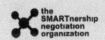
the
SMARTnership
negotiation
organization

www.smartnership.org

Bargaining	
○	Offer/counteroffer.
○	Give and take or concessions?
○	Do you negotiate in the salami method or the complete package?
○	Who got the initiative?
○	Should you ask for a break?
○	Know the agenda.

Communication	
○	Are you confident?
○	Openness?
○	How are visual aids being used?
○	Are you aware of the body language?
○	Use questions, follow-up questions and summarizing.

Negotiation style	
○	Combat, concession, compromise, collaboration, stalling?
○	Active/passive?
○	Test limits / give up easy / push too hard?
○	Locked on details?
○	Locked on own proposal / listen to counterparts proposal?
○	Ask open questions.

Closing	
○	Minimize argumentation.
○	Is closing being tried?
○	Do you need to summarize?
○	Did you miss any openings?
○	Did you split the NegoEconomics (asymmetric values)?

Post-Negotiation Audit Checklist
Negotiation Evaluation

Post-Negotiation Audit Checklist
Negotiation Evaluation

How Did it Go?

This is your opportunity to evaluate how the negotiation went. Here you can determine what went right, and what should be changed the next time. Write any specific notes in the Notes column.

_____

You can tweak or update this checklist depending on your organization's unique needs.

_____

A thorough checklist will help you easily manage your negotiation.

	Role Within the Group
☐	Did you have a lead, a note taker, and a cost calculator?
☐	Kept discipline during the negotiation.
☐	Use of SMARTnership (collaboration) to get to end result.
☐	Team members were supportive to lead negotiator.
☐	Prepared list of negotiable variables.
☐	There was consensus on the deal within the team.
	Summary of Negotiation
☐	Variables were identified, including variables other than those prepared.
☐	Achieved negotiation goal.
☐	Reached threshold of pain.
☐	Found NegoEconomics in the deal.
☐	Capitalized on NegoEconomics of the deal.
☐	Were able to choose a style and change as needed.
	Agenda
☐	Agenda was created.
☐	Agenda was followed.
	The Negotiation Process
☐	Negotiation flowed without reaching a deadlock.
	The Argumentation Phase
☐	Arguments were intelligible and credible.
☐	Focused on counterpart's values as well.
☐	There were no conflicts.

Notes:

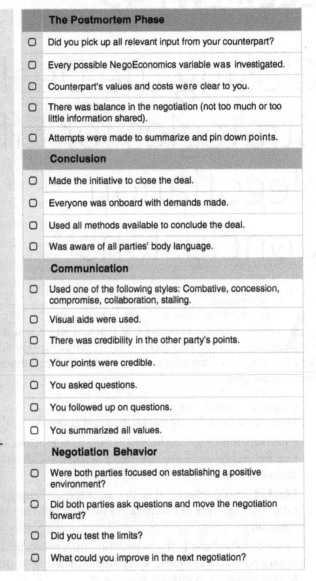

The Postmortem Phase
○ Did you pick up all relevant input from your counterpart?
○ Every possible NegoEconomics variable was investigated.
○ Counterpart's values and costs were clear to you.
○ There was balance in the negotiation (not too much or too little information shared).
○ Attempts were made to summarize and pin down points.

Conclusion
○ Made the initiative to close the deal.
○ Everyone was onboard with demands made.
○ Used all methods available to conclude the deal.
○ Was aware of all parties' body language.

Communication
○ Used one of the following styles: Combative, concession, compromise, collaboration, stalling.
○ Visual aids were used.
○ There was credibility in the other party's points.
○ Your points were credible.
○ You asked questions.
○ You followed up on questions.
○ You summarized all values.

Negotiation Behavior
○ Were both parties focused on establishing a positive environment?
○ Did both parties ask questions and move the negotiation forward?
○ Did you test the limits?
○ What could you improve in the next negotiation?

SMARTNERSHIP
NEGOTIATION ORGANIZATION

ELEMENT 45

Closing the Deal: Strategies for Effective Negotiation Conclusions

A s you approach the end of a negotiation, the crucial moment to close the contract arises. This phase is reached when you have crafted an offer that addresses the other party's needs while closely aligning with your objectives. To ensure readiness for closure, confirm affirmative answers to the following critical questions:

- **Consensus on demands:** Are all parties in agreement with the set demands? Have these been firmly established and accepted?
- **Decision-making authority (mandate):** Does the other party have the necessary authority to make a binding decision? Are key decision-makers present?
- **Market comparison:** Has the counterpart engaged with competitors or other parties? Lack of comparative insight might hinder their decision-making capability.
- **Time constraints:** Is the negotiation influenced by a deadline? Negotiations often accelerate as deadlines approach, leading to decisions driven more by time pressure than mutual agreement.

Negative Closure Tactics

There are various ways to close a negotiation, some more favorable than others. Ideally, an agreement emerges organically after thorough bargaining. However, certain tactics, which are often perceived negatively, may push the other party into an agreement and should be used judiciously.

- **Threat:** Summarize the demands and propose a compromise that only partially meets the other party's needs. For instance, offer terms with a caveat of market volatility: "Our current offer, meeting most of your requirements, cannot be guaranteed for long due to market changes." This tactic risks the other party perceiving you as bluffing or dishonest, especially if trust hasn't been fully established.

- **Proposing a new agreement:** If commitment falters, consider pausing to develop alternative solutions. This might involve reassessing your goals and presenting your offer in a more appealing way, like emphasizing quicker delivery over a price cut.

- **Unilateral concession:** In minor disagreements, offering a small, one-sided concession can be effective. Ensure that the concession has limited value and is reciprocated with a commitment, like agreeing to a specific aspect of a proposal to move forward.

- **Retracting the offer:** As a last resort, consider withdrawing a previous offer. This high-stakes tactic involves subtly altering demands during the summary phase and should only be used when no better alternatives remain.

Signing the Deal

Finalizing the negotiation involves officially signing the agreement. Celebrate your success only after the deal is sealed. Remember, verbal agreements are nonbinding and vulnerable to misunderstandings or last-minute changes. Therefore, ensuring all agreements are in writing is crucial to avoid future disputes.

Navigating Post-Negotiation Challenges

Sometimes, unexpected modifications arise even after reaching an agreement. In such cases, you might:

- Grant additional concessions within your negotiation margin.
- Stand firm on your terms, understanding the risks involved.
- Seek compensation for agreed-upon terms, especially in oral agreements.
- Stall and reassess the situation, treating it as a new negotiation phase.

The Importance of Documentation

Concluding every negotiation with a written summary of agreements is paramount. This is particularly crucial when the formal agreement is drafted by a party not present during the negotiation or in scenarios involving language barriers. Detailed notes and summaries during negotiation help in crafting a mutually agreeable and binding contract.

By following these strategies and ensuring thorough documentation, you can navigate the closing phase of a negotiation effectively, leading to successful and binding agreements.

ELEMENT 46

Working with Summaries

When you summarize, your message takes a new turn in the circuit of the sensory memory, the short-term memory, the long-term memory, and the working store. New bits become entrenched, repetition intensifies learning, and you become aware of any misunderstandings.

When your colleagues summarize, they intensify the effect. You can also ask the recipient to summarize, which is by far the best method. You get direct feedback as to how much of the message has come across and been assessed, and you can rectify any misunderstandings. Always ask the other party to summarize your proposals before they leave to consider them.

Always summarize what you've agreed to before you part company. Ask questions of the type, "What have we arrived at?" "Does this mean we have a deal?" "What does it look like?" "Could you please summarize?"

Consider this example: It's Sunday morning and your child enters the room saying,

We haven't been to the movies for a long time.

That's right.

Couldn't we go today?

We'll have to see.

But when can we go?

This afternoon.

Later in the day, the child says,

Aren't we going soon?

Where?

You promised that we'd be going to see a movie.

I didn't promise, I said we'd see ...

You promised, you promised !!!!!

If you start anything, we certainly won't be going.

But you promised !!!

The child turns to her mother to complain. She sides with her child and takes the child to the cinema. After the cinema they go to the burger place. At home the husband doesn't plan for his own dinner, and he thinks that his wife is making a mistake in siding with the child. He plans to have a serious talk with his wife concerning the importance of bringing up your child with firmness and consistency. Later when she comes back together with the child, she doesn't want to talk to him; she has a headache and goes to bed. The whole situation could have been avoided if, before going on reading his paper, the father had asked his child, Now, what did we just agree to?

The child would have told him that he had promised to take them to see a movie. The father could then have corrected the mistake and said that he would think about it. A answer with which child would probably not have been satisfied; it would have gone on pressing him to take her to the cinema.

Check by Summarizing

Summarize the message of the other party: What you're telling me is that you can't make a decision today. In this way you avoid misunderstandings, and you force the other party to send clear signals. You give the other party an opportunity to explain themselves. You can also be provoking in your summary in order to test boundaries by summarizing "incorrectly." You add things, you detract things, and you modify.

Once the summary has been made, you can empty the working store and store information again in your long-term memory. You know where it is and can retrieve it on demand.

Document the Process

If what you're looking for are constructive and efficient negotiations, you will only lose time and trust if you take the other party by surprise at the negotiating table. They can't answer your questions. They can't benefit from all the information given them all at once and they may feel insecure and unable to act. Use these tactics to avoid these misunderstandings:

- **Forward your documentation prior to the negotiation.** The other party will be more receptive to your message, better prepared, and more capable of asking questions.

- **Forward your documentation after the meeting.** Provide a full set of documents, but don't run the risk of nobody reading it. Underline the most important points in an accompanying letter.

- **Document all agreements in writing.** If disagreement occurs later, this is certainly one agreement that can be highly valuable.
- **Be efficient in how you transmit communication.** Does this sound difficult? None of these initiatives aimed at improving the efficiency of communication are difficult in that they don't call for special intellectual skills. It's chiefly a matter of practice and self-discipline on your part.

Always review your negotiations afterwards, interpret your notes, discuss things with colleagues, analyze the results, and establish new objectives. Assess your own performance and that of your colleagues. Develop a clean copy of the picture you established.

Learn How to Listen

Don't just listen with your ears. You should also establish eye contact. Concentrate your senses on the other party. If not, there is an overwhelming risk that your other sensory organs will start registering competing signals.

To be able to listen activity, you must be well prepared; if not, your thoughts will be busy preparing for the negotiation while the other party is speaking to you. You must be relaxed and shouldn't feel stressed or provoked, because then you will be preparing for fight or flight. You must ensure ample time; if not you will be chased by the hands of the clock.

Active listening requires two-way communication. You must ask questions to demonstrate your interest, to get more information on the table, to clarify, and to be able to concentrate on the other party. If you take an active part in what the other party is saying, you exclude competing signals.

Use Paper and Pen, iPad, or Computer

Don't overestimate your ability to remember everything afterwards; what was set by whom, when it was said, your perception of the other party's reaction to your signals, or emotions which the other party's signals have invoked in you. Always use paper and pen when you listen.

Experience as well as experiments have shown that the negotiator who doesn't take notes during negotiations often has an erroneous and incomplete picture of what happened. These negotiators can correctly recount only a third of what happened in the course of the negotiations.

When I say notes, I don't mean a stenographic manuscript of every word said in the negotiation. It's a matter of taking down keywords, reminders, important reactions and moves, feelings, questions, and ideas that cropped up.

All the notions that come to you during the negotiation should be jotted down in keyword format. In this way you empty the working store, and you remove the block that can otherwise hamper continued listening.

Active listening and registering the results of the negotiation mean that the conscious sensing and filtration of the other party's signals will be intensified. You now have much better control over the signals that are leaked and those stored in the long-term memory. You are no longer disturbed by competing signals. The learning curve improves.

ELEMENT 47

Anchoring in Negotiation

Scholars in negotiation have for centuries debated whether or not placing the first offer on the table gives a negotiator a benefit.

In my years of exploring the nuances of negotiation, I've come to appreciate the subtlety and power of certain tactics. One such tactic, often overlooked yet immensely influential, is *anchoring*. To me, anchoring in negotiation isn't just a technique; it's a window into the human psyche. It's based on the principle that the first piece of information offered in a negotiation—the anchor—significantly shapes all subsequent decisions and discussions.

I've observed that the true art of anchoring lies not just in numbers but in understanding its psychological roots. As humans, we are wired to give undue weight to the first information we receive. In negotiations, this means the initial offer, terms, or even the tone can set the trajectory for the entire dialogue. It's a subtle dance, where the first step can predetermine the path of the entire performance.

Grasping the concept of anchoring is a game-changer. It's not merely about learning a tactic; it's about gaining a deeper understanding of decision-making. By mastering this concept, you can better steer your negotiations toward more favorable and sustainable outcomes.

EXAMPLE | Anchoring in Action—The High-Stakes Corporate Deal

Let me share a compelling example from my experience. In a high-stakes merger negotiation between Company A and Company B, Company A, well-versed in the art of anchoring, opened with a striking offer of $500 million for Company B. This was a strategic masterstroke. This figure, though higher than market expectations, set the psychological baseline for the negotiation. Company B, aiming for a higher valuation, found itself anchored to this initial figure. The final deal, influenced by this initial anchor, was a testament to Company A's strategic acumen.

This scenario demonstrates that anchoring is more than just setting a price; it's about setting the stage for how the negotiation unfolds. It's about conveying confidence and shaping perceptions, which are as crucial as the numbers on the table.

The Everyday Salary Negotiation

Anchoring isn't just for the boardroom; it's a part of everyday negotiations as well. Take, for instance, a typical salary negotiation. A candidate, expecting a certain salary, is met with an initial offer higher than the expectation. This immediately recalibrates their perspective, setting a new mental baseline. In my advisory role, I've seen how such a tactic can favorably anchor the negotiation for the offering party, often leading to a mutually agreeable outcome that still aligns with the employer's initial strategy.

ELEMENT 48

Postmortems: Navigating the Aftermath

Congratulations on successfully concluding a negotiation! You've adeptly navigated through preparation, trust-building, argumentation, bargaining, and finally, drafting a binding agreement. However, the journey doesn't end here. It's time to engage in a critical postmortem analysis, evaluating the negotiation's outcomes and pondering the future of this business relationship.

Post-Negotiation Analysis and Relationship Continuity

Remember, the outcomes of negotiations hinge more on personal relationships than on price or other material factors. Emotions play a significant role; a sense of loss or unfairness in any party can derail even the most well-planned agreements. For sustainable implementation and enforcement, both parties must feel satisfied and victorious.

It's crucial for your counterpart to justify the financial results of the agreement within their organization. Short-term and long-term benefits must be compelling enough to outweigh any risks or costs. This necessitates assisting them in crafting a convincing narrative for their internal stakeholders.

An accompanying post-negotiation checklist is available in Element 44 for a structured evaluation.

Avoiding feelings of deception or manipulation is essential. A successful negotiation leaves both parties content not just with the outcome, but also with the process itself. Failure to maintain this balance can erode previously built interpersonal relationships, leading to reluctance in future negotiations, contract nonrenewal, price adjustments, or even negative word-of-mouth.

Historical agreements, like the Treaty of Versailles, serve as reminders that a negotiation resulting in clear winners and losers can seed future conflicts. Hence, maintaining open communication channels, established during the initial phases, is vital even after the negotiation concludes. People value ongoing consideration, not just when it's time to sign or renew agreements.

Deciding Whether to Continue the Relationship

The decision to renew or terminate a business relationship is influenced by multiple factors:

- **Changes in key personnel:** New appointees bring different perspectives and needs, affecting existing relationships and agreements.
- **Technological advancements:** Evolving solutions can alter the dynamics or necessity of the deal.
- **Shifts in the economic, political, or social landscape:** Such changes can impact the feasibility or desirability of the agreement.
- **Budgetary adjustments:** New financial constraints or opportunities can reshape the agreement's scope.

The process of ending an agreement can be complex and painful, potentially damaging professional relationships. Unilateral decisions to withdraw can provoke adversarial responses, risking the loss of a valuable business connection.

Consider a situation with a boutique hotel owner and an interior designer. They worked together for eight years and their strong partnership and mutual commitment seemed unshakable until an unexpected sale of the hotel left the designer jobless and distrustful. This scenario underscores the importance of including "divorce" clauses in long-term agreements. Establishing clear guidelines for potential separations during amicable times can prevent misunderstandings and conflicts later.

The unpredictability of post-agreement scenarios is a reality. Conducting thorough postmortem analyses of your negotiations helps navigate future uncertainties. This introspective process, combined with all the phases previously discussed, will equip you to be a discerning and successful negotiator.

ELEMENT 49

Creating a Negotiation Planner

Another valuable tool in any negotiation you have is your negotiation planner. This is a chart that shows you different possible outcomes in any particular negotiation. The purpose of this chart is to prepare you in case your negotiation isn't going the way you want. If you reach a standstill on your goal, what are you willing to concede? Where are you willing to compromise to reach your goal? If you haven't prepared ahead of time for bargaining, you'll end up making concessions that impact you negatively.

Your chart should have the following for both your own negotiation goals and your negotiating counterpart's goals:

- **Variables:** These are the terms you are negotiating, which could include things like price, delivery dates, conditions of payment, or even terms for a promotion.

- **Starting point:** Where you are starting in your negotiations? This will include specific details about your goals and desired outcomes for your end of the negotiation.

- **Negotiating space:** Where do you have wiggle room in your negotiation? If the negotiating counterpart pushes back, where do you have room to meet them halfway? This gives you an idea of how flexible you can be, and the alternatives you can take advantage of.

- **Changing of conditions:** This defines the outcome if you need to compromise on your goal. This will reveal the points that are sensitive to you, and what the consequences are if you give in, hold fast, or compromise.

Your Negotiation Goals

Here's an example of a negotiation planner for a negotiation between a client and a manufacturer.

Variable	Starting Point	Negotiating Space	Changing of Conditions
Price	$520,000	$490,000	–$30,000
Delivery Date	January 6th	February 10th	10,000/week
Warranty	2-year	1-year	+$45,000
Conditions of Payment	Net cash		Internal interest rate12%

Your Counterpart's Negotiation Goals

Negotiation Space	Changing of Conditions	Have in Mind/ Competitor
		Avoid concession
		What is the cost to the client?
		Remember to ask questions

Filling out your side of the chart is the easier part, but how do you know what your counterpart's goals are before a negotiation? You can do some research on how your counterpart has negotiated other deals in the past, or you can create many different scenarios on how a negotiation would go on their end.

Fill out this planner with an open mind. What would it look like to give in on certain points? And if you have to give in, what can you get out of the negotiation instead? Being open to finding agreement terms other than the ones you originally wanted creates confidence, because ultimately you'll be in control of which variables you can and cannot compromise on. But beware of revealing too much—you should only reveal flexibility where you absolutely must.

Asking things like "How much would you save if we could _____," opens a door to possibilities that wouldn't have originally been on the table if you hadn't been willing to find a beneficial solution for both parties. It also opens room for your negotiating counterpart to find where they can be flexible on their terms, which benefits you as well. Being willing to compromise and, more importantly, knowing what you're willing to compromise on, will give you the upper hand and set you up for success:

"Sure, I can be open to a longer delivery time. It might entail some extra expenses, but I think it would still be worth your while. Of course, delivering as early as you can will give you a leg up over other suppliers we are talking with as we compare our options. How can we come to a delivery date that would benefit both of us?"

It's hard to know how flexible another party will be in the negotiating room, and it can be even more difficult to determine the consequences of a possible change in original negotiating terms. You could compromise on the delivery date, but would that affect your inventory down the line? One of the main objectives in preparing for a negotiation must therefore be to fill out your negotiation planner as much as possible. Be sure to think about how you can ask questions in the room without revealing too much of your desired outcome too soon. If you do reveal too much, you end up losing some of your negotiation power.

ELEMENT 50

The Next Best Alternative in Negotiations

In negotiations, especially within the corporate sector, the concept of the *Next Best Alternative* (NBA) plays a pivotal role in strategy formulation. This principle, closely aligned with the Best Alternative to a Negotiated Agreement (BATNA) concept from the *Getting to Yes* book by Roger Fisher and William Ury, emphasizes the importance of having a fallback option that can be leveraged during negotiations

The Concept of NBA

The NBA, in essence, represents the alternative action a negotiator will take if the current negotiation fails to yield a desirable outcome. It is not just a theoretical construct but a practical tool that guides decision-making in complex negotiation scenarios. The existence of a well-defined NBA can empower negotiators, providing them with a sense of security and a clear benchmark against which to measure the offers on the table.

Importance in Strategy Development

Developing a clear and viable NBA is a fundamental step in preparing for any negotiation. It's a part of the broader strategy that encompasses understanding the tactics of the opponent, especially in situations where the negotiation resembles a zero-sum game. A robust NBA offers a guideline on when to walk away from the negotiation and when to push for better terms.

Application in Corporate Negotiations

In the context of corporate deal-making, the NBA is often closely tied to business objectives, market positions, and competitive strategies. The negotiation table is not just about the immediate deal but also about how this deal fits into the larger business strategy. Therefore, an NBA in this context might include alternative partnerships, different market strategies, or even a complete overhaul of the business approach.

EXAMPLE | Negotiating a Corporate Partnership

Imagine a scenario where Company A is negotiating a partnership deal with Company B. Company A's primary goal is to form a strategic alliance with Company B to expand its market reach. However, the negotiations are tough, with both parties having divergent views on the terms of the partnership.

Developing the NBA

Before entering the negotiations, Company A develops its NBA. They identify that if a partnership with Company B isn't feasible, their next best alternative is to approach Company C, a smaller but rapidly growing competitor in the market. This alternative partnership might not offer the same immediate market expansion as Company B, but it holds potential for long-term growth and innovation.

Application in Negotiations

During the negotiation, Company A finds that Company B is insisting on terms that are not favorable, potentially impacting Company A's autonomy and future growth. Company A uses this moment to reassess its position and contemplate its NBA.

Company A strategically introduces a break in the negotiation process. During this break, they evaluate the current offer from Company B against their NBA. Realizing that the partnership with Company B, under the current terms, would be less beneficial than their NBA with Company C, Company A returns to the negotiation table with a renewed strategy.

Armed with a clear understanding of their NBA, Company A confidently negotiates with Company B, emphasizing that while they prefer a partnership with them, they have a viable alternative. This shifts the dynamics of the negotiation. Company B, recognizing Company A's strong position and the risk of losing the deal, becomes more flexible in their terms.

The negotiation concludes with a mutually beneficial agreement, primarily because Company A had a well-defined and viable NBA. This example highlights how the NBA can empower negotiators, providing leverage and clarity in decision-making, and ultimately leading to more favorable outcomes in complex corporate negotiations.

The Power of Breaks

A critical but often overlooked aspect of employing the NBA effectively is the use of breaks during negotiations. Breaks allow negotiators to reassess their position, consider their NBA, and return to the table with a clearer perspective. This can be especially useful when negotiations reach a stalemate, providing a much-needed pause for strategizing and recalibration.

The NBA is a vital component of any negotiation strategy, particularly in the corporate world where stakes are high and decisions have far-reaching consequences. It's a tool that not only helps in achieving immediate negotiation goals but also aligns these goals with broader business strategies. Understanding and preparing an NBA is, therefore, not just about having a backup plan, but about ensuring strategic soundness in the complex dance of corporate negotiations.

ELEMENT 51

Testing Limits with Respect

In negotiations, pushing boundaries is essential, yet it must be done with respect to avoid alienating the other party. Seemingly straightforward statements can be perceived as aggressive, jeopardizing the relationship.

In order to make progress in generating *NegoEconomics* (see Element 20) and identify additional values, it is essential for you as a negotiator to test limits. But do it without becoming threatening.

Consider an incident involving Swedish efforts to sell JAS-Gripen jets to Finland. Elisabeth Rehn, former Finnish defense minister, recounts in her memoirs a conversation with Swedish executive Peter Wallenberg. Wallenberg implied that if Finland didn't buy the jets, the Wallenberg conglomerate might pull out of Finland, potentially leading to job losses. Rehn was offended, and when the media asked Wallenberg about this, he suggested there might have been a misunderstanding, questioning the effectiveness of threats in negotiation.

This raises two points: Did Wallenberg view his statement as a threat? And, who is responsible for misunderstandings in communication?

The Carrot vs. the Stick Approach

Resorting to threats can backfire, intensifying the other party's defenses. Imagine if Wallenberg had instead highlighted the benefits of choosing JAS-Gripen, suggesting potential job growth in Finland. This positive approach could have been more effective.

Effective negotiation methods include these:

- **Time pressure:** Negotiating with a deadline can lead to concessions, but it's stressful.
- **Budget constraints:** Making a counteroffer and seeking compromise can be effective.
- **Mutual benefits:** Offer something in return for concessions, like a cash payment for a better product.

- **Leveraging needs:** Use your counterpart's needs to your advantage, such as offering exclusivity in exchange for better terms.

Avoiding Lowball Offers

Inexperienced negotiators might misjudge their leverage, leading to unrealistic offers. I once encountered a client who expected a significantly lower rate for my first project. Initially, I reacted emotionally and almost ended the relationship. Now, I'd take a moment to cool off before responding, keeping emotions in check.

Encouraging Dialogue, Not Debate

Negotiation isn't about winning an argument but understanding each other's positions. Instead of countering every point, it's more productive to understand the other party's constraints and work toward a solution.

The Art of Saying No

Refusing negative propositions constructively is key. For example, parents denying their child's request for a moped can guide them to understand the costs and responsibilities involved, leading to a natural resolution.

Understanding Pressure Dynamics

In negotiations, pressure often begets counterpressure, escalating conflicts. The strategy should be to reduce stress and avoid emotionally charged responses. This principle is crucial in extreme situations like hostage negotiations, where the goal is to build rapport and gradually de-escalate the situation.

When you are testing boundaries and positions, you should evince firmness, stick to your guns, and motivate your demands. You should learn to do so without reverting to combative moves.

It's the rule rather than the exception that negotiations are full of surprises. It always becomes clear that the picture you had of the negotiation was incomplete and partially wrong. You must be responsive and flexible so that you can adjust to the reality that you come across at the negotiating table. Unfortunately, many negotiators are inflexible, and instead they try to force reality to adjust to their negotiation as they have designed it.

If negotiations are slipping from your grip: TAKE A BREAK!

In conclusion, effective negotiation requires a balance of assertiveness and empathy—understand your counterpart's perspective and foster a constructive dialogue.

CHAPTER 4

Tactics

Introduction: Negotiation Tactics

N egotiation approaches vary greatly among individuals. Each of us has a unique perception of negotiation, and our responses to stress and pressure during these interactions differ significantly.

Two key factors stand out in successful negotiation. Firstly, it's crucial to recognize the negotiation style of your counterpart and adapt your strategy accordingly. Secondly, and of equal importance, is understanding your own negotiation tendencies. Are you prone to confrontation? If so, what triggers this response? Could it be the attitude of the other party, influence from your management, or external stressors?

I've delineated five primary negotiation styles: Combative, Concession, Stalling, Compromise, and Collaborative.

Negotiation, as we know, is not a one-size-fits-all process; it is a science that demands a keen understanding of various tactics and the wisdom to apply them effectively.

- **Element 52: The combative negotiator.** The elements in this chapter begin by discussing "the combative negotiator," a type of behavior that unravels the aggressive, often confrontational style of negotiation. This approach, while sometimes effective, can be a double-edged sword, potentially leading to a breakdown in communication and trust. Understanding the dynamics of combative negotiation equips you with the knowledge to either employ or counteract this method when necessary.

- **Element 53: Concession.** The focus shifts to "the concession," a tactic that could be dangerous and misunderstood. Here, you learn the difficulty of giving and taking, a delicate balance that can or cannot pave the way to a mutually beneficial outcome. Concessions, when made strategically, can be a powerful tool to advance negotiations while maintaining one's core interests.

- **Element 54: Compromise.** This examines the intricate dance of give and take. Compromise is not just about splitting differences; it's about finding creative solutions that address the needs and constraints of both parties. This element highlights the importance of understanding and aligning interests to reach a satisfactory resolution.

- **Element 55: Stalling.** This element explores a tactic often used to gain time, reassess positions, or apply pressure. This technique, while sometimes perceived negatively, can be a strategic pause, offering valuable moments for reflection and recalibration in the negotiation process.

- **Element 56: The collaborative negotiator.** This is a stark contrast to the combative approach. This element dives into the principles of collaborative negotiation, where the focus shifts from competing interests to finding common ground and achieving joint gains. This approach underscores the importance of building relationships and seeking win-win outcomes.

As you traverse these varied landscapes of negotiation tactics, remember that the key to successful negotiation lies not only in understanding these strategies but in knowing when and how to apply them. Each negotiation scenario is unique, demanding a tailored approach. The wisdom lies in recognizing the dynamics at play and adapting your strategy accordingly to navigate toward a successful outcome.

However, the reality of negotiation is not so straightforward. It would simplify matters if a combative negotiator always remained aggressive, or if a concession-focused individual consistently adopted a yielding approach. Such predictability would ease preparation.

The complexity lies in the fluidity of these styles. A collaborator might suddenly adopt a combative stance, or a compromiser might shift to a concessionary approach without warning.

To excel in negotiations, it's imperative to not only recognize these various styles but also to know precisely which technique from your repertoire is most effective in addressing each specific behavior.

ELEMENT 52

The Combative Negotiator

C ombative negotiation is the dominant approach in some cultures and the first choice of some people. Combative negotiation is characterized by:

- **One-way communication:** The combative negotiator is often verbally driven and good at arguing. They work with assertions, demands, and threats. They will not or cannot answer questions, because their answers would show that they are bluffing, or that they have no cards in their hand. The answers would give the opponent valuable information—information that could upset the balance of power.
- **Conscious insults:** The combative negotiator wants to create stress for the opponent so they can knock them off balance. Negotiators choose to flee the situation by making one-sided concessions.
- **Bluffing:** The combative negotiator often appears strong and tries to seduce the opponent with promises that will never be kept.
- **Dirty tactics:** The combative negotiator wants to create uncertainty and stress by being unscrupulous, unethical, and inappropriate.
- **Loud voice:** The combative negotiator yells to distract their opponent from the fact that they have no factual arguments.
- **Threats:** The combative negotiator badgers to intimidate and create fear and uncertainty.
- **Greediness:** The combative negotiator does not want to share the added values that are created. The purpose of the negotiation is hidden—they want their opponent to open up and back themself into a corner.

Agreement Disputes

Disputes about agreements often develop into conflicts. What do you do if your opponent, who was friendly and accommodating earlier, now refuses to fulfil their obligations? Suddenly you each have very different views on the agreements you have just made.

Many disagreements can be avoided or solved to mutual satisfaction if the parties take the time to examine possible future scenarios by asking themselves: *If it happens, what have we promised each other in the agreement?*

EXAMPLE | Petersen's Electronics Fire

Petersen's Electronics has insurance that covers all damages. One night, a fire broke out in a room where, among other items, plastic packaging and cables are stored. Luckily, the fire was spotted by employees who were working late. Before the fire spread, they succeeded in getting it under control so that the adjacent stockroom did not burn. The fire department arrived and put the fire out.

The next day, the damage was inspected by a representative from the insurance company. The parties could not agree on whether the goods in the stockroom were damaged by the smoke. The only visible damage was soot on the cardboard boxes. In accordance with regulations, the insurance company only intended to pay for the cost of cleaning or repacking the goods whose cardboard boxes were damaged by soot. The owner claims that the sensitive electronics have probably been affected by the smoke and that future damages are unavoidable. He claims that the entire stock has to be scrapped. The parties have different opinions about how likely this is. The insurance company claims that, if this is the case, Petersen's is partly liable since the goods were not properly protected. If compensation is to be paid, the insurance company must keep the goods in order to assess their value. The owner cannot accept this under any circumstances, as the brand name could suffer.

The parties engage their legal departments, but they cannot agree. Finally, they come to an unfavorable settlement agreement in order to avoid a court case.

The owner comes to the conclusion that the next time there is a fire, he will wait to put it out. If the company had suffered total damage, they would have avoided discussions with their insurance company about whether the goods were damaged. This puts the parties in a dangerous spiral, as insurance premiums are rising rapidly.

Two more forward-thinking parties could have avoided this battle if they had discussed the following:

- What can be done to limit damage in case of a fire? How will it affect the premium?
- What will happen to the stock if damage occurs due to fire or flood? Who decides whether the goods should be discarded, and how?

Conflict Is Harmful

Combative negotiating can create short-term gains, but it is damaging in many ways:

- Conflict damages relationships and trust. The openness necessary to attain mutually positive results does not exist.
- Combative behavior is often not accepted by the other party in a negotiation, who may break off the negotiation. They may have an alternative, or they may choose to leave simply because of the combative behavior.
- Combative negotiators have bad reputations, which may result in fewer opportunities to negotiate.
- The insults combative negotiators hurl at their opponents will lead to blocks, because parties do not want to concede to aggressive people.
- The combative negotiator's ego plays too large a role in negotiations, and this will rouse the ego in their opponent. The insertion of the ego causes emotions to take over, which derails negotiations.
- The combative negotiator forces their opponent into an agreement that they cannot or will not fulfil. In the long term, there are two losers.

Not Seeing the Whole Picture

Combative negotiators are unaware that they do not see the whole picture, and therefore cannot judge whether they have negotiated successfully. They have forced one-sided issues, though, and feel like winners.

EXAMPLE | Being Myopic

A purchasing/sales negotiation ends with the buyer saying: That does not look so bad. We should be able to accept this agreement, but I will get the approval of my colleagues. You can count on receiving the formal order on Friday. Friday morning, they then call the seller.

Buyer: The business that I promised you went to a competitor.

Seller: Why? I thought we had an agreement.

Buyer: Yes, in theory. But this morning your competitor rang and offered us 60 days credit. Those extra 30 days are worth so much to us that we cannot turn it down. But obviously, if you can also offer us 60 days, we would rather buy from you.

> The seller knows that an extra 30 days of credit will cost their firm $30,000. But after a brief pause, the seller says, "Okay. If those extra credit days are really worth $20,000 to you, we can give them to you."
>
> The buyer received a concession without having to give anything in return. The buyer's tactics are classic, but was it a good result?
>
> If the extra credit costs the seller $30,000, how does the whole picture look? Both parties have lost $10,000 on the change in the terms. By using NegoEconomics, they could have reached a better solution – a price reduction of $25,000. If you do not look at the whole picture, including the effects on both parties' costs and profits, you will make the wrong decisions.

Don't Get Caught in the Trap

When the buyer says, "These extra 30 days are so valuable to us that we cannot turn it down," the seller must ask, "How much are those 30 days' worth to you?" If the buyer gets the answer "roughly $20,000," the seller's response should be, "I will compensate you by reducing the price by $20,000."

A basic rule of negotiation is to never give one-sided concessions. With this in mind, the seller continues: "In order for us to carry this cost, we want the agreement to run for 18 months instead of 12." With this concession from the other party, the seller should regain the $20,000 in the long term.

The buyer could continue the negotiation after receiving the 60 days: "Great that you will accept 60 days. You will, however, have to carry the cost of this; how much would that be?" If the seller says that it will be about $30,000, the buyer can continue: "Then it would be better for you if you reduced the price by $27,000." This proposal evens out the difference between you and the competitor, but it is ultimately cheaper for you.

By using NegoEconomics, both the seller and the buyer have achieved more beneficial solutions.

How to Meet a Combative Negotiator

You cannot change other people, but you can change yourself by adjusting to the other person's behavior. Depending on the opponent, the situation might require accepting the situation as it is and making the best of it. If there are equally beneficial alternatives, you do not have to accept the offers of combative negotiators.

The following are a few tactics you can employ in order to adjust to a combative negotiator:

- **Change supplier:** When the personal chemistry between negotiators works, both parties have a greater desire to come to an agreement.
- **Do not be alone:** If you negotiate alongside a partner, you will have moral support. Your partner can help you exit the situation if it becomes too tense.
- **Ask for an agenda before you meet:** An agenda signals to you how the opponents intend to negotiate and who they are bringing with them.
- **Be silent:** You do not have to answer or comment on everything immediately, not even when you believe the combative negotiator is lying. Counterarguments easily lead to conflict.
- **Try to start a dialogue:** If you think that a proposal is insufficient, suggest amendments to it, rather than abandoning it.
- **Delay and tire the opponent:** If a combative negotiator becomes exhausted, they will be less able to implement their aggressive tactics.
- **Play along:** If you come to a friendly agreement, you may be able to make it look as if the opponent has won. Many negotiators are blinded by results shown on paper. If they can negotiate some free spare parts, better payment terms, or discounts, then they (and often their managers) are happy. Why battle against a counterpart if the problem can be solved by leaving some room for negotiation? Take into account the concessions you may have to make. It may be a simple market negotiation, but if both parties are happy with the end result, where is the harm? Leaving room for negotiation is not the same as starting with a high price.

You can leave room for negotiation by taking these steps:

- Make provisos.
- Suggest payment terms, delivery time, or something else you know that the opponent wants to change.
- Offer an alternative technical solution.

Meeting Conflict with Conflict

Consider this situation: Despite all attempts to reach an agreement, your opponent is not giving way. You have tried many tactics that ordinarily succeed with combative negotiators. But nothing helps. In the end, there is nothing left for you to do but be aggressive as well. Before you do this, ask yourself a few questions:

- Am I strong enough to win?
- Have I got the resources needed to see this battle through to the end?
- Is the law on my side?
- Am I willing to pay the price?

Be sure you have affirmative answers to all of these questions before becoming aggressive.

EXAMPLE | The Property Developer

McFadden, one of my project managers, tells me the following: I have not been paid for the work I did for the property developer. The work has been inspected and approved, but there is still no payment. It is a full $1 million. Payment reminders and threats have not produced any results. I need to be paid—otherwise, I cannot pay my taxes and charges on time.

Although considering how to approach this obstacle, we both agree that debt collection is not an alternative, because it takes too long. A journalist offers to help by writing an article in the paper about the developer's business morals, which will feature a picture of the developer, accompanied by the headline: Do you have no business morals? Or do you just lack ability? With this ace up his sleeve, McFadden contacts the developer and carries out his threat: If I do not get the money you owe immediately, you will be reading about yourself in tomorrow's paper. After that you will find it hard to get credit.

The developer responds: I am sorry that you have not received your money; we made a mistake and I apologize for that. If you come over here in half an hour, I will make sure there is a check for $1 million ready for you. I will give it to you personally with my apologies.

McFadden is happy; he appears to have won. The two meet, but when the developer is about to hand McFadden the check, he says, "Before I give this to you, I would like to ask you a question. Have you really thought this through? Do you want the million dollars, or do you want more business from us?" Facing the threat of no more business, McFadden pulls back. The developer agrees to give McFadden a check for $700,000, and McFadden leaves $300,000 poorer but with the promise of a new contract. He gets a new contract, but the final amount of this new contract is also reduced.

ELEMENT 53

The Concession-Oriented Negotiator

Picture a scenario where a customer declares, "I'm sorry, but we can't use you as our supplier. You're too expensive." The seller, anxious to close the deal, hastily offers discounts without any reciprocal demands. This approach, while seemingly accommodating, is a perilous path in negotiation. It's the art of making concessions without strategy or return benefits, often seen as a quick escape from the perceived discomfort of negotiation. This is the trap of unilateral concessions.

The Domino Effect of Unilateral Concessions

When a seller admits to having little control over pricing, they inadvertently signal a weakness, suggesting a margin for reduction. This leads to a series of unilateral concessions, raising the buyer's expectations and potentially leading to a situation where the seller feels compelled to give away more than intended. This not only undermines the seller's position but also sparks a chain reaction of increasing demands from the buyer.

Common Mistakes in Concession-Based Negotiations

The seller's approach in this scenario reveals several critical errors:

- Failure to understand the customer's perspective of "too expensive."
- Negotiating solely on price rather than discussing total costs and value.
- Signaling a lower price possibility by admitting limited authorization.

Alternative Approaches: The Strategic Concession

Instead of immediately yielding to price reductions, the seller could propose conditional concessions, like offering a discount in exchange for an advance payment. This method doesn't weaken the negotiation position but shows a readiness to explore various solutions.

Unintended Use of Concessions

Unplanned concessions often stem from a desire to avoid conflict or to seek approval, leading to a string of uncalculated compromises. The solution? Request a break to regroup and reassess, thus avoiding hasty and pressured decisions.

Recognizing and Countering Unplanned Concessions

Unplanned concessions are marked by one-sided communication and lack of strategic negotiation tactics. To counter this, establish a balanced negotiation where both parties feel valued, and ensure the other party comprehends and has the resources to fulfill their end of the deal.

The Tactical Concession: A Negotiation Tool

Tactical concessions are pre-planned and form part of your negotiation strategy. They are not about compromising needs or profitability but about using built-in negotiation margins (like time, warranties, extras) to achieve various gains. This approach can unlock deadlocks, demonstrate goodwill, and balance power dynamics in negotiation.

When Concessions Are Admissions

Admitting mistakes can be a powerful negotiation tool, portraying personal strength and fostering trust. Politicians often fail in this regard, leading to public distrust.

The Art of Concessions in Negotiation

Concessions can be a double-edged sword. Used strategically, they can be powerful tools to advance negotiations. However, unplanned or unilateral concessions can be detrimental, leading to a loss of credibility and negotiation power. The key is to balance concession with strategy, ensuring mutual benefit and understanding during the negotiation process.

ELEMENT 54

Compromise in Negotiation: The Delicate Art of Balancing Interests

In the intricate dance of negotiation, compromise often emerges as a central theme, a balancing act between conceding and prevailing. This element delves into the nuances of this concept, examining its dynamics and unveiling the layers that often remain hidden in typical compromise scenarios.

Imagine a negotiation between a seller and a buyer. The buyer contests a point in the seller's quotation, focusing on the credit terms. They demand a 90-day credit period, countering the seller's offer of 30 days. This disagreement sets the stage for a negotiation where both parties cling to their positions, seemingly immovable. The seller, constrained by company policy, can only extend up to 30 days of credit. Meanwhile, the buyer insists on 90 days, deeming it a non-negotiable term.

As the dialogue progresses, the seller, sensing the risk of losing the deal, stretches the offer to 45 days, and eventually to 60 days, despite initial claims of a 30-day maximum. This shift, while appearing as a movement toward compromise, actually unveils a common pitfall in negotiations: the erosion of trust through inconsistency and perceived deception.

This scenario exemplifies a surface-level compromise, where each party begins with a firm stance, relying on arguments and sometimes threats to sway the other. The eventual agreement, often a midpoint between the original positions, might seem like a fair resolution. However, such resolutions can be fraught with underlying issues. In this case, the seller's sudden flexibility raises questions about their initial honesty, and the buyer's quick acceptance of 60 days contradicts their earlier firm stance on 90 days being non-negotiable.

This type of compromise, often reached under the pressure of maintaining a deal or relationship, can lead to an expensive resolution for both parties. The seller, in extending the credit terms, incurs additional financial costs without gaining anything tangible in return. For the buyer, despite achieving a longer credit period, the resolution falls short of their initial requirement, potentially leading to financial strain when the invoice becomes due.

What is often missed in such negotiations is an understanding and acknowledgment of the underlying needs and constraints of each party. Had the buyer been transparent about their liquidity issues and the seller been upfront about the implications of extending credit, a more mutually beneficial agreement could have been reached. This might have involved adjusting other terms of the deal, such as price, in exchange for different credit terms.

The essence of a genuine compromise lies in the ability of both parties to engage in open and honest communication. It involves a willingness to understand each other's needs and constraints and to explore creative solutions that address these needs. When parties engage in this level of dialogue, they move beyond the superficial give-and-take of traditional compromise and into the realm of collaborative problem-solving.

However, reaching this level of understanding is not without its challenges. It requires both parties to move beyond rigid positions and to view the negotiation not as a zero-sum game but as an opportunity for mutual gain. This shift in perspective is crucial for transforming a negotiation from a battle of wills into a constructive, solution-oriented discussion.

In this example, the seller, by understanding the buyer's liquidity challenges, could have explored alternative solutions such as offering a discount for early payment or adjusting the pricing structure to accommodate the extended credit terms. Similarly, the buyer, by recognizing the seller's constraints, could have proposed a phased payment plan that aligns with their cash flow while respecting the seller's credit policies.

This approach to compromise is not just about finding a middle ground; it's about expanding the ground itself. It's about discovering new possibilities and solutions that may not have been apparent at the outset of the negotiation. This requires creativity, flexibility, and a willingness to explore options beyond the conventional boundaries of negotiation.

As you delve deeper into the art of compromising, it will become evident that the key to successful negotiation lies not just in the ability to balance interests, but also in the capacity to understand and align them. This understanding leads you to explore strategies that can transform a negotiation from a rigid exchange of demands into a dynamic and creative problem-solving process.

Exploring the Depths of Each Party's Needs

A critical aspect of effective negotiation is the ability to explore and understand the deeper needs and motivations of each party. In the seller-buyer scenario, the seller's initial refusal to extend beyond a 30-day credit period was not merely a rigid policy but likely stemmed from financial constraints or risk management strategies. Similarly, the buyer's insistence on a 90-day credit term was likely rooted in their own cash flow challenges or budgetary planning.

Understanding these underlying factors can open doors to alternative solutions. For instance, the seller might offer a tiered pricing structure where longer credit terms are offset by slightly higher prices, or they could propose a discount for early payment that incentivizes the buyer to adjust their financial planning. Such solutions not only address the immediate issue of credit terms but also foster a sense of partnership and collaboration, laying the groundwork for future business dealings.

The Role of Creativity and Flexibility in Compromise

Creativity plays a pivotal role in transforming a negotiation. It involves looking beyond the apparent constraints and exploring a range of options that might satisfy both parties' needs. Flexibility, on the other hand, is about being willing to adjust one's position in light of new information or understanding.

In the context of the negotiation scenario, creativity could involve the seller offering additional services or products as part of the deal, adding value without directly impacting the credit terms. Flexibility might manifest in the buyer adjusting their payment schedule to align more closely with the seller's financial planning, thus creating a win-win situation.

Building Trust Through Transparent Communication

Trust is the foundation of any successful negotiation. Transparent communication is key to building this trust. This means openly discussing constraints, needs, and the rationale behind each party's position. In the scenario, if the seller had initially explained their credit policies and the reasons behind them, the buyer might have been more understanding and open to discussion.

Similarly, if the buyer had been upfront about their financial situation, the seller might have been more inclined to explore flexible solutions. Trust, once established, makes it easier for both parties to move beyond positional bargaining and into a more collaborative and productive negotiation.

The Long-Term Impact of Compromise

It's important to consider the long-term impact of any compromise reached. A poorly thought-out compromise can lead to resentment, a breakdown in relationships, or financial losses in the long run. Conversely, a well-negotiated compromise can lead to ongoing business relationships, repeat business, and positive referrals.

In the negotiation example, a compromise that takes into account the long-term business relationship could lead to more favorable deals in the future. It could also result in the buyer recommending the seller to other potential clients, thus expanding the seller's business network.

Compromise as a Strategic Tool in Negotiation

In conclusion, compromise in negotiation is not just about finding a middle ground; it's about creating a new ground where both parties can stand together. It's a strategic tool that, when used effectively, can lead to mutually beneficial solutions, stronger business relationships, and long-term success. By approaching negotiations with an open mind, a willingness to understand the other party's needs, and a readiness to be creative and flexible, negotiators can turn potential conflicts into opportunities for collaboration and growth.

ELEMENT 55

Stalling

Imagine you're in the final stages of a contract negotiation. Everything appears settled, the terms outlined clearly. Suddenly, the other party queries, "Is this your best offer?" Despite your belief that you've met all their demands, this question throws you off balance. You respond with uncertainty, seeking clarification, but the other party merely sets another meeting for a later date, leaving you in a state of doubt and confusion.

The Art of Stalling: A Calculated Move

Stalling, or intentionally delaying decision-making in negotiations, is a common tactic. It can manifest as postponing a conclusion, introducing new alternatives, or insisting on additional documentation. The reasons for stalling vary—from hoping the other party lowers their demands to creating time for gathering information or examining other options.

Recognizing and Responding to Intentional Stalling

When stalling is a deliberate strategy, it aims to strengthen the staller's position. It might involve avoiding conflict resolution, putting time pressure on the opponent, or creating uncertainty to elicit a better offer. You might notice it when the other party dwells on trivial details, postpones decisions, or hints at a more favorable offer in the future.

The Risks and Countermeasures of Tactical Stalling

Tactical stalling can backfire, leading to missed opportunities or being perceived as noncommittal. Counter it by applying pressure, waiting out the other party when advantageous, ensuring negotiation alternatives, or setting clear timelines.

Unplanned Stalling: A Sign of Conflict Avoidance

Sometimes, stalling happens unintentionally, often as a result of conflict avoidance or decision-making difficulties. This can lead to misunderstandings, mistrust, or losing deals to competitors. The signs include indefinite responses, hiding behind formalities, and reshaping the negotiation's purpose.

Strategies to Overcome Unplanned Stalling

To manage unplanned stalling, it's crucial to clarify negotiation objectives, prepare the other party for the topics to be discussed, and ensure you're dealing with decision-makers. Having alternative negotiation options can also provide leverage.

Conclusion: Navigating Through Stalling in Negotiations

Stalling, whether intentional or not, presents a significant challenge in negotiations. Recognizing the signs and understanding the underlying motives are key to developing effective countermeasures. Be it through creating time pressure, employing ultimatums, reaching partial conclusions, or exploring alternative solutions, a strategic approach to stalling can help steer negotiations back on track.

Stalling characteristics:

- Indecisiveness, excessive focus on details or procedural matters.
- Postponement of decisions, promises of future advantages.

When used intentionally:

- To gain time, strengthen positions, or create uncertainty.
- To exert time pressure and manage emotions.

When used unintentionally:

- Out of conflict avoidance or decision-making difficulties.
- To delay confronting unsatisfactory negotiations or conflicts.

Risks involved:

- Negative perceptions, growth of problems, entry of competitors.
- Withdrawal of offers, misunderstanding of party positions.

Countermeasures:

- Apply time pressure and ultimatums.
- Seek partial conclusions and informal negotiations.
- Have alternative solutions ready.

Stalling is used as a tactic or stems from hesitation. Understanding and addressing it effectively is crucial for successful negotiation outcomes.

ELEMENT 56

The Collaborative Negotiator

T wenty-first century negotiators are discovering that cooperation leads to better solutions and longer-lasting relationships than aggression does. By using cooperative methods, the pie can grow larger before it is shared. This approach is called *NegoEconomics*. When employing NegoEconomics tactics, look for alternatives that will result in increased profits and reduced costs and risks. This will increase the value of the proposals from both sides of the negotiation. Often, though not always, you will achieve a better result when using NegoEconomics. When the pie is large enough, it is possible to reach a solution with two winners. A cooperative negotiation has the following characteristics:

- The parties are willing to be open, but they are not naïve.
- Openness allows the parties to see the alternatives and add value to the pie.
- There does not have to be *total* openness. Withhold information that will be to the opponent's advantage when the pie is shared.

   To encourage a cooperative negotiation, you must:

- Create a dialogue. Listen to the opponent even though you do not agree with them. Instead, ask questions. Be honest and treat your opponent with respect.
- Avoid making threats. Demands, emotions, and evaluations should be put forward without threats or insults. The negotiators should use their energy for solving problems. Both parties are looking for long-term, solid, and rewarding relationships.

Share the Profit

Must your demands be solely based on the costs, or do you have the right to get a share of the advantage you give the opponent? Now and then, possibilities will arise where you can meet the customer's requirements without any cost to you. Should you give without getting something back?

> **EXAMPLE** | Hotel Stay
>
> You have to book a conference in a hotel on Wednesday and Thursday, 17 and 16 May. The hotel responds: *Okay, yes, 17 May. . . . Yes, we have to try and solve that somehow.*
>
> You: Is there a problem?
>
> Hotel: We have a large group for lunch on that Thursday, so we are a bit short of space. We will solve it somehow.
>
> You: Would it be better if we were there Tuesday and Wednesday instead?
>
> Hotel: Yes, that would be a great help.
>
> You: I will try to persuade my customer to change the dates. What do you think I should tempt her with?
>
> Hotel: How about we give you free wine with dinner?
>
> It is important to find and use the possibilities that show themselves. In the case with the hotel, it is not greed – it is business. Offering free wine with dinner does not cost the hotel very much, but the customer will appreciate it. In other cases, a negotiator may want to give without getting anything back. They may want to help the opponent, want to build a relationship, or feel sorry for them. Being business-like is not always easy. If a negotiator gives too much away too easily, the negotiator will appear naïve and risk being taken advantage of. If they want too much, they will appear greedy, and people will prefer not to do business with them.

See the Whole Picture

Demands can be seen as costly, risky, threatening, and degrading. A negotiator may feel like they have received an offer that is far too low. If you relax a little bit, keep your emotions in check, and ask questions, you will probably be able, eventually, to see the whole picture. You will then discover that risks can also lead to interesting possibilities.

> **EXAMPLE** | Worthington and Wong
>
> Worthington and Wong are discussing a project. They both contribute, trust each other, and mutually gain from one another's experience. The workload that they agree to take on for the project is fairly equal. Before the distribution of the profits, Worthington makes the demand: *My company must get 75 percent of the gross income, otherwise our management will not approve the project.*

A normal reaction to this demand would be: That is unreasonable. My group is spending just as much time on the project as your company, so the income should be shared 50/50. Emotions may come into play once a party realizes an offer is too low. However, waiting for more information is more beneficial than making an immediate counterargument.

Wong: How did you get to 75 percent?

Worthington: We must be able to earn a profit of €500,000.

Wong: What is your estimation of your costs?

Worthington: €700,000.

Wong: Let me see if I understand you correctly: If we can agree on a distribution that gives you €500,000 plus €700,000, a total of €1.2 million, will you be happy?

Worthington: Yes.

Wong: How did you come to the 75 percent figure that you want?

Worthington: Our management does not believe that we will sell more than 1,000 of the 2,000 units. The price per unit is €1,600. So 1,000 units will give us a gross of €1.6 million, and 75 percent of this gives us the €1.2 million that we would need to participate in the project.

Wong predicts that at least 1,800 units will be sold. Instead of arguing about how many units will be sold in the future, Wong sees that there is an opportunity to increase his profit, if everything goes well. His counter suggestion is: *We will consider taking a greater risk and let you keep maybe 65 percent, if not 75 percent, of the first 1,000 units. But we then want 90 percent of all sales above 1,000 units.*

If this is accepted, Wong will get 60 percent of the pie.

CHAPTER 5
Emotions
Introduction: The Role of Emotions in Negotiations

The elements in this chapter dive into a topic close to my heart and crucial in the art of negotiation—the role of emotions. Throughout my career, I've observed and experienced first-hand how emotions profoundly influence negotiation outcomes. This chapter is an exploration of that intricate dance between our feelings and the strategic moves in negotiation, aiming to demystify the emotional landscape that underpins these interactions.

All Business Is Human

My point with this statement is that we need to recognize that negotiations most of the time happen between people. Not organizations or governments, but individuals like you and me. People are irrational since we are emotional, and the emotional impact in negotiations is considerable.

The elements in this chapter examine emotions not just as mere reactions, but as pivotal elements that can either hinder or enhance our negotiation strategies. From the anxiety that grips us when stakes are high to the empathy that builds bridges, each emotion carries a potential impact on the negotiation table. I'll share insights and stories from my own experiences, illustrating how emotions can sway the direction of a negotiation.

Element 67 of this chapter is dedicated to emotional intelligence in negotiations. It delves into techniques for recognizing and managing not only your own emotions but also interpreting and responding to the emotions of others. This understanding is a powerful tool, offering a way to connect, build trust, and ultimately, reach more satisfying agreements.

By the end of this chapter, my goal is for you to not only recognize the importance of emotions in negotiations but also to have a toolkit for harnessing them. Whether you're a seasoned negotiator or just starting out, mastering the emotional aspect of negotiations is a game-changer, one that I believe can transform your approach and success in this fascinating field.

ELEMENT 57

Argumentations

What characterizes the *argumentation* phase is that the arguments are established in general terms, and that the negotiation may easily slip into verbal combat. The negotiation grows into a test of strength between the parties. The party who argues well and credibly may win the initiative and reach a conclusion without having to make any concessions. What we get is a zero-sum game in which everything is done at the expense of the other party. They will have to be satisfied with a smaller share of the profits and bear more of the costs and risks.

Let me start off by saying that argumentation as a collaborative negotiation is generally bad for the development of values. In the argumentation phase, the parties try to exert influence on each other's ambitions and perceptions of each other's negotiation strength. They position themselves for the forthcoming negotiation.

Many arguments are rigid and will have to be further developed before constructive negotiations will become possible.

The argument is: We thought we'd get more for our money.

The argument is further developed: What is it that you're missing?

Don't reply: This is a standard offer. Any additions will have to be charged as extras.

The argument is: The operating costs for your plant are too high.

The argument is further developed: What did you expect them to be? How had you arrived at that figure?

Don't reply: Our documented useful effect is as high as 92 percent. No company is more efficient than we are.

To achieve another and better negotiated solution, you should ensure that the discussion is open and constructive. The purpose of the negotiation is to locate the *NegoEconomics*, that is, alternative sub-solutions that increase the size of the pie to be shared (see Element 20 for more). NegoEconomics arises if a seller who offers to shorten their delivery times only has to bear costs that are lower than the profits achieved by the buyer. By making an extra effort, the supplier can increase the quality of their services/products. If the benefit accruing to the customer exceeds the costs accruing to the supplier, NegoEconomics is created.

If you analyze the arguments of the other party and find them very rigid, this might make you suspect that they are bluffing.

They mention the name of your competitor; the details that distinguish themselves from what you're offering are not mentioned; they don't specify the price gap, nor do they explain why they suspects a possible miscalculation. The negotiation resembles a game of poker. If someone wants to appear credible, they must clarify and substantiate their arguments.

Don't merely say, That is too expensive! Say, I can buy the same living room suite from Milmo; they will give me a 10 percent discount plus free transportation. As you might have seen from their ads, they always grant a 5 percent discount on any purchase over 20,000 euro. I have the ad right here.

Dealing with Argumentations

Lock Down the Other Party

It's important to have a good balance in the negotiation. This can be achieved in the following way:

- **Listen without answering questions.** If you counter everything you hear directly, the negotiation will very likely deteriorate into verbal combat. Pressure engenders counter pressure.

- **Note that arguments are not the same as demands.** A claim to the effect that something is too expensive need not be identical with a demand for a price reduction. It might just as well mean, *Please, show me what it is I'll be getting for my money.* You must get more information about what the other party wants. Ask questions: *Could you please explain/go into further detail about your ideas?* Ensure that you get concrete counterproposals, so that you can determine how far apart you really are, and what you're in agreement about. Never try to guess what the other party wants or would like to accept.

- **Don't make up your mind about the requirements one by one.** Then you'll get a negotiation in which the other party plucks you like a chicken, feather by feather. You must have a full picture before you can determine what is best so that you can move forward. Make sure that you know all the objections and demands before you make your decision. Summarize these demands and objections. Lock down the negotiations and try to get confirmation that you're in agreement, *Provided I can meet your demands, do we have a deal?* If you haven't locked in the other party, you run the risk of new demands cropping up all the time.

- **Before you decide how to accommodate the other party, you need more information.** What consequences will the demands have for you? What solutions do you envisage? What should you demand in return? Why does the other party make these demands? What are they worth to the other party? What are their alternatives? In which ways will it be possible to negotiate with them? Would they benefit from having more?

- **When you've obtained the answers you need, you should take a break before choosing your way forward.** The demands may be unexpected—they can be accommodated in many different ways and lie inside or outside the boundaries within which you have to stay. Knowing what way to move calls for a detailed analysis.

- **Make sure you are heard.** When you present and develop your own proposal, you must make sure that the other party receives it in an easily intelligible way.

- **It may be necessary to repeat and clarify your arguments.** If possible, try to illustrate them visually and be ready to substantiate them. Make simulations and try to demonstrate in an easily intelligible manner what the results of your proposals would be. If the other party can save a lot of money, it's not enough simply to claim, *If you accept our proposal you'll earn a lot of money*. How much is a lot of money? Go to the flipchart or blackboard and use a simple example to show how much it could actually be. This enhances credibility. Motivate your counterclaims and conditions.

Make No Concessions

Remember that the argumentation phase is a test of your respective positions of strength; therefore you shouldn't concede any important points. Points that are conceded prematurely are often wasted points. If you concede a point, never do so without getting something in return. If you do, you run the risk of the other party gaining the upper hand in the negotiation, psychologically speaking.

Negotiate according to the following stringent rule: *Never give anything away without getting something back.*

Here's a summary of the argumentation phase:

- Summarize the point of departure anew. Specify the things you agree about, the common ground you've found, and which problems and needs you should try to solve between you.
- Listen without providing answers to questions put to you!
- Reinforce your own negotiation position by obtaining more information!
- Don't decide about the requirements one by one!
- Get all the requirements out in the open! Lock in the other party!
- Develop your own alternative!
- Summarize the point of departure before pursuing the negotiations!
- The most important thing: Make no concessions without something in return!

ELEMENT 58

Building Rapport with Your Counterpart

F irst, talk about the weather or sports. Take an interest in the other party. Tell them about yourself and ask questions about who they are. Discuss the news headlines or sports. Share a meal, or have a drink and enjoy each other's company. In some countries, no one would think of beginning serious negotiations without sharing a meal first, or at least a drink. Though these tactics may sound simple, many people find this approach incredibly difficult. Others feel it is a total waste of time.

The Role of Oxytocin in Enhancing Negotiation Outcomes

Negotiations, at their core, are a complex interplay of human emotions, rationality, and behavioral nuances. Understanding the biochemical underpinnings that influence human interactions can be crucial in strategizing effective negotiation tactics. One such biochemical factor is *oxytocin*, a hormone predominantly linked to social bonding and trust.

Oxytocin, often termed the "love hormone" or "trust hormone," is produced in the hypothalamus and released into the bloodstream by the pituitary gland. Its influence extends to various social behaviors, including empathy, trust, and relationship-building—all of which are critical elements in negotiations.

In the context of negotiations, oxytocin plays a pivotal role in building rapport and trust between parties. Research suggests that elevated oxytocin levels increase the likelihood of parties reaching mutually beneficial agreements. It fosters a sense of social bonding and trust, which can be instrumental in breaking down barriers and overcoming impasses.

Several studies have illuminated the role of oxytocin in negotiation settings. For instance, experiments involving simulated negotiation scenarios have shown that participants administered with oxytocin were more likely to exhibit cooperative behaviors and reach agreements. This correlation underlines the hormone's potential to enhance negotiation outcomes.

According to ancient Chinese wisdom, negotiations should never be pursued on an empty stomach. Only when good food and drink have been served should negotiations begin. This rule is not based on etiquette, it is based on hard core science. When people eat and drink together, the brain produces oxytocin, which promotes likeability and trust. The chances of creating a good relationship are improved when dinning! Within the first 15 minutes of interplay with a counterpart, I can predict with reasonable precision whether a negotiation will be successful or not.

How Long Should You Talk about the Weather?

When negotiators meet, they often have limited information about each other. The negotiator rarely has answers to these questions:

- How does my counterpart look at things?
- How interested are they in the outcome?
- What decisions have been made previously?
- What priorities have been set?
- What do they want to achieve?
- Do they have an alternative?

If the negotiators do not spend time building rapport, then the first few minutes of the negotiation often are characterized by combat over who gets the floor and who takes the initiative. This combat will likely lead to early deadlock. Instead of a constructive dialogue, the parties will be speaking at cross-purposes and find themselves in destructive verbal combat.

Your emotions and the mood you are in affect your ability to communicate and develop rapport. In order to be a successful negotiator, it is essential to keep your cool. In some cases, the negotiation situation may even require you to hide your feelings altogether.

When parties are very anxious and expectations are high, the exchange of information is reduced. You are inclined to push forward your own proposals and not listen to the other party. Only when the other party has been able to say what is on their mind, and understands that you are listening, will they listen to you. You do not have to be the first to present a solution.

When you are negotiating with people you know well, the deal can be made in a few minutes. In other circumstances, it can take weeks. In some cultures, attempts to skip the opening phase and quickly get into hardcore bargaining can constitute a serious breach of etiquette. Breaches of protocol can render further negotiations impossible.

People who come from a technical background and those who do not regularly deal with new contacts in their day-to-day work environment sometimes have difficulty establishing rapport with strangers. This reluctance can cause problems, especially in international negotiations, where socializing between the parties is far more common than in North America. Irrespective of nationality, we tend to do business with people we know and like. Personal relations can mean more to the transaction than technical matters, presentation style, or financial terms.

EXAMPLE | The Importance of Good Personal Relations

One of the big commercial banks investigated why some loans were granted and others were refused. The banker responsible was asked the following:

Which factor was the most important in your decision whether or not to comply with a request for a loan?

A: The borrower presented good collateral.

B: The borrower presented a financial calculation proving that they could service the loan.

C: The borrower seemed trustworthy.

Most respondents answered C. A follow-up question was asked: Why did you choose C?

The response: I need to see that I can trust the borrower as a person. You can always reach an agreement on the technical details such as collateral and servicing of the loan.

ELEMENT 59

Small Talk

No deal without socializing! Whether a decision is made often depends on whether the personal chemistry is working rather than on rational, measurable factors like price and performance. This is even more true in international negotiations than in negotiations at home. It's easier to be rational when negotiating within familiar frames of reference. Time and time again, internationally experienced negotiators will stress the importance of personal relations. People want to know whom they're doing business with. They want to meet the people they've dealt with before, people whom they trust and on whose word they rely. This is where socializing enters the picture, and here it will be determined if the personal chemistry works out.

Socializing is regulated by written as well as unwritten rules that are more or less entrenched in the culture in question. A small mistake on your part can, at worst, mean that you're seen as impossible in a business context, whereas in other cultures much forbearance is shown vis-à-vis exotic visitors.

In some countries, the old rules governing social behavior have been watered down over the years. Anyone observing the old norms runs the risk of being perceived as a museum piece. A social mistake made in our culture will rarely lead to a deal falling through.

Be careful to observe when a negotiation should be conducted online or when it should be a face-to-face session. Creating a social bond is obviously harder on a Zoom call than over lunch.

For some people, small talk is a challenge—something unpleasant or even unnecessary. However, you need to understand that talking about the weather, kids, hobbies, or something else creates a relationship and generates trust. Remember, at the end of the day, all negotiations are human.

ELEMENT 60

Positive and Negative Emotions

Emotions play an important part of how we make decisions. We are all impacted by both positive and negative even before the negotiations begin.

The Impact of Positive Emotions in Negotiations

Positive emotions play a pivotal role in the realm of negotiations. Emotions like happiness, satisfaction, and excitement can significantly influence the dynamics of a negotiation, often leading to more constructive and successful outcomes. The presence of positive emotions tends to facilitate a more amicable atmosphere, fostering trust and openness between parties.

Happiness and satisfaction in a negotiation context can lead to greater collaboration. Negotiators who exhibit these emotions are often perceived as more cooperative and trustworthy, traits that are crucial for building a strong negotiation relationship. Moreover, positive emotions can enhance creative problem-solving. A negotiator who feels positive is more likely to think creatively, be open to different perspectives, and explore innovative solutions.

Excitement, another powerful positive emotion, can be contagious in negotiation settings. It can stimulate enthusiasm and energy in the negotiation process, encouraging all parties to engage more deeply and persistently. This heightened level of engagement often results in more thorough exploration of the issues at hand, leading to more effective negotiation outcomes.

However, it's essential to balance the expression of positive emotions. Over-exuberance or unwarranted optimism can sometimes be misinterpreted as insincerity or naivety. The key is to harness these emotions to build a positive, yet realistic, negotiation climate.

Navigating Negative Emotions in Negotiations

Dealing with negative emotions like anger, frustration, and fear is one of the most challenging aspects of negotiations. These emotions, if not managed properly, can derail the negotiation process, leading to impasses or suboptimal outcomes.

Anger and frustration are common in negotiations, especially when parties face deadlocks or feel their interests are being threatened. It's crucial for negotiators to recognize and manage these emotions, both in themselves and in others. Techniques such as taking a break, rephrasing contentious points, or employing active listening can help de-escalate negative emotions. The goal is to shift the focus from emotional reactions to problem-solving.

Fear is another emotion that can significantly impact negotiations. It often stems from the uncertainty of outcomes, the potential of losing something valuable, or the pressure of reaching an agreement. To navigate fear, negotiators should seek to build a safe and open environment where concerns can be openly discussed.

Providing reassurance, seeking common ground, and demonstrating empathy can mitigate fear and lead to more fruitful negotiations.

Dealing with negative emotions in negotiations is a nuanced and critical aspect that can have a significant impact on outcomes. When negative emotions like anger, frustration, fear, or resentment arise, they can cloud judgment, impede communication, and derail the negotiation process. Here's a quick overview on how to effectively manage these emotions:

- **Recognize and acknowledge emotions.** The first step in dealing with negative emotions is to recognize and acknowledge them, both in yourself and in others. It's important to understand that these emotions are a natural part of human interaction, especially in high-stakes situations like negotiations.
- **Understand the underlying causes.** Often, negative emotions are symptoms of underlying issues. It could be a perceived threat, a past negative experience, or a misalignment of interests and expectations. Digging deeper to understand these causes can provide valuable insights into how to address the emotional aspect of the negotiation.
- **Maintain emotional control.** Practicing self-regulation is key. Techniques such as deep breathing, taking a moment to pause, or even excusing oneself for a short break can help in regaining composure. The goal is to respond rather than react.
- **Listen empathetically.** Active and empathetic listening can go a long way in diffusing negative emotions. By showing genuine interest in the other party's

concerns and viewpoints, you create a more collaborative atmosphere. This approach helps build trust and understanding.

- **Reframe the situation.** Reframing involves changing the perspective on a situation to view it in a more positive or neutral light. This can shift the focus from confrontational to problem-solving, helping both parties to see the issue from a different angle.

- **Communicate effectively.** Clear and assertive communication is essential. Avoid language that might be perceived as accusatory or confrontational. Instead, use "I" statements to express how you feel about the situation without placing blame.

- **Seek common ground.** Find areas of agreement or common interests as a foundation to build upon. Focusing on common goals can help in redirecting the conversation away from emotionally charged topics to more neutral or positive ones.

- **Use humor wisely.** In some situations, appropriate humor can lighten the mood. However, it's important to be sensitive to the context and ensure that it's not at the other party's expense.

- **Employ professional mediation.** In cases where emotions are too high and impede progress, it might be beneficial to involve a neutral third party or mediator. They can facilitate communication and help in finding mutually acceptable solutions.

- **Know when to walk away.** If negative emotions are overwhelming and productive dialogue seems impossible, it may be wise to adjourn the negotiation. Sometimes, a break or postponement can provide the necessary time for emotions to settle.

Incorporating these strategies requires practice and patience. It's also important to remember that every negotiation and every negotiator is unique. Flexibility in approach and a deep understanding of human behavior and emotions are key in effectively managing negative emotions in negotiations.

Understanding and managing negative emotions is not about suppressing them but rather about acknowledging and channeling them constructively. The ability to navigate through these emotional waters can be the difference between a failed negotiation and a successful one.

ELEMENT 61

Maintaining Emotional Control

Negotiations can be high-stress environments where emotions run high. The key to navigating these emotions effectively lies in self-regulation, a component of emotional intelligence that involves controlling one's emotional responses to situations. This element delves into various techniques and strategies to maintain emotional control during negotiations.

- **Understanding emotional responses:** The first step in self-regulation is recognizing one's emotional triggers. Understand what situations or behaviors in negotiations make you anxious, frustrated, or angry. Self-awareness allows you to anticipate and prepare for these emotional responses.

- **Deep-breathing techniques:** When emotions start to escalate, one of the simplest and most effective methods to regain control is deep breathing. Deep, controlled breaths can help lower stress levels, reduce anxiety, and promote a clear mind. This physical response directly impacts emotional state, allowing for more rational thinking and decision-making.

- **Taking a moment to pause:** Sometimes, the best response is no immediate response. When emotions are high, taking a moment to pause before responding can prevent reactions that are purely emotional. This pause can be a few seconds to gather thoughts or a deeper reflection on the implications of the emotional response.

- **Excusing yourself for a break:** In situations where emotions become overwhelming, it may be necessary to take a short break from the negotiation. This physical separation from the negotiation environment can provide the space needed to calm down, reassess the situation, and plan a more effective response.

- **Practicing mindfulness:** Mindfulness involves being fully present in the moment and aware of yourself and your surroundings. Practicing mindfulness can help negotiators stay centered and calm, reducing the likelihood of emotional overreactions.

- **Developing a response, not a reaction:** The goal of emotional control is to respond thoughtfully rather than react impulsively. A response is considered and takes into account the broader context and potential consequences, whereas a reaction is often immediate and driven by emotion.

- **Seeking constructive outlets:** Having an outlet for emotions outside of the negotiation can be beneficial. This could be discussing the situation with a mentor or colleague, engaging in physical activity, or practicing relaxation techniques.

- **Managing emotions long-term:** Developing long-term strategies for emotional control is crucial for professional growth. This can include regular stress-management practices, seeking feedback on emotional responses, and continuous learning about emotional intelligence.

Maintaining emotional control is not about suppressing emotions but managing them effectively. By practicing self-regulation, negotiators can ensure that they are responding in a way that is conducive to constructive negotiation, leading to better outcomes and more productive relationships.

ELEMENT 62

Cheating, Bluffing, and Little White Lies

Honesty is a precursor to trust. Cheating is the opposite of honesty and therefore precludes trustworthiness. The use of bluffing, white lies, and the belief smart people cheat those who are not so smart appear to be increasing at an alarming rate. In fact, there is a widespread belief that business goes hand-in-hand with dishonesty, cheating whenever you can get away with it, and bending the rules.

The Epidemic of Cheating

My research shows that up to 50 percent of people surveyed believe they ought to bluff just a little bit in a negotiation. This becomes an endless spiral. The boundary between the permissible and the nonpermissible begins to shift, slowly but surely.

A study conducted by Robert Feldman at the University of Massachusetts, Amherst, found that 60 percent of people lied at least once during a 10-minute conversation and told an average of two to three lies. However, if you only look at participants from the educated middle class, lies are told more frequently than that: on average with this group one in every three minutes of conversation consists of lies. It is thought this difference has a lot to do with the fact that the better a person's education is, the wider their vocabulary. Along with that, the educated person tends to be self-assured, making it easier to lie. People with a higher level of education can more easily see the advantages of a well-placed fabrication, which is why they are more likely to elaborate the truth. This research also shows that men in 68 percent of cases lie or cheat at a job interview, whereas 62 percent of women do the same.

Studies conducted by Dan Ariely, a professor of behavior economics at Duke University, have persuasively shown that cheating is much more widespread—and infectious—than we commonly believe. An anecdote Ariely shares in a *Wall Street Journal* article quotes a locksmith, who quips that "one percent of people will always be honest and never steal. Another one percent of people will always try to pick your lock and steal your television. The purpose of locks is to protect you from the 98 percent of mostly honest people who might be tempted to try your door if it had no lock."

In the studies Ariely conducts, which typically entice people to cheat by showing them potential financial gain in doing so, he claims he "lost hundreds of dollars to the few big cheaters in our experiments—but lost thousands to the many little cheaters." The picture that emerges from these studies is that it is not merely Madoff-like characters that lie and steal and damage the global economy—it is rather the countless dishonest acts that 98 percent of us commit. Ariely claims as long as we can convince ourselves we are basically honest when we look in the mirror—that is, as long as we don't go too far with our lies—we will continue to commit little dishonest acts here and there.

Ariely believes that these little acts only reinforce others' bad behavior, building a culture of dishonesty. The variables that increase dishonesty include knowing others are behaving dishonestly, an easy ability to rationalize, and previous dishonest acts. The more a person excuses themself, the more they damage others through insidious little white lies.

If the business community committed to a policy of total honesty and increased practices such as honor codes, moral reminders, and signature requirements, we could reinforce overall practices of ethics and fair-dealing in the business world, creating a new culture of honesty.

Is Bluffing So Bad?

Bluffing may yield good results but the decision is always uncertain. The person who subsequently discovers their partner is a liar will not be forgiving.

The short-term gain you have achieved through bluffing may turn into a painful defeat in the long run. In negotiations, things are rarely black-and-white. Carefully assess the facts before you claim you are better able than the other party. More often than not, negotiators function in a gray zone.

Individuals, industries, and cultures impose different limits on the acceptability of bluffing in the course of negotiations. Be responsive and do not cross the line of what is acceptable, especially if you think there is a chance your bluff will be called.

ELEMENT 63

Perseverance

I magine you're sitting at the negotiation table, asking the counterpart a question such as, "What is the your value if we change the delivery date?"

Your counterpart is quiet for a moment and then replies, "That would be beneficial, but changing terms of payment is . . ."

Your assignment as a professional negotiator is to chase the opening and show perseverance. Many negotiators give up if they don't get a reply to their question. Your counterpart is often not willing to admit the financial benefit of changing the delivery date just like that. It may take several questions. According to my studies, sometimes you'll need to ask the same question up to four times before your counterpart will either share the data or tell you they won't.

This persistence is crucial in negotiations because it demonstrates your commitment to understanding the full picture. Moreover, it shows respect for the complexity of the situation your counterpart is in. By asking the same question multiple times, you're not merely repeating yourself; you're allowing space for the other party to reflect and respond more thoughtfully.

Negotiators should understand that the first response is often a reflex, not a well-considered answer. People are instinctively guarded, especially in situations where they feel they might lose something. This defensive mechanism can cause them to hold back information that could be mutually beneficial. Your perseverance helps them move past this initial resistance.

Use Tact and Patience

Perseverance must be balanced with tact and empathy. You're not interrogating your counterpart; you're engaging in a dialogue. Your tone should remain respectful, and your questions should be phrased in a way that's not accusatory but rather exploratory. It's about creating an atmosphere where both parties feel comfortable to discuss and negotiate openly.

Additionally, when you persist, do so with the intent to understand and not just to win. The aim is to build a smart partnership where both parties gain something valuable from the negotiation. This approach often leads to creative solutions that weren't apparent at the start of the discussion.

In cases where the counterpart remains resistant, it's essential to read the situation correctly. Know when to push and when to step back. Sometimes, giving the counterpart some time to ponder over the question and returning to it later in the conversation can yield better results.

Perseverance in negotiation is about patiently and respectfully peeling back the layers of a conversation to discover the core issues and opportunities. It's a skill that, when mastered, can transform an ordinary negotiator into an exceptional one. Through thoughtful persistence, you not only uncover hidden opportunities but also build a foundation of trust and respect, essential elements for successful long-term business relationships.

ELEMENT 64

Pacing, Rapport, and Lead

Think back to a time when you and another person saw completely eye to eye about something and were completely in tune with one another. This may have been a friend, a colleague, a member of your family, or someone you met by chance. Cast your mind back and work out what it was that gave rise to those feelings of absolute concord and unanimity.

Perhaps the reason for this was identical thoughts, or you had the same views of a book, a film, or a play. Perhaps you did not notice this, but you are bound to have had identical breathing patterns, body language, and manner of speaking. No matter what it was, the thing you experienced was something called rapport. This is called being "in rapport." What is rapport? *Rapport* is a harmonious, empathetic, or sympathetic relationship or connection between two people. Rapport means identifying the ability to perceive the world as another person. In other words, it means communicating on the same channel as another and thereby being better at communicating with that person.

You Have a Choice

You can consciously choose to establish rapport. The activity of establishing rapport is called *matching*.

Rapport is the ultimate tool for producing results with other people, no matter whether they are individuals or groups. The ability to establish rapport is one of the most important talents any human being can have in life. You can achieve amazing results by utilizing rapport.

Rapport can be the mediator in nonverbal communication. One word of warning: Rapport must be used in an ethical manner. Manipulating another person with dishonest or unfair motives can cause havoc. In most cases, body language is a giveaway, and that is why rapport should also be used scrupulously.

To achieve rapport, you need to maintain a consistent speed when you are speaking and breathing. Notice people who agree on the subject that they are discussing. These could be your colleagues standing around the coffee machine or a married couple in a restaurant.

They will either sit or stand in a more or less identical fashion. If one of them has their arms crossed, it is likely that the other will be doing this too. If one of them is leaning up against a wall, it is likely that the other one will be doing the same. This is called *pacing*—conscious or unconscious imitation of the opposite number's total communication pattern, body language, verbal, and non-verbal behavior.

By establishing rapport with another person, you can create a basis for effective exchange of thoughts and ideas regardless of whether you are negotiating, giving a consultation, selling something, or talking to someone who you know. There is often natural rapport between close friends or between married people. They automatically complement each other. As humans, we tend to be attracted to those who are nearly identical to ourselves. How do we build up a rapport with another person? The most crucial factors are as follows:

- Physiology—that is, posture and movement
- Voice, tone, and speed
- Language and representative system (auditory, visual, kinesthetic)
- Experience, common background
- Breathing
- Beliefs and values

It is important to behave naturally and use our innate qualities when we match rapport. Every one of us has our own ways of sitting, standing, and reclining. We should be true to ourselves; otherwise, the person who we are communicating with will perceive us as being affected and insincere.

One well-known cliché is that opposites attract. Just like the majority of clichés and myths, it is mainly incorrect, but it does have a grain of truth. In your mind, who is the most appealing? Who would you like to spend time with or do business with? People who you completely disagree with and who have completely different interests and goals? Of course not—you want to be with people who are similar to you. When people are similar, they tend to like each other. Are different people with different interests involved in the same type of club work, for instance?

The flimsy evidence about opposites attracting one another is based on the fact that two people who agree on most things can find that there is an element of excitement with their differences. Think of someone you really do like. What makes you like this person? Isn't it because this person is like you? Or is this person a prototype of how you would like to be? You perceive that person to be clever and smart. They perceive the world in this same way. Then think about someone who you do not like. You think to yourself, what an idiot. Do they think in the same way you do?

Physiological Matching

Physiological rapport often occurs automatically without us realizing it. Should you intentionally acquire the physiological characteristics of the other person and match them? For example:

- Adopting a similar way of standing or sitting, following suit if people lean up against a wall on one arm
- Crossing arms or not crossing arms, depending on the other person, and the same applying to legs
- Using the same gestures with arms and hands and assuming an equivalent facial expression
- Adopting the same posture
- Hands relaxed or stretched out
- Eyes—open or screwed up
- Eye movements (see the section on language and representative systems in this element)
- Shoulders raised or slouched

With matching, you should never mirror another person exactly. Do it at a steady pace, one thing at a time. An example could be body language. Notice the tone and speed of their voice. Try to match and establish rapport early on in a dialogue in order to create a common basis for further communication.

There is also the concept called *crossover matching,* which means that what we do is equivalent, but not exactly the same. If the person you are speaking to crosses their arms, you should cross your legs. If they fidget with a cup, you can click your pen, and so on. A good way of establishing rapport is to have the same document, page, diagram, or flip-over chart. This object creates a neutral basis and brings you closer together, as both of you are responsible for the development of the writing, the drawing on the paper, or the flip-over chart.

What happens if the person you are talking to becomes aware of what you are doing? This happens very rarely if you follow my advice to do things at your own pace in a respectfully serious and scrupulous manner.

If the person you are communicating with is familiar with this technique, they will often be able to acknowledge your efforts and recognize your professionalism in communication as a goal for a win-win situation.

Voice Matching

Physiological matching is not possible on the telephone. You cannot see each other. That is why we need to find other ways to identify each other. These could be:

- The volume of your voice—do you talk loudly or softly?
- Tempo—how fast do you speak?
- Tone of voice—what emotions does tone conjure up? Is your voice high pitched or low pitched?
- Phrases—what expressions does the other person use?
- Rhythm—does the voice flow, is it a steady or a jerking voice producing words in groups? Is it legato or staccato?

Avoid imitating dialects or other ways of speaking that could come across as if you were extemporizing and being amateurish.

Matching Language and Representative Systems

You can establish a good rapport if you match the other person's representative system. In actual fact, this complements the other person's way of thinking (see Element 64).

- **Visual thinking:** People who think visually use expressions like "I can see it in front of me" and "Let us have a look at this."
- **Auditory thinking:** In the same way, these people use expressions like "I hear what you are saying" or "That sounds good."
- **Kinesthetic thinking:** These people use expressions like "I feel this is going well" or "Things are running smoothly!"

By matching and using equivalent expressions, you achieve rapport with the person in question.

Matching Experience and Finding Common Ground

If two people from the same profession meet each other—for instance, two nurses or two lawyers—they will strike up a friendly conversation and build some rapport.

Their situation is identical in many respects. You can consciously use the same basis to establish rapport with other people whose background you are not familiar with. If you arrive at a meeting or a presentation, there is every chance that each participant has:

- Driven through the traffic to reach the meeting
- Left the office with unfinished work
- Been motivated in a specific way and has reasons for attending
- A need to talk about "the weather"

If you are the chairperson, it is a good idea to use this common ground by saying something like, "Now you are all going to need a day to . . . " You generate a type of parity with everyone present and by doing that establish rapport. Other statements may include:

- "Since we would both like to achieve a beneficial result, we prefer to have a win-win dialogue with our negotiations."
- "I believe we can reach an agreement very fast, since neither of us should lose out."

Skillful salespeople take note of the surroundings of the person they are speaking to. These may include pictures of their children, boats, or something else that is of interest to the person they are speaking to.

Matching Breathing

Some people breath quite overtly; you can see their chest or their shoulders moving. When you have established eye contact, you can easily identify the other person's breathing pattern by looking at their shoulders. Then you can establish rapport by matching or by crossover matching, by nodding your head in accordance with their breathing.

Matching Beliefs and Values

The level of common values is determined by matching the effect. If you can establish that each person has the right, or a common set of values about money, honesty, or friendliness, you have already created a platform for imparting other methods of rapport. Other expressions could be "We had better not waste any more time" or "We should all participate in the project."

A good introduction for establishing rapport is to speak about a subject that you know will interest the other party. Create what is called a "yes stream." A "yes stream" consists of some well-chosen questions, which you know the recipient will probably say "yes" to. For example. "Did you all travel here by car?" "Did you all receive the course book?"

Using Rapport, Pace, and Lead

Imagine that you are having a discussion with a rather aggressive person. They attack you continuously and act very angry. When you identify this character's behavior, you can actually pace this person by mirroring their aggression (e.g., excessive use of kinesthetic words and phrases). After you have paced them, you gradually tone down your use of body language and verbal expressions.

If successful, you can now lead the person into agreeing with your point through visual representation—and make them see the situation from your point of view. The previous aggression is now no longer present, nor easy to recall.

Try to think back on a situation where you were particularly agitated or very angry with another person. Recall the pictures from the tense situation and listen to the voices. Feel the anger that you reacted with. The feeling is now gone because you lead your emotions onto another channel. Try smiling at the same time. This can be very hard because your state of mind is changed immediately.

Try to test this behavior. Try to change your behavior slowly and see if the other person follows. Try to see and listen to whether they follow your behavior and adopt body language, voice speed, and tone. If they don't, you need to go back to the beginning and try to establish rapport again.

You can use lead as a tool when you have a desire to influence other people's emotions, opinions, decisions, and attitudes. For instance, if a person's body language indicates a bad mood or depression, you might be able to lead them into psychological and emotional harmony. After this, you can again try to change your body language and express joy and enthusiasm.

When to Use Rapport, Pace, and Lead

You can use this technique in multiple situations:

- In conversations with your superior
- When handling a difficult customer
- In negotiations
- When convincing others of your ideas
- When building team spirit
- When cooling down a tense situation
- When delivering bad news

Try to imagine that you are in the middle of a very tough negotiation and facing an angry counterpart. The cause is not really of any importance, but in negotiation feelings can tend to take over. Many communication experts claim that in a situation like this, you must speak slowly and act calmly to cool down your counterpart.

But what happens? We all know the situation where you might be at home angrily laying out a grievance with a spouse, friend, or child and the other party remains calm. It can make you even more agitated and angry.

We need to develop as the discussion proceeds. Therefore, you need to pace the other person's body language, tone of voice, and speed. When the person registers the empathy from your side, you will build rapport. For instance you could say, "I know exactly how you feel; I would feel the same."

You build rapport, and thereafter you can lead the person in the direction you want, using a lower tone of voice and a calmer use of body language.

Numerous studies made on very successful people show that consciously or subconsciously, they all have a strong talent for building rapport with other people. Those who are flexible in all three areas can influence people regardless of whether these are public people, business people, or "just" regular people. You will never be a natural talent or gifted with this talent from birth. All you need to master these skills is a little practice where you measure your own success.

When Should You Break Rapport?

Rapport can end anytime you want to:

- End a relationship
- Get attention
- Move attention to other areas

How do you break rapport? Everything should be done opposite to the approach previously described. Take on another body language, use another level of voice, and use conclusive words. You know how dismissed you feel when you are having a conversation with another person and they check their watch, pull out their phone, or put their palms on the table. Breaking rapport can damage the trust, so it is imperative that your mismatching actions are carried out in a calm way. Do not break off rapport abruptly!

ELEMENT 65

Likeability in Negotiations: Insights from Research

Likeability plays a crucial role in the dynamics of negotiations, profoundly affecting outcomes. Drawing on the findings from the findings in this chapter on small talk, emotions, emotional control, perseverance, pacing, rapport, leading, personal chemistry, decisions, and bias, it's evident that the human aspect of negotiation is as critical as it is strategic. Likeability, often cultivated through effective small talk, emotional intelligence, and the establishment of personal chemistry, significantly influences the negotiation process. It's not just about the logical aspects of the deal but also how parties perceive and relate to each other on a personal level.

Engaging in small talk and demonstrating genuine interest in the counterpart's background and interests can break down barriers, building a foundation of trust and likeability. Emotional intelligence, including the awareness and control of one's emotions and the ability to empathize with others, further enhances this likeability, making negotiators more adept at creating a positive atmosphere. Perseverance, coupled with emotional control, shows resilience and commitment, traits that are often admired and can lead to increased likeability.

Pacing, rapport, and leading are techniques that, when used skillfully, can align negotiation rhythms and build a collaborative, rather than adversarial, relationship. Understanding and adapting to the other party's communication style fosters respect and likeability. The concept of personal chemistry cannot be underestimated; it can sometimes override the more tangible aspects of a negotiation, such as price and terms.

Finally, an awareness of decisions and biases is crucial. Likeability can mitigate negative biases and facilitate more favorable decisions. However, it's essential to recognize that likeability should not overshadow the importance of a fair and equitable negotiation outcome. It should be used ethically and in balance with rational negotiation strategies.

Likeability is a multifaceted attribute that, when effectively integrated with negotiation strategies, can lead to more positive outcomes. The ability to be liked and to foster personal connections in a negotiation context is a powerful tool, one that requires careful cultivation and genuine interaction. The research underscores the importance of likeability, suggesting that the most successful negotiators are those who can blend strategic acumen with genuine interpersonal skills.

The intriguing questions of whether it's possible to like someone you don't trust, or trust someone you don't like indeed have a nuanced answer: yes. This perspective is supported by extensive feedback from thousands of students and clients, highlighting the complexity of human emotions and relationships. It underscores the necessity of recognizing and understanding our subconscious biases. This insight prompts a deeper exploration of the interplay between likeability and trust, suggesting that while they are interconnected, they can exist independently within the realm of personal and professional relationships.

ELEMENT 66

Personal Chemistry

Many years ago, I was traveling through Europe to learn about different countries and their cultures. I was very young and completely inexperienced as a negotiator.

I entered a carpet shop in Istanbul, asking to be shown a particular carpet. First thing, the shop owner asks me to sit down and offers me a drink. He doesn't get out the carpet, praising all its qualities. I accept the drink. He is about to have tea himself. It's time for his tea break, and his assistant prepares the tea on a primus stove placed on a tray in front of us.

I'm interested in the small ceremony taking place, and the shop owner explains to me how and why his assistant follows a particular ritual. In this way, he establishes a good rapport with me and gains my trust.

After a while, the conversation turns to other matters. While we are having tea, he obtains information about me. Some of the questions he asks are:

How long have you been in Istanbul?

When will you be leaving?

Where have you come from, and where are you going?

What hotel are you staying at?

Have you been to the bazaar before?

I tell him that I've been in Istanbul for four days, that I'm staying at the Hilton, that I've come from Bulgaria and shall be going on to Romania on the following day. I've not been to the bazaar before, but have spent my time visiting other tourist attractions in Istanbul.

He warns me against pickpockets, and I check that my money is still in my pocket. The owner knows that he has before him a customer who has little time and much money, one who hasn't spent a lot of time bargaining in the bazaar. He needs to know more about me before negotiations can begin.

He asks his assistant to go and get out the carpets that I'm interested in. In the meantime, he asks me if I would mind being shown a few other carpets.

A little farther into the shop three carpets are spread out on the floor. He asks me: How do you like these carpets? I look at them and my comments immediately reveal that I don't know a great deal about carpets. I make comments on the colors and point out that the one in the middle is commonly found in Denmark. The owner asks: How much would such a carpet be in my home country? I replied, $1,000 to $2,000.

A little later, the assistant brings forward the carpet I've been asking about, and negotiations begin. The owner, armed with all the information he needs, skillfully steers the negotiation toward a conclusion satisfactory to both him and me. He has built up his position of strength by obtaining information about me. What this example illustrates is that I never perceived this interaction as a negotiation. I encountered a very pleasant individual who seemed to sincerely show interest in me and my background. I liked the carpet salesman, and he succeeded in creating positive chemistry between us.

ELEMENT 67

Emotional Intelligence: The Foundation for Effective Negotiation

Humans are all illogical! We do not use logic to decide, or for that matter, to think. Unfortunately, all our decisions come from emotions. Emotional intelligence guru Daniel Goleman explains that our brain's decision-making center is directly connected with emotions, and then with logic. Therefore, as any good salesperson will tell you, we decide with emotions and justify (we deceive ourselves) with logic.

Emotional intelligence is the foundation of human manipulation. High levels of emotional intelligence will lead to more successful negotiations and success. Emotional intelligence is not a fixed size but a mix of core changeable beliefs, attitudes, and competencies.

If you are emotionally intelligent, you:

- Possess a high level of self-awareness (how you affect others)
- Are sensitive to the needs and emotional states of others
- Know how to become aware of your emotions and control them in a healthy way
- Can handle setbacks and mistakes in a positive, constructive manner
- Can control stress and other destructive symptoms of negative emotions
- Possess a high level of personal power and control over your decisions

- Are goal-oriented and focused
- Are flexible and open to new ideas and changes
- Communicate openly and form strong connections with others
- Are trusted by others
- Have a healthy belief in others, while remembering to protect yourself
- Have a realistic approach to negotiations without being too optimistic or too pessimistic
- Can handle conflicts in a confident, consistent manner
- Have a healthy surplus of independence and recognize the additional benefits of working with others

All of these qualities stem from two core qualities: possessing high self-esteem and an equally high regard for other people. If you are an emotionally intelligent person, you are open to self-reflection and new learning opportunities.

Relevance for Negotiators

Emotional intelligence (EI) is particularly crucial for negotiators for several reasons:

- **Understanding and influencing others**: High EI enables a negotiator to read and understand the emotional states and needs of the other party. This insight can be used to influence the negotiation in a direction that is beneficial for all involved.
- **Managing emotions**: Negotiations often involve high-stakes and high-pressure situations. The ability to manage one's emotions and remain calm and clear-headed is vital in making rational decisions and maintaining a professional demeanor.
- **Building trust and rapport**: EI helps build trust and rapport with the other party, which is essential for successful long-term relationships. A negotiator who can empathize and connect on a human level is more likely to secure favorable outcomes.
- **Resolving conflict**: Effective conflict resolution, a key element in any nego-tiation, requires understanding both sides' perspectives and emotions. High EI equips negotiators with the skills to navigate conflicts and find mutually beneficial solutions.
- **Being adaptable**: Negotiations can be unpredictable. An emotionally intel-ligent negotiator is better equipped to adapt to changing situations and dynamics, maintaining a flexible and open mindset.

In essence, emotional intelligence is not just an advantageous trait but a fundamental skill set for any successful negotiator. It enhances every aspect of the negotiation process, from preparation to conclusion, ensuring more effective, empathetic, and beneficial outcomes.

ELEMENT 68

Decision-Making and Emotional Biases in Negotiations

In the complex landscape of negotiations, decision-making is often influenced by a range of factors, among which emotions play a significant role. Emotional biases can subtly, yet powerfully, sway the direction and outcome of negotiations, often without the negotiator being fully aware of their impact. This element explores how emotions can lead to biases in decision-making and offers strategies to mitigate these effects for more rational, objective decision-making in negotiations.

- **Identifying emotional biases:** Emotional biases in negotiations can manifest in various forms, such as overconfidence, escalation of commitment, or adverse reactions to perceived losses. Recognizing these biases is the first step toward mitigating their impact. For instance, a negotiator might continue to pursue a losing course of action due to the *sunk cost fallacy*, driven by the emotional investment in the decision rather than rational analysis.

- **Understanding the role of self-awareness:** Enhancing self-awareness is key to understanding and controlling emotional biases. By regularly reflecting on their emotional states and decision-making processes, negotiators can become more aware of when and how their emotions are influencing their choices.

- **Cultivating emotional neutrality:** Striving for emotional neutrality helps in reducing the impact of emotional biases. This doesn't mean ignoring emotions but rather acknowledging them and ensuring they do not dictate decision-making. Techniques like mindfulness and meditation can aid in maintaining a balanced emotional state.

- **Implementing structured decision-making processes:** Utilizing structured decision-making processes can counteract the sway of emotional biases. This might include defining clear objectives, using data and evidence to inform decisions, and considering a range of alternatives before making a choice.

- **Seeking diverse perspectives:** Involving individuals with diverse perspectives in the negotiation process can provide a check against emotional biases. These differing viewpoints can challenge assumptions and emotional impulses, leading to more balanced decision-making.

- **Developing emotional intelligence:** High emotional intelligence (EI) can be a powerful tool in identifying and managing emotional biases. EI involves not only being aware of one's own emotions but also understanding the emotions of others, which is crucial in negotiation contexts. You can develop your EI awareness through practice and studies.

- **Providing regular review and feedback:** Regularly reviewing past negotiation decisions and seeking feedback can help in identifying patterns of emotional bias. This practice encourages continuous learning and improvement in decision-making skills.

- **Including case studies and role-playing exercises:** Including real-world case studies where emotional biases impacted negotiation outcomes, along with role-playing exercises, can provide practical insights into recognizing and mitigating these biases.

- **Balancing emotion and logic:** Try to establish the difference between your emotions and logical thinking throughout the negotiation.

Understanding and mitigating emotional biases in decision-making is crucial for successful negotiations. By employing strategies such as increasing self-awareness, implementing structured decision-making processes, and developing emotional intelligence, negotiators can make more rational and objective decisions, leading to more favorable outcomes in their negotiation endeavors.

CHAPTER 6

Things to Consider

Introduction: Things to Consider

In this comprehensive chapter, you embark on a journey through things to consider. This chapter explores the innovative approach of NegoEconomics, which combines economic principles with negotiation tactics for maximized value. The role of mediators and facilitators in conflict resolution is then examined, highlighting their importance in guiding toward mutually beneficial outcomes. This chapter also considers the strategic thinking and holistic view necessary to grasp "the big picture" in negotiations.

This chapter further delves into essential negotiation skills, cost-effective strategies, and methods for addressing misunderstandings. The concept of Total Cost of Ownership (TCO) is analyzed, alongside the flexible approach of contingent contracts. It also discusses the significance of post-negotiation audits for evaluating and learning from each negotiation experience.

Adding to these insights, the chapter emphasizes the critical skill of listening and compares the dynamics of face-to-face or virtual negotiations. Additionally, it examines various negotiation platforms, providing a detailed analysis of their strengths and weaknesses. This chapter thus presents a holistic view of the skills, strategies, and tools essential for successful negotiations and mediations in diverse contexts.

CHAPTER 6

Things To Consider

Introduction: Things to Consider

ELEMENT 69

Implementing NegoEconomics

To illustrate the process of NegoEconomics, this element follows a process that you can see in your mind's eye—buying a coffee table. But you have to go back to the late 1950s.

Buying a Table in the 1950s

Say that I have stepped back into the 1950s and I need a new coffee table. So I head to the furniture store. Where were all the furniture stores located in the '50s? At the city center.

Advantages: It was easy for customers to get there, and all the stores were in the same place. This made it easier to compare products and prices.

Disadvantages: The furniture stores had to pay very high rents. To make financial sense of things, selling prices were high, and stores could not afford to carry large stocks of finished furniture. Instead, they had displays where customers could choose and compare tables manufactured by different factories. This led to long delivery times.

I make my decision, and the order is written out.

Once the order is written out, I pay a deposit. I am told that the time of delivery will be at least five weeks. The store sends the order to the factory.

Advantages: A down payment made by customers served to finance some of the furniture store's activities. The store never ran any risk of being stuck with large stocks of unsold products.

Disadvantages: It took an awfully long time to get the product. Frequently, information of delivery times turned out to be incorrect, which caused a great deal of irritation. The seller would contact the factory to speed things up and to get the new delivery times.

Next step: The factory books an order for a table. As it was not worthwhile manufacturing one table at a time, and if the factory did not have a finished table on stock, it waited until such a time as it could manufacture a short series of the tables.

Advantages: The factory did not have to invest in costly stocks of finished tables, and it did not risk being left carrying a lot of unsold tables.

Disadvantages: Short series and low stocks made it difficult to use advanced machinery. There was a lot of craftsmanship and short series. The evolution of new materials was held back. In part, this explains why the table was so expensive.

Next, the table was transported to the furniture store. Since it was a matter of an expensive table and long transportation, in the course of which the table had to be trans-shipped a few times, it was important to use packaging that would protect the table from harm. To keep down transport costs, attempts were made to group as many items as possible into the same shipment.

Disadvantage: Groupage took a long time. The alternative was costly: shipping one table directly to the end user.

Next, the table arrived in the furniture store. The store would check to see if it was, in fact, the correct table, and then I would get a phone call to set up an appointment for delivering the table by their own furniture van. The service included carrying the table into the customer's living room, polishing the table, and removing and taking the packaging material with them when they left. After eight weeks, I would finally get my coffee table and pay the balance of the price to the store.

Advantages: High service level

Disadvantage: Costly handling

What Was in the Cartons?

I would like to ask you a question, a question that few people can answer correctly. What was in the carton coming all the way from the furniture factory to my home?

The answer most people give is "a table." Indeed, there was a table in the carton, but most of the space in the carton was taken up by something completely different: 90 percent of what was in the carton was air. It is very costly to package, transport, and stock air. The creative individual who originally realized this approached the designer. They were assigned with the task of designing a table that was capable of being packaged in a box without air.

The solution was several hundred years old, but had probably been forgotten. British officers had had a thing constructed that they referred to as a campaign table. A brilliant construction of a dining table that they could take with them into the field and that would seat 20 people around it. The table was collapsible and the legs were detachable—they could be screwed into the table. The table top, which could be folded in the middle, constituted the flat and robust package into which the whole table, with detachable extensions and legs, could be packaged and transported.

The first furniture designers to be approached would probably have replied: Sorry, it can't be done. They only saw the problems. A table always has a number of legs, so naturally there will always be a lot of air. The legs have to be affixed at the factory, they have to be glued in—not a job that the customers can do for themselves, because they do not have the requisite tools. What was in short supply was creative thinking.

However, a couple of furniture designers had come up with the solution. The point was to *not* affix the table legs at the factory. Instead, this work should be left to the end user. The legs should not be glued on, they should be screwed on. Apparently, IKEA trusted those furniture designers, and the foundation of the multibillion company, IKEA, had been cast.

By 2001, the founder of IKEA, Mr. Ingvar Kamprad, had an estimated fortune of more than $37 billion.

This change in construction that was developed and made commercially viable by IKEA changed an entire industry. It entailed a great deal of NegoEconomics:

- The factory can get around an entire manufacturing element, thus reducing manufacturing costs. Today the work and responsibility involved in fitting the table legs rest with the end customer. You buy a table at $225, and you have to affix the four legs. How much do you add to the price by way of compensating you for your work? Nothing. You set the value of your own work at 0 dollars.

- The tables can be packaged in flat boxes, and 90 percent of the air can be dispensed with. Costs involved in packaging, stocking, and transporting the table are considerably reduced.

- By moving the furniture store away from an expensive address at the city center and to the periphery of the city, the store manages to reduce rent to a level that makes it financially interesting to carry the finished tables in stock. A furniture giant has been born.

- Customers can take their newly purchased table with them the same day; they do not have to wait for it for several months. Availability increases notably, which, in turn, leads to more decisions to buy and thus to larger turnover volumes.

- The table is packaged so as to allow customers to transport it themselves. The costs connected to the store's furniture van have disappeared.

- The furniture giant does not place an order for a table one at a time—it places orders for 10,000 tables at a time. This allows rationalization of production, the deployment of modern machines, and a more efficient purchasing of raw materials.

- The furniture giant and various factories begin working together to develop better machines and materials. The furniture giant begins transferring know-how between factories.

- The furniture giant has established its activities in Sweden; these have been tested, developed, and routines have been evolved. It can begin exporting this activity to the whole world.

- The welfare state can start furnishing people's homes with good-quality furniture at reasonable prices.

What Are the Disadvantages?

There are disadvantages to this system, as nothing is perfect:

- This coffee table can be seen in 100,000 other homes.
- From time to time, quality has been less than terrific, and we have all been forced to go back to the furniture giant because a screw was missing from the carton.
- Small factories, exclusive design, high quality, and excellent craftsmanship are finding life difficult. Some of them were knocked out, but the ones who managed to innovate are still in the market, and they are flourishing. They have all found their target groups, and they have adjusted their undertakings to these groups.
- A dominating actor now runs things and dictates conditions to many of its suppliers.

What Can You Learn from Developments in the Furniture Industry?

As long as you stay in a rut, business will be conducted as so-called zero-sum games. If you want to make more money through a deal, you have to squeeze some of the other parties in the chain to take upon themselves higher costs, risks, or liabilities.

In the furniture manufacturer chain, some of the links are the designer, the manufacturer, their employees, the owners, and other sources of financing, sub-suppliers of machines and raw materials, forwarding agents, packaging suppliers, retailers, and end customers. They have not all been involved in negotiating, but one way or another they are all part of the process of change.

This chain of different stakeholders is also found in many other types of enterprises—enterprises in which no special change has taken place for decades. Production takes a long time, time is money, and what is being produced is too expensive. Distribution is inefficient and costs money. Is the key to improved efficiency to transfer responsibility to the customer? Or is it flat cartons, low prices, long series, poor quality, and production in third-world countries? Or are design changes needed? The answers are to be found in your own enterprise. You and your colleagues have the necessary industry knowledge to know what it takes.

Analyses in keeping with this model have contributed to the development of undertakings in different lines of industry.

Benchmarking—or Whom Can You Copy?

The companies that have come the longest way are normally the ones that have been exposed to competition. Study the companies that have been facing tougher demands.

No doubt it will be possible to find NegoEconomics creating ideas in other industries, ideas that you can use both internally and in business relationships with other partners. Do not make the mistake of looking at your part of the enterprise exclusively. It is very important that you follow the whole stream, from the idea stage to the time when the product is no longer used, and that you ask yourself the following question: How can the other party benefit from this in other contexts?

Question the division of responsibility between the different partners; in other words, find out if unnecessary duplication of effort is taking place.

- Where, along the chain, are costs generated? Which party has the best cost efficiency?
- Where are the risks located? Who is best suited to handle and run risks?
- Does it take long? Who can or how can time factors be reduced?
- Where are gains generated by way of money, experience, and goodwill? Who will benefit most from these gains?
- Are there any superfluous intermediaries? Might ecommerce suit you? Element 32 includes a number of examples, illustrating how enterprises in various lines of industry have found their way to the NegoEconomics. Perhaps you can find inspiration in some of these examples.

ELEMENT 70

The Role of Mediators/ Facilitators

I often act as a facilitator or mediator in a negotiation, assisting two or more parties in reaching an agreement.

Professional mediation/facilitation is an effective way to manage complex negotiations, particularly when negative emotions or deep-seated conflicts stall them. A mediator, as a neutral third party, can facilitate communication, offer fresh perspectives, and help parties find common ground.

Mediators are trained professionals who specialize in conflict resolution. They don't take sides but help all parties understand each other's positions and interests. Their primary role is to facilitate dialogue, encourage open communication, and help parties reach a mutually acceptable agreement. This element covers various aspects of mediation.

When to Use Mediation

Mediation is particularly effective when negotiations reach a deadlock due to emotional conflicts, when there is a breakdown in communication, or when the parties need to preserve their relationship post-negotiation. It's also useful in complex negotiations where multiple parties or issues are involved.

Benefits of Mediation

Mediation can save time and costs compared to litigation. It's a confidential process, which makes it easier for parties to be open and honest. Mediators can also introduce creative solutions and alternatives that parties might not have considered.

The Mediation Process

Generally, the process involves an initial meeting where the mediator explains the rules and goals. This is followed by joint and individual sessions with the parties. The mediator helps clarify issues, explores underlying interests, and guides the parties toward a resolution.

Skills of an Effective Mediator

Key skills include active listening, empathy, neutrality, patience, and the ability to ask probing questions. A mediator must also be adept at reading nonverbal cues and managing high-emotion situations.

Challenges in Mediation

Challenges include dealing with parties who are unwilling to compromise, managing high levels of distrust, and ensuring that the process is perceived as fair by all involved.

Ethical Considerations

Mediators must adhere to ethical standards, including confidentiality, impartiality, and informed consent. They should not impose solutions but facilitate the parties in finding their own.

The Outcome of Mediation

The outcome can be a formal agreement, which is legally binding, or an informal understanding, depending on the nature of the negotiation.

Training and Selecting Mediators

Choosing the right mediator is crucial. Parties should look for mediators with experience in the relevant field, strong interpersonal skills, and appropriate training and certification.

Professional mediation is a powerful tool in the negotiation process, offering a pathway to resolution when direct negotiation fails. It harnesses the power of neutral facilitation to bridge gaps, manage emotions, and lead to solutions that respect the interests of all parties involved.

ELEMENT 71

The Big Picture

If there is motivation, an open mind, and enough freedom for individuals in an organization to look for and find new paths, considerable NegoEconomics can be created if only negotiators know in which direction they are to look. NegoEconomics increases the room for negotiation and the pie that can be divided.

Room for Negotiation

The traditional room for negotiation can be defined as the difference between the highest price that a buyer is willing to pay and the lowest price to which a seller is ready to come down. For a deal to be struck, there must be a positive room for negotiation—the buyer must be willing to pay a price above the seller's threshold of pain.

If the maximum price that a buyer can pay is 12,500 and the lowest price to that a seller can come down is 11,900, the difference of 600 constitutes the room for negotiation within which a deal can be struck.

But the actual room for negotiation is normally larger. It consists of the sum of the traditional room for negotiation plus the NegoEconomics you can create. This allows you to reach an agreement even if the highest price that the buyer can pay is below the lowest price to which the seller can come down.

Simple NegoEconomics Model

Consider this simple model to help you locate the NegoEconomics. Good preparation is extremely important in your search for NegoEconomics. Very often we see negotiators making the following preparations when making an offer.

The Offer

- How are you going to submit and explain your offer?
- What questions and objections are the other party likely to put forward?

- What terms, conditions, and price should you open with?
- Where lies the threshold of pain?

If your opening price is 118,000 and the threshold of pain is 103,000, then the room for negotiation is 15,000.

The aim of the negotiation is to get the deal and at the same time give away as little as possible of the 15,000.

If you formulate your objective in this manner, you see the negotiation in a much too narrow perspective and you risk finding yourself in a zero-sum game. The last thing you should do as a seller is give away money in return for getting a deal. If you reduce your price by 5,000, you reduce your profits by 5,000, and the other party makes a deal that's 5,000 better than the original deal. The effect is as 1:1.

You should learn to view the negotiation from a broader perspective. You should do so when preparing so that you are ready for future bargaining.

The Four-Step Model

1. The offer. You have a room for maneuver of 15,000. The central question to ask yourself is: How can you spend the money rather than lower your price?
2. What else do you have to offer, other than money? What can you add to the offer by way of extra services and products?
3. Can you reduce the scope of the package? Which services and products can you take out of the deal? What are the elements that the other party can do for themselves? Is there a simpler solution?
4. The ultimate way out if the other party is not interested in more nor in less. Try to get something by not giving away money—aim for a compromise. Make sure you get a counteroffer. You want 118,000, the customer is offering 88,000. If you split the difference, you will land on 103,000. This is the customer's likely objective. Split the difference once again, and you will land on 110,500. This is the customer's likely threshold of pain.

Place your offer at 107,500 and see how the customer reacts.

If you do not follow this model, but start with cautious one-sided concessions and move down to 115,000, there is a serious risk that you will have to go on making concessions until you reach the bottom.

The smart thing about providing extra services or products is that the costs to you associated with this may be considerably lower than their value to the other party. In other words, you are getting leverage. The effect might even be high enough for you to raise your price.

Imagine a negotiation in which the buyer receives an offer for 10 computers with the software included. The software is to be installed and the computers are to be delivered to the customer's premises. The asking price of the seller for this package is 118,000. The buyer has obtained an alternative offer for similar computers and demands that the seller must reduce their price to a little under 100,000. The seller's threshold of pain is 103,000.

Instead of attempting to accommodate the buyer's demands through a unilateral price reduction to see if the difference can be split around 110,000, the seller asks:

> What services and products can I add to the package? If I offer the customer training for five of their staff in Word for Windows, one of the programs in the software package the customer is buying, what would that mean for my company? We hold courses every week, and the standard price for these courses is 4,500 per person. However, usually one or two places are vacant in any one course. If I offer these surplus places to the customer, it will not cost me anything.

The seller tells the customer that if there are free places on a course, they can send two of their employees on the course each week. The offer is good for five people. These five participants will get a discount of 50 percent on the ordinary course fee. If the customer does not think the offer is good enough, the number of people who can participate on these terms can be raised, or the discount can be raised. As an alternative, the seller can offer to supply bigger screens or other types of hardware upgrades at discount prices.

If the customer does not perceive this as providing them with any NegoEconomics, they are not likely to be interested in increasing the package and getting as much as possible for their money. If this is a customer who would rather buy at the lowest possible price, the seller will have to see if they can reduce the package. If the customer installs the programs and collects the computers at the seller's premises, the seller can save 4,000 in working costs. If the buyer takes over these jobs, they can be offered a reduction of 3,000. The seller attempts to hold on to 1,000 to bolster their own net profit on the transaction. If the customer does not bite, the seller can suggest to the customer that if they pay cash in advance instead of getting 30 days' credit, they can get a price reduction. A price reduction that is somewhat lower than the interest gain achieved by the seller.

If this does not work, all that is left is haggling. But at least try to take the advice in Step 4.

Locating the NegoEconomics

In a project there will be many areas in which you can look for NegoEconomics. Why does it look the way it does? What could be done differently? What would the outcome be?

Follow the entire process—from the birth of the idea to the time when the end user can no longer benefit from the product. Who can do what in the course of this long chain? Consider:

- Financial variables and conditions
- Quality and performance, technical specification of requirements

- Economies of scale
- Time
- Purchasing patterns
- Rights

Following the Entire Process

Many years ago the film *From Ear of Corn to Loaf of Bread* was produced. Step by step, we could follow the lengthy chain that starts with the farmer ploughing a field, and ends when we leave the bakery shop with the newly baked loaf under our arm. Many hands were involved along the path. The film was very instructional and provided the uninitiated with a good impression of the entire process needed to get to a loaf from an ear.

Carefully follow the courses of events that you embark upon from beginning to end and ask yourself, why are we doing this? What could we be doing instead? What would be the outcome? Can responsibilities be shared differently? Will this make things better or worse? Where are the opportunities and risks? Can you see something no one has seen before?

Start by getting yourself an overview of the current situation. Make a sketch of your findings. The overview is necessary for the pieces to fall into place, and for you to be able to see the whole picture. This picture is the point of departure with which all conceivable modifications should be compared. Often, it is necessary physically to follow events step by step to see what is happening, and for every step to ask yourself these questions:

- Why do we do things this way? Never accept answers such as, "That's how we've always done it," "That's normal practice in the industry," "We just follow our routines," or "It works."

- What will happen when the need no longer exists and the production or the service is to be abandoned? Will the machine be scrapped? Can its life be prolonged? Can it be sold off? Is the system flexible? Can it be extended and modernized?

- How does it work today? What are the individual elements? How do they affect costs, risks, and profits? How do they affect time, reliability, and useful life? Define the factors that have a negative impact on time, costs, reliability, and useful life.

- What could we do instead? What would happen in that case? Positive or negative change? Where are the opportunities and risks and problems? Compare these to the point of departure.

- Who will do the work that has to be done? The most cost-effective party, the one who will benefit most from the experience gleaned, or the most risk-oriented party who can sustain adversity? How do we solve the problem if it becomes necessary to transfer the responsibility? Do we need to redesign the product, or will anyone have to get extra training?

- What advantages can new technology provide us with? The emergence of the internet as a channel of information and distribution is an example of new technology that opens up new opportunities and that constitutes a threat to much traditional commerce.

ELEMENT 72

Typical Skills to Improve

I n my extensive experience with over 35,000 participants in numerous negotiation simulations, coupled with my involvement in countless real-life negotiations, I've identified a range of skills that typically need enhancement. These
skills, though not ranked in order of importance and varying across negotiators, are
areas where I've noticed that many can benefit from improvement.

Key Skills for Negotiation Enhancement

- **Questioning:** Enhance your negotiation by asking more and better questions.
- **Openness:** Balance is key; avoid being too reserved or overly transparent.
- **Structural approach:** Implement a structured framework to avoid wasting time and resources.
- **Agenda setting:** Work on mutually agreed agendas, serving as a blueprint for both parties.
- **Persistence:** Continue probing until you receive satisfactory answers.
- **Role definition:** Clearly define roles when negotiating in a team.
- **NegoEconomics:** Understand and leverage asymmetric value for mutual gain.
- **Creative thinking:** Adopt out-of-the-box approaches, introducing varied variables.
- **Mandate clarity:** Ensure that both parties have the proper authority to negotiate.
- **Combative behavior:** Recognize and avoid combative tactics in collaborative negotiations.
- **Negotiation rules:** Agree on the rules of negotiation beforehand.
- **Listening:** Focus on the underlying value, not just the words.

- **Counterpart consideration:** Consider the other party's costs, values, risks, and liabilities.
- **Team discipline:** Respect defined roles within the negotiating team.
- **Small talk:** Build a positive environment to foster trust and gather information.
- **Initiative:** Taking the lead often results in greater negotiation success.
- **Honesty:** Honesty simplifies communication, as you don't need to track your words. It also instills trust between parties.
- **Visual aids:** Use tools like flipcharts and whiteboards to enhance negotiation effectiveness.
- **Stress management:** Recognize and manage your stress triggers.
- **Effective communication:** Ensure clear communication to keep negotiations on track.
- **Emotional intelligence:** Understanding EI is crucial to becoming an adept negotiator.

These skills, when honed, can significantly enhance your negotiation capabilities, leading to more successful outcomes.

ELEMENT 73

Navigating the Cosmos of Negotiation: Lessons from John Glenn's Insight

In a single frame, the juxtaposition of a soaring 1970s space rocket against the infinite backdrop of space, overlaid with astronaut John Glenn's poignant reflection, speaks volumes about the science of negotiation. It's a visual embodiment of the tension between ambition and pragmatism, risk and trust—a tension that sits at the heart of every negotiation table.

"As I hurtled through space there was only one thought in my mind. That every part of the capsule was supplied by the lowest bidder," John Glenn mused. This candid admission from an icon of space exploration serves as a potent reminder of the gravity that decisions hold in the negotiation.

In the pursuit of space, as in negotiation, the stakes are sky-high, and the margin for error is slim. Glenn's words ring out as a cautionary tale: When the goal is to reach the stars, cutting corners on the ground can have dire consequences.

The Gravity of Trust

Trust is the fuel for any negotiation. Just as astronauts must trust in the integrity of their vessel, built piece by piece from countless contracts and agreements, so must negotiators have faith in the bonds they forge. The lowest bidder might offer an alluring shortcut in terms of cost, but the true negotiator must weigh every factor, from quality to reliability, to ensure a successful mission.

The Vacuum of Low Cost

Focusing on cost alone creates a vacuum in which the value of partnership, quality, and long-term gains are sucked away. Glenn's reflection warns us that the allure of immediate savings is a siren song that can lead to a perilous journey. True negotiation isn't about finding the cheapest route; it's about navigating to the best *value*—a concept that balances cost with the assurance of safety, quality, and performance.

The Atmosphere of Strategy

Negotiation is an atmospheric re-entry—a strategic maneuver that demands precision. Every decision, like every component of a spacecraft, must work in perfect harmony to achieve the objective. The successful negotiator, much like the aerospace engineer, understands that the whole is greater than the sum of its parts, and that every element must be selected with an eye toward the ultimate goal.

The Orbit of Mutual Benefit

In space, orbits are a delicate balance of forces. In negotiation, the same principle applies. Striking a deal that benefits all parties requires an understanding that while cost is a gravitational force, it cannot be the only one. A successful negotiation orbits around mutual benefit, shared success, and the recognition that the journey—and the relationship—is as important as the destination.

In the final analysis, the image and the quote encapsulate a universal truth: Whether we are negotiating our way through the cosmos or around the conference table, the decisions we make are the thrusters that propel us forward. May we all aim for the stars with the wisdom to know that the best decisions, like the best spacecraft, are built not on the foundation of cost alone but on the bedrock of value, trust, and shared vision.

ELEMENT 74

Addressing Misunderstandings

ased on my extensive studies and experience in the field of negotiation, I've found that one of the primary reasons negotiations fail to reach a mutually beneficial outcome is often rooted in simple misunderstandings. These risks become even more pronounced when cultural and language differences enter the equation.

Misunderstandings in negotiations are not just minor hiccups; they can significantly derail the process. Misinterpreted words, overlooked cultural nuances, or even assumptions can lead to a breakdown in communication. This often results in each party walking away with different interpretations of what was agreed upon, or worse, no agreement at all.

As a negotiator, it's crucial to ensure that you and your counterpart are on the same page. This means actively listening, clarifying intentions, and confirming understanding. It's not enough to assume that your message is clear; ask for feedback and be open to clarifying your points. Remember, effective communication is a two-way street.

When negotiating across different cultures and languages, the potential for misunderstandings increases exponentially. Every culture has its nuances, from nonverbal cues to the way certain phrases are interpreted. Similarly, language barriers can lead to words being lost in translation. It's essential to be culturally sensitive and, when necessary, employ the services of a competent interpreter.

Emotional intelligence plays a significant role in navigating misunderstandings. Being able to read the emotions of the other party, as well as manage your own reactions, is key. This awareness can help in identifying when a misunderstanding is occurring and addressing it before it escalates.

Strategies for Overcoming Misunderstandings

- **Active listening:** Pay close attention to what is being said, and more importantly, what is *not* being said. This can help in identifying potential areas of confusion.

- **Clarifying and paraphrasing:** After your counterpart speaks, paraphrase their points to ensure you've understood them correctly. Similarly, encourage them to do the same.

- **Documenting agreements:** Keep a written record of agreements and decisions made during negotiations. This can serve as a reference point if any confusion arises later.

- **Building rapport:** Establishing a connection beyond the transactional aspects of negotiation can foster better understanding and empathy.

- **Continuous learning:** Every negotiation is a learning opportunity. Reflect on instances where misunderstandings occurred and how they were resolved. This reflection will enhance your skills for future negotiations.

Addressing misunderstandings is not merely about fixing communication errors but about building a foundation of trust and clarity. As negotiators, we must be diligent in our efforts to understand and be understood, recognizing the cultural and emotional layers that impact our interactions. By mastering these skills, we can turn potential obstacles into stepping-stones toward successful negotiations.

ELEMENT 75

The Total Cost of Ownership (TCO)

Negotiation is an intricate dance where each step, each turn, can either lead to a harmonious partnership or a discordant outcome. In this delicate interplay, understanding the Total Cost of Ownership (TCO) is not just important—it's crucial. TCO is the sum of all costs associated with the purchase, deployment, use, and retirement of a product or service. Beyond the price tag, it includes the costs of service, maintenance, training, infrastructure, and the opportunity cost of alternative options. It is particularly significant in the realm of collaborative negotiations and the formation of SMARTnerships. In fact, it's the key to successful collaborations and SMARTnerships.

TCO and Collaborative Negotiations

Collaborative negotiation is a process where the involved parties seek outcomes that offer mutual gains. The focus is on building relationships, understanding each other's needs, and working together to achieve more. Here's where TCO becomes pivotal. It provides a comprehensive framework to assess not just the immediate costs but also the long-term implications of a deal.

In the realm of collaborative negotiations, every decision has a ripple effect. A low initial price might seem attractive but can lead to higher costs down the line if it results in lower quality, increased downtime, or more frequent replacements. By considering TCO, negotiators can make informed decisions that ensure long-term satisfaction and avoid the pitfalls of short-sighted gains.

TCO in SMARTnership

The concept of SMARTnership, which goes beyond traditional partnership to leverage the collective intelligence and resources of all parties involved, is heavily reliant on the thorough understanding of TCO. A SMARTnership is not merely transactional; it is transformational, creating additional value for all stakeholders. It moves beyond the "win-lose" or even the "win-win" to a "win-more" situation where the combined efforts of the parties result in greater innovation, efficiency, and profitability.

In a SMARTnership, TCO is not just a number—it's a strategic tool. It helps identify and minimize hidden costs and uncover opportunities for value creation that might not be immediately apparent. For example, if two companies collaborate on a technology solution, a comprehensive TCO analysis might reveal that sharing resources for R&D or jointly investing in a bespoke solution could lead to significant savings and better performance over time.

Strategic Considerations of TCO

When negotiating a SMARTnership, the TCO is integral to the strategic considerations of both parties. It impacts contract terms, the allocation of resources, and the management of the relationship over time. A low TCO can be a competitive advantage, making an offer more attractive compared to alternatives. However, the goal should not be to minimize TCO at the expense of quality or performance. Instead, the aim is to optimize TCO to enhance the strategic position and the benefits of the partnership.

TCO and Sustainability

Sustainability is another critical aspect where TCO plays a vital role. In a world increasingly focused on environmental impact and social responsibility, the TCO extends to include the cost of environmental compliance, waste disposal, and social implications. A SMARTnership that recognizes and incorporates these elements into its TCO calculations will not only be seen as more responsible but will also be better positioned for future regulatory changes and consumer expectations.

TCO and Innovation

Innovation is at the heart of any SMARTnership. Here, TCO is a driver for innovation as it challenges the parties to think long term and holistically. By understanding the full life cycle costs, partners are encouraged to innovate to reduce costs over time, improve efficiency, and enhance the overall value proposition of their offering.

TCO is not just a buzzword; it's a vital component of successful negotiations, especially when it comes to collaborations and SMARTnerships. It ensures that decisions are made with a full understanding of their financial implications over time.

This comprehensive approach to cost allows for more sustainable, innovative, and strategic partnerships that yield greater benefits for all parties involved. As you continue to navigate the complexities of the modern business landscape, TCO stands as a beacon, guiding the way to smarter, more collaborative, and mutually beneficial negotiations.

ELEMENT 76

Listening, Summarizing, and Locking (LSL)

LSL is a powerful tool to avoid positional negotiation (zero-sum) and move a negotiation in a more collaborative direction.

For example, say you are negotiating a partnership with another company. The other party, represented by their CEO, is concerned about the distribution of responsibilities and profit sharing.

CEO: "I'm concerned about how we're dividing the responsibilities. We feel like we're taking on a larger share of the work, but the profits are split evenly. This doesn't seem fair to us."

You (applying LSL):

1. **Listen:** You listen attentively, nodding and maintaining eye contact, showing that you are fully engaged in what the CEO is saying.

2. **Summarize:** "I understand your concerns. You feel that your company is being asked to handle a more significant portion of the workload, yet the profit sharing remains equal. You're looking for a more equitable distribution that reflects the effort put in by each party. Is that correct?"

3. **Lock-in:** "Let's see how we can address this. We definitely want a fair partnership. How about we revisit the task distribution and adjust the profit sharing accordingly? We can draft a proposal that outlines a more balanced approach and discuss it in our next meeting. Does that sound like a good way forward?"

Outcome: By using the LSL technique, you demonstrate active listening, ensure mutual understanding, and propose a collaborative solution to lock in agreement, moving the negotiation toward a more positive and productive outcome.

ELEMENT 77

Contingent Contracts

Contingent contracts in the context of negotiations are agreements that are designed to take effect only when certain conditions or "contingencies" are met. They are a way to deal with uncertainty during a negotiation by specifying in advance how certain future scenarios will be handled. This type of contract is particularly useful when negotiating parties have different predictions about future events or outcomes and want to come to an agreement that acknowledges these uncertainties.

Here are some key aspects of contingent contracts:

- **Risk management:** Contingent contracts allow parties to manage risks associated with future uncertainties. For instance, a seller and buyer may disagree on the future price of a commodity; a contingent contract can specify a price adjustment mechanism based on market indices.

- **Future performance:** Contingent contracts stipulate performance or actions that are dependent on future events. For example, a bonus might be paid if the company's earnings exceed a certain threshold by a specified date.

- **Disagreement bridging:** Contingent contracts can bridge disagreements about uncertain future events by providing a "bet" on the outcome. If one party is confident in a particular outcome, they can agree to conditions that are favorable to the other party if their prediction is incorrect, and vice versa.

- **Motivation and goals alignment:** Contingent contracts can align incentives and motivate performance. For example, in employment contracts, contingent bonuses or stock options are used to align the interests of employees with the company's performance.

- **Flexibility:** These contracts provide flexibility and adaptability to changing circumstances without the need for renegotiation. They are crafted to automatically adapt to the specified contingencies.

- **Measurable and observable:** The conditions set in a contingent contract must be clear, measurable, and observable to both parties to prevent disputes when triggering the clauses.

- **Legally enforceable:** Contingent contracts, like any contract, must be legally enforceable. The contingencies should be reasonable and in compliance with legal standards to ensure they can be upheld in a court of law if necessary.

In negotiation theory, contingent contracts are a solution proposed by Roger Fisher and William Ury of the Harvard Negotiation Project in their book, *Getting to Yes*. They suggest the use of contingent contracts when parties are facing a stalemate due to differing predictions about future events. By agreeing to a contingent contract, both parties can proceed with an agreement that takes into account their differing forecasts, allowing them to share the risks and rewards of future outcomes.

ELEMENT 78

Post-Negotiation Audit

Post-Negotiation Audit
Negotiation Evaluation

How did it go?

Want to make sure that everything went well and as expected?

To negotiate is a major responsibility for the negotiation team. They need to pay attention to detail while planning the negotiation.

You can tweak or update this checklist depending on your organization's unique needs.

A thorough checklist will help you easily manage your negotiation.

---

the SMARTnership negotiation organization

www.smartnership.org

Role within the group

☐	Who did what?
☐	How was the discipline during the negotiation?
☐	SMARTnership (collaboration)
☐	Were the team members supportive to the head?
☐	Prepared list of negotiable variables
☐	Consensus and agreement within the team

Summary of negotiation

☐	Were variables identified?
☐	Were additional variables identified other than those prepared?
☐	Did you follow the agenda?
☐	Did the negotiation achieve your aim?
☐	Was the threshold of pain reached?
☐	How did the negotiation develop?
☐	Did you find the NegoEconomics and capitalize on it?

Agenda

☐	Was a joint agenda created?
☐	Did you "win" the agenda?
☐	Was the agenda adhered to?
☐	Were the items in the correct order?

The Negotiation Process

☐	How was time organized between each phase? Did the negotiation reach a deadlock or did it flow?

The Argumentation Phase

☐	Were arguments intelligible and credible?
☐	Was there focus on the counterparts situation?
☐	Did you experience any verbal conflicts?
☐	How much time did the argumentation phase take?
☐	Did the argumentation produce results or was it wasted?
☐	Were the breaks used effectively?

Post-Negotiation Audit
Negotiation Evaluation

Notes:

The Analysis Phase

☐ Were new openings created?

☐ Was every possible NegoEconomics variable investigated?

☐ Were the counterpart's values and costs clear to you?

☐ Was too much or too little information shared?

☐ Were attempts made to summarize and pin down?

☐ Did you need more breaks?

Conclusion

☐ Were attempts made to conclude?

☐ Were opportunities missed?

☐ What methods were used for concluding?

☐ Are you aware of the body language?

☐ Who had the initiative in closing?

Communication

☐ Combat, concession, compromise, collaboration, stalling?

☐ How do you evaluate your counterpart's credibility on a scale from 1–10 (10 is high)

☐ How do you evaluate your own credibility on a scale from 1–10?

☐ How was the openness in the negotiation, from 1–10?

☐ How were visual aids used?

☐ How was the body language interpreted?

☐ How were the questions, follow-up questions, and summarizing?

Negotiation style?

☐ Were both parties equally active in establishing a favorable atmosphere?

☐ Were parties equally active/passive?

☐ Were the limits tested?

☐ **What should be changed for the next negotiation?**

the
SMARTnership
negotiation
organization

www.smartnership.org

ELEMENT 79

Face-to-Face or Virtual Negotiations

"Can you hear me?," "I can't hear you!" "Can you see my screen, I'm trying to share it?"—these phrases have become a staple in the realm of online meetings. A study I conducted with World Commerce & Contracting reveals that approximately 70 percent of commercial negotiations are now conducted virtually, with around 41 percent occurring via email. As technology evolves, the traditional face-to-face negotiation is increasingly giving way to virtual formats.

Embracing the New Normal in Negotiations

Despite this shift, 96 percent of respondents in our survey still believe that in-person meetings are more effective and valuable. Face-to-face interactions allow for physical gestures like handshakes, eye contact, and the subtle nuances of body language that are often lost in digital communication. This loss can affect the effectiveness and success of negotiations conducted online.

The Challenges and Benefits of Virtual Negotiations

Research by Michael Morris, Michael Janice Nadler, Terri Kurtzberg, and Leigh Thompson, published by the American Psychology Association, highlights the shortcomings of online negotiations:

- Difficulty in reaching agreements and a higher likelihood of impasses.
- Challenges in building and maintaining trust.
- Reduced rapport development compared to in-person negotiations.

So, does this mean we should avoid virtual negotiations entirely? Not at all. Virtual negotiations can be effective and efficient, especially when combined with in-person meetings. The key lies in using various methods—emails, phone calls, video conferences—intelligently.

Email Negotiations: A Double-Edged Sword

Email is convenient and cost-effective but fraught with risks of misinterpretation. Professor Albert Mehrabian's study at UCLA in the 1960s showed that only 7 percent of emotional communication is conveyed through words, with tone of voice and body language accounting for the rest. This underlines the limitations of email for emotional or conflict-laden discussions. It's important to use email judiciously, primarily for exchanging data and setting agendas, and to exercise caution and empathy in every interaction.

The Role of Phone Negotiations

Phone conversations, according to UCLA studies, contribute significantly to building trust, accounting for about 38 percent of the trust factor in communication. While phone negotiations lack the visual cues of face-to-face or video meetings, they are superior to emails for discussing complex issues or building rapport. It's crucial to prepare adequately for phone negotiations and to be mindful of vocal tones and inflections.

The Advantages of Video Conferences

Video conferencing is the closest digital alternative to in-person meetings. It allows for some degree of nonverbal communication and is preferable to emails and phone calls for more nuanced negotiations. However, challenges such as technology preferences, connectivity issues, and the inherent limitations of digital communication make thorough preparation and testing essential.

ONLINE NEGOTIATION

VARIOUS NEGOTIATION PLATFORMS

Comparison Chart

Legend: ⊙ It's a successful platform ⊙ May or may not work ⊙ Will NOT work for you

MEETING	RELATION AND TRUST	VALUE CREATION	VISUAL AIDS	COST OF MEETING	STRUCTURE	TEAM EFFICIENCY	TIME EFFICIENCY	RISK OF BULLY	MEMORY	COLLABORATION	LONG TERM	HANDLING CONFLICTS	COMBINATION
FACE TO FACE	⊙	⊙	⊙	⊙	⊙	⊙	⊙	⊙	⊙	⊙	⊙	⊙	⊙
VIDEO	⊙	⊙	⊙	⊙	⊙	⊙	⊙	⊙	⊙	⊙	⊙	⊙	⊙
PHONE	⊙	⊙	⊙	⊙	⊙	⊙	⊙	⊙	⊙	⊙	⊙	⊙	⊙
TEXT	⊙	⊙	⊙	⊙	⊙	⊙	⊙	⊙	⊙	⊙	⊙	⊙	⊙

KJ Keld Jensen

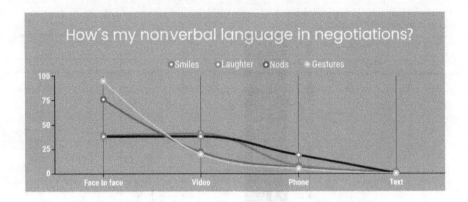

Virtual Negotiation Strategies

Regardless of the medium, understanding and agreeing on the negotiation strategy is vital. Whether adopting a zero-sum or collaborative approach, clarity in communication and process is key. Assumptions can be dangerous, especially in virtual settings where information is limited.

Caution in Digital Communication

Avoid negotiations on social media platforms and be wary of the permanence of digital records. Ethical considerations are paramount in virtual negotiations, as the ease of misrepresentation is greater.

Generating Value in Virtual Negotiations

In virtual negotiations, extra effort is needed to create value. Timing and manner of presenting offers, using breaks effectively, and choosing the right communication channel are critical. Developing a personal negotiation style that complements the chosen medium can enhance the effectiveness of virtual negotiations.

- In email negotiations, clarify ambiguities and avoid assumptions.
- Use phone negotiations to supplement digital and face-to-face interactions.
- Establish face-to-face relationships before delving into virtual negotiations.

- Choose the most effective communication channel for each stage of the negotiation.
- Adapt your negotiation style to fit the communication medium.

In conclusion, virtual negotiation is an evolving art that requires adaptability, awareness of its limitations and advantages, and a strategic approach to communication.

ELEMENT 80

Ability to Anticipate

An important aspect of negotiation is the ability to anticipate. This involves understanding and predicting the needs, intentions, and behavior of the other party to achieve a more favorable negotiation outcome. Anticipation in negotiation requires thorough preparation, which includes researching the other party's background, interests, negotiation style, and potential constraints. Everything is covered in our pre-negotiation checklist. It also involves developing a deep understanding of the negotiation context, including market conditions, legal considerations, and cultural factors.

Effective anticipation allows negotiators to plan their strategies and tactics more effectively, identify opportunities for creating value, and prepare for potential challenges. It can lead to more creative solutions that satisfy the interests of both parties, enhancing the possibility of achieving a win-win outcome. Furthermore, by anticipating the other party's moves, a negotiator can better manage the negotiation process, control the pace, and steer the negotiation toward favorable terms.

In practice, anticipation involves not just planning for expected scenarios but also preparing for unexpected turns in the negotiation. This requires flexibility, adaptability, and the ability to think on one's feet. Successful negotiators use anticipation to build trust and rapport, making it easier to navigate difficult conversations and find mutually beneficial solutions.

The ability to anticipate is a crucial skill in negotiation, enabling negotiators to be more strategic, proactive, and effective in achieving their goals. Through diligent preparation, understanding of the negotiation context, and development of flexible strategies, negotiators can leverage anticipation to improve their negotiation outcomes significantly.

It is well documented that flexibility in negotiations increases with higher levels of trust between parties. Conversely, a lack of trust can significantly reduce the willingness of negotiators to be flexible. This relationship underscores the importance of building and maintaining trust in negotiations. When trust is present, parties are more open to sharing information, considering alternative solutions, and adapting their positions, which can lead to more effective and mutually beneficial outcomes. Therefore, fostering trust is not just a matter of ethical negotiation practice but a strategic approach to enhancing negotiation flexibility and success.

ELEMENT 81

Soft vs. Hard Variables

Understanding and leveraging both soft and hard variables is key to becoming a great negotiator. *Hard variables* are the tangible, measurable elements that often form the backbone of negotiation discussions. These include terms of payment, warehouse costs, transportation fees, discounts, installation charges, warranty terms, currency considerations, and more. They are concrete, quantifiable, and often directly impact the economic outcome of the negotiation.

However, a great negotiator understands that focusing solely on hard variables can be a limited approach. This is where soft variables come into play. *Soft variables* are the intangible elements that exist in negotiations. They are often not immediately measurable and can be overlooked, yet they are crucial in influencing the negotiation's direction and outcome.

Soft variables encompass the emotional and relational aspects of negotiation. They include factors such as the perceived value of an item or service, the emotional reasons behind wanting a particular outcome, and the interpersonal dynamics between the negotiating parties. For instance, in a property negotiation, a tenant might prefer an apartment on a higher floor for the view it offers, even if it means a higher rent. In this case, the location and view (soft variables) could be more influential than the price (a hard variable).

The power of soft variables lies in their ability to tap into the psychological and emotional aspects of decision-making. A negotiation is not just a transaction; it is a human interaction where feelings, perceptions, and relationships play a significant role. For example, the relationship with the other party, the trust level established, and the emotional state of the negotiators (like anxiety over losing a deal or excitement about a potential partnership) can dramatically sway the negotiation process and outcome.

Furthermore, soft variables include timelines and flexibility in negotiations. A tight deadline might push a party to concede more than they would under normal circumstances, or a negotiator's ability to offer flexible terms might sweeten a deal in ways that purely financial concessions cannot.

A nuanced understanding of soft variables also aids in creating value in negotiations. When negotiators are able to identify and address the underlying emotional and relational needs of their counterparts, they open up possibilities for creative solutions that satisfy both parties beyond the conventional give-and-take of hard variables.

While hard variables are undoubtedly important in negotiations for their clear, measurable impact, the soft variables often hold the key to unlocking truly successful and mutually beneficial agreements. A skilled negotiator is one who adeptly balances both, recognizing that the art of negotiation lies as much in understanding human psychology and emotions as it does in the numbers and terms.

CHAPTER 7

Ultimate Level

Introduction: The Pro Level

Welcome to a pivotal chapter in your journey toward becoming a master negotiator. This chapter delves into the nuanced realms of negotiation, transcending traditional tactics to explore the profound impact of psychological and strategic elements. This exploration covers seven critical topics, each offering unique insights and powerful techniques to enhance your negotiation skills.

- **Element 82: Negotiation mastery: techniques of the experts.** Negotiation mastery is the culmination of skills, strategies, and mindset. This part of the chapter provides you with advanced techniques used by expert negotiators. From strategic planning to in-the-moment decision-making, you will learn to handle any negotiation scenario with confidence.

- **Element 83: Silence: the unspoken power.** We begin with the art of silence, a tool often overlooked yet immensely powerful in negotiation. Silence isn't just a pause; it's a strategy. Learn to harness its potential to create space for reflection, encourage your counterpart to reveal more information, and control the pace of the discussion.

- **Element 84: Teach others and multiply your impact.** As you develop your negotiation skills, it's essential to pass on your knowledge. This element guides you on how to effectively teach negotiation principles to others, thereby amplifying your impact and fostering a culture of effective communication and conflict resolution.

- **Element 85: Expand the pie: find creative solutions for mutual gain.** The next element shifts the focus to "expanding the pie." This concept challenges the conventional zero-sum approach, encouraging you to think creatively to find solutions that benefit all parties. By expanding the pie, you're not just winning; you're crafting outcomes where everyone feels like a winner.

- **Element 86: The power of subtext: reading between the lines.** Understanding the subtext in negotiations is crucial. This element teaches you to read the unspoken messages and underlying emotions that often dictate the course of a negotiation. Grasping the power of subtext allows you to respond not just to what is said but also to what is meant.

- **Element 87: Human engineering: the psychological dimension.** Human engineering in negotiation involves understanding and influencing the psychological factors at play. This element explores how emotions, biases, and personality types can be navigated and even leveraged to steer negotiations toward favorable outcomes.

- **Element 88: Conflict handling: turn challenges into opportunities.** Finally, the chapter addresses conflict handling. Negotiations often involve conflicts, but these challenges can be transformed into opportunities for growth and understanding. Learn to navigate conflicts with grace and turn potentially adverse situations into win-win outcomes.

Embark on this chapter with an open mind and a willingness to learn. The skills and insights you gain here will not only elevate your negotiation abilities but also enrich your understanding of human interaction in all spheres of life. Let's begin the journey to negotiation mastery.

ELEMENT 82

The Essence of Negotiation Mastery

Negotiation is not just about experience or repetition of formulas; it's about adaptability, strategic thinking, and the ability to unearth hidden values in every situation. Great negotiators understand that each negotiation is unique and requires a fresh approach. They recognize the importance of listening, probing with questions, and focusing on understanding and leveraging the values and costs relevant to their counterparts, as well as finding NegoEconomics (asymmetric values) and distributing these values.

Effective negotiation involves a thorough analysis of variables, identifying areas of value and understanding the impact of each variable on the overall deal. It requires a nuanced approach that considers not only economic factors but also *soft* variables, such as interpersonal relationships, timelines, and emotional factors.

A skilled negotiator knows how to prioritize and balance these variables, often using them to gain an advantage in other areas. For instance, in negotiations involving delivery times and pricing, a nuanced understanding of the interconnectedness of these variables can lead to more favorable outcomes.

However, negotiation isn't a one-sided pursuit of victory. It's about understanding mutual needs and finding solutions that benefit all parties involved. For example, in the case of an employee seeking a remote work arrangement, a better approach is to propose a compromise that aligns with company policies while addressing personal preferences.

Great negotiators also excel in clear communication, making effective use of visual aids, and showing initiative through proactive listening and information gathering. They stand out by their ability to communicate their points confidently and listen for unspoken values, leading to more effective and collaborative solutions.

Furthermore, setting realistic goals and being methodical in approach are key traits of a great negotiator. They enter negotiations with well-defined strategies but remain flexible to adapt as situations evolve. This includes being prepared with alternative solutions and creating a positive climate for negotiation.

In team negotiations, role clarity is crucial. Assigning specific roles such as a negotiation leader, an observer, and an economic manager can significantly enhance the effectiveness of the negotiation process.

Lastly, great negotiators don't succumb to time pressure. They take the necessary time to evaluate offers thoroughly, ensuring that the final agreement aligns with their goals and benefits all parties involved.

In conclusion, the art of negotiation is a blend of strategic thinking, effective communication, emotional intelligence, and a deep understanding of the variables at play. It's about finding balance, creating value, and forging agreements that stand the test of time and mutual benefit.

ELEMENT 83

Using Silence Effectively

Silence is an underutilized but effective tactic. Many negotiations have failed because someone spoke too much, but few negotiations have failed because of silence.

Not everything that is said in the course of a negotiation requires a response or comment. The objective of a negotiation is not to be right on each and every point or to persuade others to abandon their views. The objective of the cooperative negotiator is to find a solution that meets the requirements of all parties involved. Learn to master silence and seek to understand why the other party is silent when they have chosen this approach. Is it because they do not want to answer your question and have run out of arguments, or is it because they hope that you will break the silence and start negotiating with yourself?

Silence, or the absence of a reaction, creates insecurity and stress. The supplier who introduces their offer with the words: *I think it will be possible for us to come down 3–4 percent,* and is met with silence, will be more likely to say: *We can probably give you 4 percent. The payment conditions can also be changed. . . .*

EXAMPLE | A Moment of Silence

Rupert decided to sell his house. After six months, the real estate agent had not found a serious buyer willing to make an offer at his asking price. The agent made it clear that if Rupert wanted to sell the house, he had to reduce his asking price by $10,000. Once Rupert agreed to the reduction, the realtor produced a buyer almost immediately.

Rupert made his calculations and found that there was enough of a margin to go through with the deal at the lower price. He played out in his head several alternative arrangements for the financing that would leave him with the cash he needed. His threshold of pain was a reduction of $13,000. Rupert considered himself prepared for the negotiations, which were to be held the next day.

Later in the evening it struck him that he knew nothing about the buyers and their situation. What were their objectives, and what must happen for them to be comfortable moving forward with the purchase? He tried to put himself in the role of the buyer. He asked, "If I were the buyer, what would be my concerns?" The following points occurred to him:

- Cash for the down payment
- Monthly mortgage cost
- Selling their old house
- Move-in date
- Possible renovation or improvements
- Schools and childcare facilities
- Public transportation and distance to work

Rupert realized that he didn't know enough about the buyers to be able to properly prepare for the negotiation. He didn't know their names, how many children they had, what they did for work, and where they were currently living. He realized that he had to get more information before the price discussions began. He decided to remain silent—a classic tactic to get the other party talking.

It worked. The buyers told him that they have a house they have not yet been able to sell. The wife was worried about the time it might take them to get it sold. She was also worried about their ability to make both mortgage payments in the interim. She said that Rupert's house was perfect when it came to style, location, and size. When she was speaking, Rupert could see that mentally she had already moved into the house and had arranged her furniture in the rooms. The only problem was affording the double mortgage payments. The buyers intended to solve this problem by bargaining on the purchase price.

Rupert saw a different solution and decided to put it on the table. If the buyers would accept his original asking price, he would continue to be responsible for the mortgage payments on the house until they were able to sell their old house, building in some time limit. On hearing Rupert's offer, the wife turned to her husband and said: *That would solve all our problems.* Her husband replied: *Will we agree to his original asking price then? We really cannot afford to pay both mortgages.*

Rupert left the room so the husband and wife could negotiate between themselves. Since he had given them a direct solution to their problem, they accepted the offer. Completing the transaction was more important to them than squeezing Rupert down on the price.

Taking a minute to think about the circumstances of the other party, plus a moment of silence, turned out to be worth $10,000 to Rupert. At the same time, the buyers got a satisfactory solution to their problem. When their house sold, the parties made the final settlement and Rupert was reimbursed for the payments he had made, plus interest.

This example illustrates the usefulness of being silent and biding your time. After a few seconds of silence, most people will start talking. Let them! Question, listen, work with hypotheses, prompt them to suggest solutions, and draw your conclusions on the basis of what you've learned! Take your time and do not make up your mind right away.

As the expression goes, sometimes silence truly is golden. There is no danger in listening to the other party. Knowledge and information will provide you with a stronger bargaining position. Listening does not mean that you have to agree with the other party and abandon your own point of view.

It is essential to avoid misinterpreting silence for agreement. Do not make the mistake of believing that you have reached an agreement just because the other party listens to you without stating any objections. Silence in a negotiation does not automatically equal consent.

Do not become threatened when your opponent is using silence as a tactic. Question, summarize, or take a break. If you want to provoke the other party into breaking their silence, you only have to summarize incorrectly, and they will correct you.

ELEMENT 84

Teaching Others

In the world of negotiation, the journey toward proficiency is ongoing. It's a path that involves not only acquiring knowledge but also sharing it. As you delve into this element, you explore the symbiotic relationship between teaching and learning in the realm of negotiation skills. The act of teaching doesn't just benefit the learner; it significantly enhances the teacher's understanding and retention of the subject. This phenomenon is backed by research, which indicates that individuals who teach or share information are more likely to remember and understand that information themselves.

The Power of Teaching: Enhancing Personal Retention and Understanding

A study by the Learning Pyramid model suggests that the average retention rate for those who actively teach others is around 90 percent, a stark contrast to the 5 percent retention rate for those who only listen to a lecture. This model highlights the effectiveness of active engagement in learning processes. By teaching negotiation techniques to others, you're not just imparting knowledge; you're also reinforcing and deepening your own understanding. This process of teaching creates a powerful feedback loop, where you can reflect, refine, and solidify your negotiation strategies. Clearly, the cycle of learning and teaching is a path to mastery.

Negotiation Skills: A Collective Benefit

While the personal benefits of teaching negotiation are clear, there's also a broader, societal advantage. Negotiation is not a secret art meant for a select few. Its principles and techniques can be widely beneficial in various aspects of life, from professional to personal relationships. By spreading this knowledge, we create a more collaborative and understanding society. When more individuals are equipped with effective negotiation skills, it leads to more productive discussions, fairer outcomes, and reduced conflicts.

Practical Tips for Sharing Negotiation Knowledge

To put this into practice, here are some actionable strategies to teach negotiation skills effectively. This includes:

- **Structured learning sessions:** Organizing workshops or informal sessions where you can discuss and teach negotiation principles to your colleagues, suppliers, clients, and so on.
- **Mentoring:** Taking on a mentorship role for individuals who are new to negotiation.
- **Active learning tools:** Using role-playing scenarios to teach real-world negotiation tactics.
- **Feedback and reflection:** Encouraging feedback from those you teach to further refine your understanding and approach.

A Continuous Journey of Growth

The journey of learning and teaching negotiation is a continuous cycle of growth. By sharing your knowledge, you not only empower others but also enhance your own skills and understanding. This chapter underscores the importance of this cycle, not just as a means to individual improvement but also as a tool for fostering a more skilled and understanding community.

Through this exploration, you not only affirm the value of teaching as a learning tool but also reinforce the notion that negotiation skills are vital for everyone. By passing on what we learn, we not only grow as individuals but also contribute to a more harmonious and effective society.

ELEMENT 85

Expanding the Pie

Y ou will have a bigger pie to share if you find alternatives where the costs and risks are smaller, or where the profit is greater. This is not magic; there are examples of this in our everyday lives. Consider the following ideas and try to adopt them into your organization.

The IKEA Idea

IKEA's customers have to pick up the furniture they have bought from the store and take it home to assemble it. Their furniture is produced in a different way: the legs are not glued on in the factory; the customers have to put the piece together themselves. The packaging is smaller, and the factory's production costs are smaller, along with the transport and storage costs.

The Ryanair Discount Airline Model

When Michael O'Leary created Ryanair, an innovative discount airline, he first looked at how traditional airlines operated, then changed things to suit himself. He made the following changes and observations:

- The length of the contract between the company and supplier is often overlooked; three-year contracts are now the norm, rather than one-year contracts.
- A supplier who is not ready on time must pay a fine, and the supplier who provides more than was agreed to will receive a bonus.
- The customer researches and buys through the internet.
- Free office space is offered in exchange for looking after the company's accounts.
- Early orders receive a discount.
- Organizations concentrate on their own core activities. The organization that can deliver the best quality at the lowest cost will get business.

- O'Leary also studied other industries. He noticed that when the telecom industry stopped invoicing small amounts and instead asked for payment in advance from customers, the sale of mobile contracts increased drastically.
- The telephone company does not own all the equipment anymore. Now customers are permitted to buy their own telephones. More calls were made and the revenue increased.

Creative Service Provider Solution

A large service provider is faced with a possible conflict. The employees have demanded pay increases of 8 percent, but the current agreement does not allow more than 2 percent. The compromise of 5 percent is unthinkable for the organization. Strike warnings have been issued. After conversations with the involved parties, the following issues become clear.

The employees have been unhappy for several years—this has affected profits. The costs for materials and machines have been increasing in an alarming way. Quality has deteriorated. It is becoming more and more difficult to hire staff. The turnover of staff is large. Employees are separated into groups of three people, but because absenteeism is about 25 percent, each of the groups must have a fourth person on standby. Many of the employees have chosen the work because it gives them more freedom: they do not have to start or finish at a certain time. When they have completed the work for the day or week, they can go home.

With a wage increase of more than 2 percent, the employer would be forced to outsource the work. If nine employees want to earn more, they have to make the pie bigger. You cannot change the income side—that leaves the costs. The annual costs for materials and machines are already known, and there are nine employees who can work to bring them down.

Solution: Institute a bonus system where the organization and the nine employees share the savings they create. Consider if a working group of nine people can make do with a single person on standby. The cost of the two now-obsolete employees is shared between the organization and the employees. In order to do this, the employees must cover for each other and do the work of the person who is absent. The employees' working day will be a bit longer. If they can make this plan work, they will have a larger pie to share and the wage increase may end up being close to 15 percent. As it has been difficult to hire staff, the number of employees can be reduced by attrition.

Result: The employees accepted the proposal, which resulted in reduced absenteeism and a wage increase of 14 percent. The employees were given more responsibility for planning and carrying out the work. The turnover of employees was reduced. In this case, both parties won by using cooperative negotiation tactics.

ELEMENT 86

Subtext Awareness

S ubtext awareness in negotiation refers to the ability to recognize and understand the underlying messages, intentions, or emotions that are not explicitly stated in the conversation. It's about being attuned to the unspoken elements of communication, which can be as important, or sometimes even more important, than the actual words used. This can include body language, tone of voice, facial expressions, and other nonverbal cues.

Here's why subtext awareness is crucial in negotiations:

- **Uncovering real interests and concerns:** Often, what people say isn't the whole story. By reading the subtext, you can gain insights into their actual interests, concerns, and motivations, which might not be directly expressed.

- **Building relationships:** Understanding the subtext helps in building rapport and trust. Recognizing emotions like frustration or enthusiasm allows you to respond more empathetically, strengthening the relationship.

- **Preventing misunderstandings:** Misunderstandings in negotiations can lead to conflict or failed deals. By being aware of the subtext, you can clarify ambiguities and ensure both parties are on the same page.

- **Gaining strategic advantage:** Detecting subtext can provide strategic advantages. For example, if you sense hesitation in a counterpart's nonverbal cues, it might indicate they are unsure about their position, which you could leverage in your favor.

- **Adapting your approach:** Subtext awareness helps you adapt your negotiation strategy in real time. If you sense the other party is becoming defensive, you might choose to soften your approach or address their concerns directly.

- **Enhancing communication effectiveness:** Ensures that your communication is not just about the words but also about how those words are perceived and understood, leading to more effective and meaningful exchanges.

In a negotiation scenario where one party says, "We would like to move the delivery," this request could be carrying a subtext that's influenced by financial benefits they are not openly sharing.

Understanding the Subtext

Negotiation is not just about what is said but how it's said, and what is not said at all. The subtext includes nonverbal cues, hidden agendas, and emotional undercurrents. It's the realm where true intentions and unexpressed concerns reside. For a negotiator, being attuned to this subtext is akin to having a sixth sense—it provides a deeper understanding of the situation, allowing for more strategic and effective decision-making.

The Silent Conversations

- **Revealing the unspoken:** Often, the most crucial aspects of a negotiation are not directly articulated. Subtext awareness helps in discerning these underlying interests and aligning negotiation strategies to address them.
- **Building trust through nonverbal communication:** Trust and rapport are the foundations of successful negotiations. A nod, a shift in tone, or a change in posture can speak volumes about the other party's comfort or distress levels, providing insights into their true feelings and attitudes.
- **Emotional intelligence in action:** Subtext is deeply entwined with emotional intelligence. Recognizing and responding to emotions—both your own and the other party's—is crucial in steering negotiations toward a positive outcome.

Navigating the Undercurrents

- **Uncovering hidden agendas:** Every negotiation has layers. Understanding the subtext helps to peel these layers back, revealing any hidden agendas or constraints that might be impacting the negotiation.
- **Resolving conflict:** Subtext awareness is key in identifying potential conflict points before they escalate. Recognizing early signs of frustration or dissatisfaction allows for timely intervention and resolution.

Enhancing Communication Effectiveness

- **Strategic communication:** Being aware of the subtext enables negotiators to communicate more strategically, often using implication and suggestion to guide the negotiation toward desired outcomes.
- **Adapting communication styles:** A good negotiator adapts their communication style to match the other party. This adaptability, informed by subtext awareness, enhances comprehension and persuasiveness.

Decision-Making and Creative Problem-Solving

- **Informed decisions:** By understanding the underlying dynamics of the negotiation, decisions are more comprehensive and considerate of all parties' interests.

- **Crafting win-win solutions:** Awareness of the subtext often leads to identifying unaddressed issues, paving the way for creative and mutually beneficial solutions.

As you navigate the complexities of negotiation, the awareness of subtext stands as a beacon, guiding you to deeper understandings and more fruitful engagements. It is not merely an additional skill but a fundamental aspect of any effective negotiation strategy. Consider the following example, which illustrates this concept.

EXAMPLE | Early Delivery Negotiations

Suppose you're negotiating a contract with a company for the delivery of certain goods. During the negotiation, the company's representative says, "We would like to move the delivery to an earlier date."

Surface level: On the surface, this seems like a straightforward request to expedite delivery. You might interpret it as them needing the goods sooner for operational reasons.

Subtext and potential financial benefit: However, the subtext might be that moving the delivery date could have financial implications that they are not openly discussing. For example:

- **Cost savings:** They might have a financial incentive to receive the goods earlier. Perhaps they are running low on inventory and by getting your goods earlier, they avoid the cost of having to source from a more expensive supplier.

- **Contractual penalties:** They might be facing penalties from their clients for delays in their projects, and getting your goods earlier helps them avoid these penalties.

- **Market advantage:** The early receipt of goods might enable them to launch a product sooner, giving them a competitive edge in the market, which could translate to significant profits.

- **Financial reporting:** They might be trying to manage their financial reporting. By advancing the delivery, they could record the inventory or assets in the current financial quarter, impacting their financial results positively.

Why It Matters:

Understanding this subtext is crucial for several reasons:

- **Negotiation leverage:** Knowing their underlying motivation gives you leverage. You might be able to negotiate better terms if you agree to expedite delivery.

- **Cost implications for you:** Accelerating delivery might increase your costs, which you should factor into the negotiation.

- **Long-term relationship:** If you understand and accommodate their underlying needs, it could strengthen the business relationship.

In summary, when a negotiator requests changes like moving a delivery date, it's important to consider the subtext and potential hidden financial benefits. This awareness can significantly influence your strategy and outcomes in the negotiation.

ELEMENT 87

Human Engineering

The Carnegie Institute of Technology conducted a groundbreaking study that revealed a surprising aspect of professional success: only 15 percent is based on professional or technical knowledge, while a staggering 85 percent hinges on an understanding of human behavior, negotiation, and effective communication. This study underscores the significance of interpersonal skills (also called human engineering) in the workplace, highlighting the transformative power of functional, two-way communication.

Core Findings of the Study

The study's findings emphasize the importance of soft skills, particularly communication, in achieving professional success. In a world where technical expertise is highly valued, this revelation shifts the focus to the human element of business interactions. Effective communication is not just about conveying a message, but also involves listening, understanding, and respecting different viewpoints.

The Dynamics of Functional Communication

Functional communication is inherently two-way. It involves listening, asking questions, discussing alternatives, and using the answers constructively. This approach fosters mutual respect and understanding, crucial for productive negotiations and conflict resolution. The absence of this dynamic can lead to deadlocks, where parties become entrenched in their positions, leading to a breakdown in cooperation and understanding.

The Pitfalls of Ineffective Communication

Ineffective communication often stems from a failure to establish a common ground at the conversation's onset. This failure can lead to withholding information, misunderstandings, and a lack of willingness to negotiate. When parties lock themselves into their proposals without considering others' viewpoints, communication reaches a deadlock and interest in cooperation diminishes.

Credibility in Communication

The effectiveness of communication is largely determined by the exchange of credible information. The perception of credibility is always in the hands of the listener. Misunderstandings arise when the sender fails to convey the message effectively, leading to one-way communication. This situation highlights the sender's responsibility in ensuring the message is understood, not just delivered.

Exploring One-Way vs. Two-Way Communication

One-way communication often leads to misunderstandings and hinders mutual comprehension. To understand the effects of one-way and two-way communication, simple experiments can be conducted. These experiments demonstrate how reciprocal communication enhances understanding and problem-solving, while one-way communication creates barriers.

The Carnegie Institute of Technology study profoundly impacted our understanding of professional success. It showed that technical knowledge, while important, plays a smaller role compared to the mastery of soft skills, particularly effective communication. In the modern professional landscape, the ability to engage in functional, two-way communication is not just an asset but a necessity for success. This study serves as a clarion call for professionals and educators alike to prioritize and cultivate these vital interpersonal skills.

ELEMENT 88

Mastering Conflict Resolution Skills

I n the realm of negotiations, conflicts are not just inevitable but can also be instrumental in achieving deeper understanding and more robust agreements. This element delves into the art of conflict resolution within the context of negotiations, highlighting essential skills and strategies that can transform conflicts into opportunities for creating value and strengthening relationships.

Understanding the Nature of Conflict

Conflict in negotiations often arises from differing interests, values, perceptions, or goals between the negotiating parties. It's crucial to understand that conflict is not inherently negative. Instead, it can be a catalyst for exploring new ideas, uncovering underlying issues, and fostering innovative solutions.

Active Listening and Empathy

The first step in resolving conflict is active listening. This involves fully concentrating, understanding, responding, and then remembering what the other party is saying. It's about listening not just to the words but to the emotions and underlying concerns behind them. Empathy plays a key role here—it's about seeing the world through the other party's eyes and understanding their perspective.

Effective Communication

Clear and open communication is vital in conflict resolution. This means expressing your own perspective honestly and constructively while also being open to the viewpoints and feelings of others. Avoiding accusatory language and focusing on using "I" statements can help in expressing your position without triggering defensiveness. For example, instead of blaming the counterpart by saying "Your prices are too expensive," you could instead say, "I feel the price is too high."

Problem-Solving Approach

Adopting a problem-solving approach to conflict involves identifying the underlying issues and interests of both parties. It's about moving away from a position-based negotiation, where the focus is on what each party wants, to an interest-based negotiation, where the focus is on why they want it. This approach facilitates finding common ground and crafting solutions that address the needs of all parties involved.

Managing Emotions

Negotiations can be emotionally charged, so managing emotions is a critical aspect of conflict resolution. Recognizing and regulating your own emotional responses, as well as responding appropriately to the emotions of others, can prevent escalation and keep the negotiation on track.

Seeking SMARTnership Outcomes

The goal of conflict resolution in negotiations should be to achieve a SMARTnership/collaborative outcome, where the interests of all parties are met to the greatest extent possible. This requires creativity, flexibility, and a commitment to finding mutually beneficial solutions.

Building and Maintaining Trust

Trust is the foundation of any successful negotiation. Resolving conflicts in a respectful, fair, and transparent manner can strengthen trust between parties. This not only resolves the immediate conflict but also lays the groundwork for more effective and collaborative negotiations in the future.

Conflict resolution skills are essential in negotiations. They enable negotiators to transform conflicts from obstacles into opportunities for understanding, growth, and mutually beneficial solutions. By mastering these skills, negotiators can navigate complex negotiations more effectively, build stronger relationships, and achieve better outcomes.

CHAPTER 8

The Foundation

Introduction: Foundational Basics for Negotiations

This chapter focuses on the actual foundations for negotiations. These are the basics, and often something the professional negotiator doesn't even think about.

Success often hinges on a deep understanding of not just the mechanics of negotiation but also the human elements that drive these interactions. This chapter delves into the intricate tapestry of negotiation, exploring various facets that collectively shape the outcomes of any negotiation process. From the foundational role of trust to the creative maneuvers that break deadlocks, each element of this chapter offers a unique lens through which to view and understand negotiation.

- **Element 89: Love of negotiation.** The chapter begins with an exploration of the love of negotiation, delving into the passion and dedication required to excel in this field. Negotiation is not just a skill but an art form that requires a deep appreciation of its nuances and subtleties.

- **Element 90: Building trust.** Trust is the bedrock upon which successful negotiations are built, acting as a catalyst that can significantly enhance or, if absent, impede the negotiation process.

- **Element 91: Creativity.** In negotiation, creativity is then brought to the forefront. In the "Creativity" element, I discuss how thinking outside the box can lead to innovative solutions that satisfy all parties involved.

- **Element 92: Empathy.** This is closely tied to empathy, another vital component of effective negotiation. Understanding and relating to the emotions, perspectives, and needs of the other party can lead to more compassionate and mutually beneficial outcomes.

- **Element 93: Practice.** This element emphasizes the importance of honing negotiation skills through continuous application and learning. This is essential for adapting to the ever-evolving landscape of negotiation.

- **Element 94: Argumentation.** This element explores the art of presenting and defending a position persuasively and rationally, a critical skill in any negotiator's toolkit.

- **Element 95: Adaptability.** This element then examines the prerequisites for successful collaboration and co-creation, highlighting the importance of flexibility and responsiveness in negotiations.

- **Element 96: Ethics in negotiations.** Here, you navigate the moral complexities and responsibilities inherent in negotiation, underscoring the need for integrity and ethical considerations in all negotiation scenarios.

- **Element 97: Choose a strategy.** Strategic thinking in negotiation is covered in the "Strategy" element, which highlights the importance of planning, foresight, and tactical approaches to negotiation.

- **Element 98: Brainstorming.** This is presented as a technique to generate creative and effective solutions during negotiation impasses.

- **Element 99: Consider gender.** The element then addresses the influence of "gender" in negotiation, exploring how gender dynamics play a crucial role in shaping negotiation strategies and outcomes.

- **Element 100: Make sure you get something in return.** The "something in return" element encapsulates the essence of negotiation—the principle of reciprocity. It underscores the importance of ensuring that all parties feel valued and that concessions are balanced, reinforcing the notion that successful negotiation is about creating win-win situations.

- **Element 101: The power of habit.** Continuing with the theme of personal development, the "Habits" element discusses the behaviors and routines that contribute to becoming an effective negotiator, emphasizing the role of consistency and discipline in negotiation practice.

- **Element 102: Reflect.** The "Reflection" element offers insights into the typical skill sets and behaviors needed to improve and become a great negotiator, encouraging self-assessment and continuous improvement.

- **Element 103: The choice to negotiate.** Finally, the "It's a Choice" element provokes you to think about negotiation as a mindset and not a skill. Is a "standard" really a standard and when is a price negotiable?

In sum, this chapter is a comprehensive guide to understanding the multifaceted nature of negotiation. It blends theory with practical insights, aiming to equip you with the knowledge and skills needed to navigate the complex world of negotiation successfully.

ELEMENT 89

The Love of Negotiation

Let me make one thing clear: Negotiation is a skill we all need to master to varying degrees, and it's a skill everyone can learn. Negotiation is predominantly a skill, in contrast to the notion of it being an art. If negotiation were purely an art, some people would be born great negotiators and others, not so much. However, this is not the case.

Having acknowledged that we can all learn to negotiate, I have observed that approximately 20 percent of all professional negotiators (those for whom negotiation is a part of their job) are inept. They shouldn't be negotiating, simply because they are not adept at it. This means that, alarmingly, one in every five professional negotiators is unqualified.

You may think this figure is high—and it is. Disturbingly so. The pressing question is not so much about the number of less qualified negotiators, but rather why so many professionals are inadequate in the science of negotiation.

One obvious reason is the lack of education. I recently came across a study by Contract Nerds, revealing that 55 percent of contract professionals have never received formal education in negotiation. I met a business executive who wholeheartedly agreed that negotiation training is crucial for success. He recounted with enthusiasm the two-day training he underwent 18 years ago.

Negotiation is a skill that evolves, and if your last training was 18 years ago, it might be time for a refresher.

But here's the main reason why 20 percent are not qualified to negotiate: our investigation revealed that the majority of these unqualified individuals share a common trait—they dislike negotiating.

Think about it. None of us will excel at something we dislike. To be good at something, we need to have an affinity for it.

Raise your hand if you dislike negotiating. If you did, you should either stop doing it professionally or delve into why you have an aversion to negotiation. Many view negotiation as confrontational, but true negotiation is something entirely different.

Your immediate task is to reflect on why you like or dislike negotiation.

ELEMENT 90

Building Trust

In my professional journey, which includes extensive research culminating in my doctoral thesis, I have delved deeply into the dynamics of trust in business relationships and negotiations. This exploration aligns with findings from A. T. Kearney, emphasizing the pivotal role of trust in negotiations and strategic alliances. Their study highlights a direct connection between trust and profitability, illustrating that honesty and openness in communication not only foster trust but also enhance the quality and outcomes of agreements.

EXAMPLE | Trust Is Good, Control Is Better

This is an old Russian saying. This maxim very much permeated the view taken on negotiations and choice of strategy that typified the former Soviet system.

The difference between trust and control isn't just a question of hidden microphones and unfair methods. In negotiations based on an adversarial philosophy, mutual trust isn't required.

From the point of view of the Kremlin, combat was perceived as an excellent strategy. If the other party was accommodating and reasonable, this only encouraged the Soviet negotiators to pursue the fight.

According to the Soviet mentality and philosophy, you withdraw if you encounter serious opposition. If you encounter someone with a reasonable attitude, you exploit the situation to your own advantage. This behavior shows how dangerous it is to make unilateral concessions. The attitude was, according to Arkadij Sjevtjenko, ambassador and vice-secretary general of the United Nations, fundamental to Soviet behavior in connection with negotiations.

I'll leave any moral judgment to my reader. Remember that an agreement concluded between two satisfied parties will always be the best agreement in the long run. Unfair methods are short-sighted. If you hoodwink the other party, you're going to pay for it sooner or later.

When choosing your strategy and tactic, you should adapt to the norms of the market in which you find yourself. A high degree of morality based on your norms and values could constitute a handicap in many international contexts. We are too naive and gullible; we behave like nice guys in markets where greater toughness is required.

Learn to be mild in manner, firm in substance: *suaviter in modo, fortiter in re.* The objective is to get as much as possible from the negotiation without being perceived as a combative negotiator.

Tru$tCurrency

My doctoral research focused on the value buyers place on trust in their suppliers. It revealed a willingness to pay a significant premium—up to 20 percent more—for products or services from a supplier they trust over one they do not. This insight underscores the tangible economic value of trust in commercial transactions—I have named that *Tru$tCurrency*. Building such trust requires time and consistent effort, but it is a worthwhile endeavor. In today's competitive environment, the ability to establish and maintain trust is increasingly seen as a key differentiator. However, it's crucial to note that trust, once established, is fragile and easier to break than to build.

> Consider this perspective: In any collaborative endeavor, when trust is high, transactional costs tend to decrease, leading to an increase in profits. Conversely, if trust is low, transactional costs are likely to rise, resulting in a reduction in profits.

The role of trust extends beyond negotiation tables to the very foundation of business relationships. It's hard to imagine a successful business arrangement with a supplier lacking trustworthiness, or a productive working relationship with an unreliable colleague. Similarly, personal relationships, like marriage, hinge on trust. Establishing and sustaining a business in an environment devoid of trust is not only challenging but also unsustainable. Trust is not just important in long-term relationships; it's indispensable, affecting every interaction, leaving lasting impressions and shaping future outcomes.

Cultivating Trust

The question then arises: What engenders trust? The answer lies in the congruence between what we say and what we do. Initial impressions are often guided more by nonverbal cues than by words. The presence or absence of trust and respect can either facilitate smooth relationships or create insurmountable barriers. An agreement based on trust has a much higher chance of successful implementation and longevity.

In the absence of trust and mutual understanding, agreements are reduced to mere formalities without real value. The institution of marriage serves as a prime example, where the lack of trust often leads to dissolution. In the realm of negotiations, whether in business or critical situations like hostage negotiations, honesty and sincerity emerge as the only viable approach. Aggressive, domineering tactics are not only ineffective but can also lead to disastrous outcomes.

To cultivate trust, you need knowledge, awareness, and a willingness to be open and take risks. In scenarios where trust is lacking, parties resort to formal securities like warranties and guarantees. However, for truly effective negotiations, trust is paramount. It is, arguably, the only way forward.

Reflecting on the evolution of business transactions, one wonders about the days when a handshake was enough to seal a deal. What did we do before the advent of extensive legal contracts and agreements? While these legal instruments protect interests, they cannot replace the need for personal trust, ethics, and morality in business dealings. The real challenge lies in understanding the true essence of trust and the responsibility that accompanies it.

In our daily interactions, we face numerous opportunities to demonstrate our trustworthiness. Our actions and words, often observed unconsciously by others, reveal our character. Upholding promises, playing fair, and adhering to ethical standards are true tests of credibility. Trustworthiness involves more than fulfilling agreements; it reflects a deep-seated respect for others and the value we place on our relationships.

To build trust, understanding the principles of honesty, integrity, and commitment to agreements is crucial. Honesty is the foundation of trust; without it, trust cannot exist. Trustworthy individuals do not manipulate truth or offer misleading information. Their integrity is unshakeable, grounded in a strong ethical framework that guides their actions.

When considering trustworthiness, we often think about the person's ability to keep promises and fulfill agreements. But trustworthiness extends beyond mere agreement fulfillment; it signifies that one's word is their bond, reflecting a fundamental loyalty to others. Trustworthiness communicates how we value others and the importance we place on relationships. The greatest obstacle to being perceived as trustworthy is often ourselves. Greed, self-centeredness, lack of self-control, or low self-esteem can sabotage our efforts to build trust. Once lost, trust is extremely hard to regain.

Every day, we demonstrate our credibility through small actions and decisions. Whether making a promise to a colleague, a family member, or a customer, each instance is a test of our credibility. Adhering to ethical standards, even when it's more profitable to do otherwise, is another test of our integrity and moral values. To truly understand the foundations of trustworthiness, ethics, and morality, we must consider the importance of sincerity, integrity, and commitment to agreements.

The journey to building trust is not a quick one. In another survey I conducted with over 5,000 professionals, the importance of trust in relationships and transactions was universally acknowledged. Interestingly, a significant majority believed that trust could be established rapidly, even within minutes of a first meeting. This perception highlights our ability to quickly "read" others based on various factors such as appearance, body language, and initial impressions. It underscores the importance of our nonverbal communication in establishing trust from the outset.

In summary, trust is the bedrock of all successful relationships, both in business and in personal life. It is a powerful tool that transcends external factors like social status, education, or wealth. Trustworthiness starts with our words and actions, and the promises we keep. It cannot be bought or feigned; it must be earned through consistent, ethical behavior. Understanding that ethics and morality are the foundation of trust between people is crucial. We may not always label our assessments as such, but we are constantly evaluating others based on our ethical and moral standards to determine their trustworthiness.

Trust is essential in every aspect of life. It influences every interaction and shapes every relationship. The journey to building and maintaining trust is continuous, requiring consistent effort and commitment to ethical principles. It is a journey well worth undertaking, as the rewards of trust are immeasurable in both our professional and personal lives.

ELEMENT 91
Unleashing Creativity

In the dynamic world of NegoEconomics, success often hinges on altering traditional assumptions and embracing creativity. This shift faces challenges from individuals resistant to change, those who settle quickly to avoid conflict, people reluctant to consider a wide range of options, and opponents disinterested in creative solutions.

As an experienced negotiator, enhancing existing business relationships can be challenging, particularly when counterparts adhere to the adage, "If it ain't broke, don't fix it," or are unable to think beyond a price/quantity-focused model. Reinventing and improving preexisting relationships is key to building trust; creativity is crucial in a troubled economic climate. The creative negotiator uncovers hidden values in established relationships and develops innovative ways to generate value through new relationships.

EXAMPLE | Transforming Competition into Collaboration

Let's explore a real-life scenario illustrating the power of creative negotiation. A close associate was on the verge of selling his business. He received three distinct offers: Buyer A proposed $14.3 million, Buyer B $11.1 million, and Buyer C a seemingly underwhelming $8.5 million for a company valued at $11 million.

The apparent choice was Buyer A. However, my friend was advised to delve deeper, to understand each bidder's motivations and plans for the company. This inquiry revealed that:

- Buyer A aimed to acquire the company's established brand, intending to shift production offshore.
- Buyer B was interested primarily in the company's state-of-the-art equipment, with plans to sell it for profit.
- Buyer C aspired to transform the company's premises into an industrial school, with no interest in its production equipment.

By recognizing these unique interests, an innovative solution emerged. Instead of selling the company as a whole, each buyer acquired only what they truly needed, at a price below their initial bids. This strategic partitioning led to the seller amassing over $14.4 million, surpassing Buyer A's offer for the entire business. This negotiation culminated in a rare scenario with four winners, demonstrating the transformative impact of creativity in negotiation.

In expanding the role of creativity in negotiations, it is crucial to consider various aspects. Creative negotiators often redefine problems, identifying new areas for agreement and value creation. Integrative bargaining, focusing on mutual gains, can enlarge the "pie" before it's divided. Brainstorming and ideation during negotiations can lead to innovative solutions. Embracing diverse perspectives at the negotiation table can spark creativity, leading to richer ideas and solutions. *Scenario planning*—considering a range of possible futures—helps identify unforeseen opportunities and risks. Using analogies and metaphors can clarify complex issues and bridge understanding gaps. In today's fast-paced, technology-driven world, negotiators need to be creative in adapting to new tools and platforms.

Creativity in negotiation is about thinking beyond conventional constraints and embracing new possibilities. It's not just about winning or losing but redefining the rules of the game to create mutually beneficial outcomes. As negotiators navigate the intricacies of NegoEconomics, let creativity guide you in crafting solutions that transform challenges into opportunities for collaborative success.

ELEMENT 92

Conveying Empathy

E mpathy is about understanding things from another person's perspective. It involves not just putting yourself in the shoes of another person but also comprehending their emotional and rational needs. This understanding is crucial in negotiations as it helps build trust and leads to mutually beneficial outcomes.

However, empathy goes beyond mere understanding; it's about actively responding to the other party's needs and emotions in a business context. As soon as we start to judge another person, we hinder our ability to understand them fully, thus becoming incapable of seeing things from their perspective.

> John and Sally took their three-year-old son, Ben, to the zoo. Ben really wanted to see the lions, so the first place they went to was the lion cage. John told Ben that he was to look at the lions and he asked him what he thought. Ben reacted by looking upset, which frustrated his father who repeated: "Come on, Ben, do as I tell you. Look at the lions." Sally realized immediately that Ben could not see the lions properly because of the high wall, so she went over to him and lifted him up. Ben immediately started to smile and point at the lions.

How often do you see things from your own perspective?

Intuition: Your Moral Compass

We notice it when we have done the right thing. In the same way we notice it when we have done something that we do not feel is right. Our "emotional brain" communicates this via emotions or sensations in our bodies. This is intuition. Our intuition cannot communicate in words, so it has to do it in another way. It could be a certain muscular tension, a headache, an unpleasant feeling in our stomachs, loss of appetite, sleepless nights, and many other physical signs. If you are in contact with your emotions and listen to them (self-awareness), they tell you whether you have done the right thing or the wrong thing. The problem is that our "rational brain" is good at deceiving us.

EXAMPLE | An Important Business Decision

Jesper is a negotiator and the procurement head of his company. He has to buy 20,000 new valves for some important equipment that his company manufactures. He has negotiated with two important salespeople. Salesperson A sells valves at a unit price of 15 euros. Salesperson B sells the valves at a unit price of 13 euros. After several meetings with both salespeople, Jesper notices that he always feels good when meeting with salesperson A—these meetings seem to fly by. But when he has meetings with salesperson B, he feels drained and has an unpleasant nervous sensation in his stomach. After having thought everything through, Jesper persuades himself to ignore his uneasiness and do the rational thing—take salesperson B with the lower unit price. "After all, this is business." Some weeks after making his decision, Jesper still feels ill at ease and nervous about this new supplier. After working together for three months, the supplier stops replying to Jesper's communications. When Jesper finally manages to track him down, he explains that he had recruitment problems and was not in a position to supply the agreed number of valves within the next two months.

Would you have done the same?

Jesper's decision to purchase valves from a lower-priced supplier, despite his intuition signaling discomfort, serves as a cautionary tale. Ignoring his intuitive misgivings, he faced significant supply issues later. This example highlights the importance of balancing rational analysis with intuitive signals in business decisions.

Self-Awareness: Listen to Your Intuition

Being in tune with your emotional state and listening to your intuition is crucial. Recognize the physical manifestations of emotions and understand their implications in negotiations. High self-awareness enables better understanding and empathy toward others, leading to more effective negotiation strategies.

Emotions do not reside in your brain; they are experienced throughout your entire body. Do you listen to the signals that your body sends to you? Have you ever found yourself sweating or having back pains when you are tense or nervous? What about that person at the meeting whose voice seemed to tremble when he got up and started to talk to the group?

Evaluate Your Empathy Level

Use the following checklist to find out whether your empathetic skills are good and whether there are areas you can improve. In each area, decide whether you are:

- Good: You do it frequently.
- Medium: You do it sometimes but could improve.
- Poor: You do it seldom or never.

Use this checklist to assess your empathetic skills in a negotiation context:

☐ Do you ask others how they are and genuinely care about the answer?

☐ Do you acknowledge and respond to other people's feelings appropriately?

☐ Can you handle anger or other negative feelings in negotiations?

☐ Can you tolerate periods of quietness and use them effectively in negotiations?

☐ Are you aware of your own body language and how it affects negotiations?

☐ Do you encourage others in negotiations to express their feelings and concerns?

☐ Are you comfortable with closeness and affection in professional relationships?

☐ Do you help others in negotiations to articulate their feelings and interests?

☐ Can you pick up and decipher the body language of your negotiation counterparts?

☐ Are you receptive to others expressing their feelings during negotiations?

Empathy, intuition, and self-awareness are interconnected and vital in the art of negotiation. Understanding and improving these skills can significantly enhance your ability to negotiate effectively and build successful business relationships. Embrace these skills to navigate the complexities of negotiation and strategic partnerships with greater insight and success.

Empathy is not a strategy or tool. It's about being sincere and honest and truly trying to understand your counterpart's chain of thoughts.

ELEMENT 93

Practicing

In negotiation and strategic partnerships, one fundamental truth stands out: There is no ultimate, unchanging solution. This dynamic business landscape requires a flexible approach, constantly adapting strategies to meet evolving needs and scenarios.

The Importance of Personal Insight in Negotiation

Success in negotiation begins with a deep understanding of oneself. Recognizing and leveraging your strengths while acknowledging and improving your weaknesses forms the foundation of effective negotiation. It's not just about what you bring to the table but also about understanding your limitations and working proactively to address them.

Focusing on a select few issues at a time ensures you don't spread yourself too thin, allowing for a more profound and impactful engagement in each area. Reciprocity is a vital aspect of negotiation—expecting and demanding something in return is not just fair but necessary for balanced and productive outcomes.

Communication is key. Summarizing discussions helps keep track of progress and clarifies mutual understanding. Asking questions is a sign of engagement and intelligence—it shows you're actively involved and seeking deeper insight. Breaks are not merely pauses in conversation; they are opportunities to reflect, strategize, and come back stronger.

Practicing and Reflecting on Negotiation

Negotiation is a science honed over time through practice and reflection. Each negotiation encounter is a learning opportunity. It's essential to take a step back after each session to analyze how it went, understand the underlying factors of its success or failure, and identify areas for improvement. This self-reflection is crucial for the growth and development in negotiation skills.

Collaboration and Discussion

Negotiation is not a solitary endeavor. Engaging with colleagues and mentors about your experiences in negotiation opens up new perspectives. These discussions can offer invaluable insights, allowing you to see aspects of your negotiation style that you may not have noticed. They also provide an opportunity to learn from others' experiences, further enriching your understanding and approach.

ELEMENT 94

The Nuances of Argumentation

In my extensive experience with negotiations, I've consistently observed that the argumentation phase (introduced in Element 57) is both critical and delicate. However, I've come to advocate a significant shift in this phase: replacing traditional argumentation with a more question-centric approach. This subtle yet powerful change transforms the negotiation from a potential battleground into a collaborative exploration of mutual interests and solutions.

The Dynamics of Argumentation

Typically, the argumentation phase involves influencing the other party's ambitions and perceptions of negotiation strength. While a well-argued point can shift the balance of power, it often leads to a zero-sum game. Instead, I propose a different strategy: using questions to guide the conversation. By asking insightful and strategic questions, negotiators can uncover underlying needs, potential compromises, and areas for joint gains, steering the negotiation toward a more positive and productive outcome.

The Shift from Argumentation to Inquiry

Replacing arguments with questions serves several purposes. It helps avoid the pitfalls of subservience, where one party might concede under pressure. Questions encourage a more open and constructive dialogue, focusing on understanding each other's needs and exploring NegoEconomics—solutions that enlarge the value pie for all parties involved (see Element 20).

For instance, instead of challenging a seller's pricing directly, a buyer could ask about the factors influencing the price, alternative pricing models, or options for added value. This approach not only maintains a respectful tone but also opens avenues for creative solutions.

Strategies for Effective Use of Questions

Incorporating questions into negotiation requires specific strategies. Open-ended questions encourage expansive thinking and detailed responses. Information-gathering questions help in understanding the full implications of demands and objections. Clarifying questions ensure that all parties are on the same page. Solution-oriented questions focus on collaborative problem-solving, exploring possibilities that could lead to mutual benefits.

The Art of Strategic Inquiry

Strategic inquiry involves not just asking questions but also listening actively to the answers. This approach fosters a more balanced negotiation, transforming potential confrontations into opportunities for SMARTnership. Each question should be a step toward understanding and addressing the core issues, moving away from the traditional adversarial dynamics.

While traditional argumentation has its place, I recommend a shift toward a question-centric approach in negotiations. This strategy enhances the effectiveness of the negotiation process, fostering a more respectful, understanding, and ultimately productive dialogue. It's about transforming the negotiation from a series of arguments to a journey of mutual discovery and agreement.

ELEMENT 95

Adaptability

What are the prerequisites for a successful cooperation agreement? In the world of negotiation, adaptability and flexibility are not just beneficial traits; they are essential for success. This element delves into the significance of these qualities in negotiation, highlighting how they can influence outcomes and foster more effective and dynamic negotiation strategies.

The Fluid Nature of Negotiations

At its core, negotiation is a fluid process, characterized by changing dynamics, evolving interests, and unforeseen challenges. The ability to adapt to these changing circumstances is crucial. This means being open to new information, adjusting strategies in response to the other party's actions, and being willing to explore alternative paths to agreement. Adaptability allows negotiators to pivot when necessary, turning potential obstacles into opportunities for mutually beneficial outcomes.

Flexibility in Strategy and Approach

Flexibility in negotiation involves more than just a willingness to change tactics; it requires a mindset that values creative problem-solving and open-mindedness. This approach includes:

- **Exploring multiple options:** Being flexible means considering a range of possibilities and not being fixed on a single outcome. This approach opens the door to innovative solutions that might satisfy both parties more effectively.
- **Responsive communication:** Adaptability in communication is about actively listening, understanding the other party's perspective, and adjusting your messages accordingly. This responsiveness can build trust and rapport, crucial elements in successful negotiations.

- **Balancing firmness with accommodation:** While it's important to have clear goals, being too rigid can lead to impasse. Flexibility involves knowing when to stand firm and when to make concessions.

Cultural Adaptability in Global Negotiations

In today's globalized business environment, negotiators often encounter diverse cultures and practices. *Cultural adaptability*—the ability to navigate and respect these differences—is indispensable. This includes understanding cultural norms, communication styles, and decision-making processes, which vary significantly across cultures.

Embracing Technological Changes

Technological advancements are continuously reshaping the negotiation landscape. Adaptability in this context means staying abreast of and proficient with new negotiation tools and platforms, such as virtual meeting software, digital contracts, AI, and data analysis tools. These technologies can enhance efficiency, provide valuable insights, and facilitate negotiations in a digital era.

The Role of Emotional Intelligence

Adaptability and flexibility are deeply intertwined with emotional intelligence. Recognizing and managing one's own emotions, as well as perceiving and responding appropriately to the emotions of others, are key components of successful negotiation. This emotional agility allows for more empathetic and effective communication.

Continuous Learning and Development

The final aspect of adaptability and flexibility in negotiations is the commitment to continuous learning and self-improvement. The best negotiators are those who view each negotiation as a learning opportunity, reflecting on their experiences to refine their approach continually.

Adaptability and flexibility are not just tactics in negotiation; they represent a philosophy of openness, responsiveness, and continuous growth. By embracing these qualities, negotiators can navigate the complexities of negotiation with greater skill, creating more successful outcomes and fostering stronger, more collaborative relationships.

ELEMENT 96

Ethical Negotiations

E thical negotiations are the cornerstone of sustainable SMARTnerships. In the arena of negotiation, ethics plays a pivotal role in building trust, credibility, and long-term success. This module explores the concept of ethical negotiation, underscoring its importance in fostering sustainable business relationships and strategic partnerships.

The Essence of Ethical Negotiation

Ethical negotiation goes beyond mere compliance with legal standards; it embodies honesty, integrity, and fairness in every interaction. It involves being transparent about intentions, respecting the interests of all parties, and ensuring that outcomes are mutually beneficial. The essence of ethical negotiation lies in creating value not just for oneself but for all involved.

Trust and Reputation in Negotiations

The cornerstone of ethical negotiation is trust. A negotiator's reputation for fairness and integrity can open doors to new opportunities and partnerships. In contrast, a reputation tarnished by unethical practices can lead to long-term detrimental effects on business relationships. Trust is hard-earned and easily lost; hence, maintaining ethical standards is crucial for a negotiator's credibility and success.

Balancing Interests Fairly

Ethical negotiation involves a balanced approach to interests. It's about understanding and respecting the needs and constraints of the other party, avoiding exploitation, and striving for agreements that are fair and reasonable. This balance ensures that negotiations are not just about winning at the expense of others but about finding solutions that are acceptable and beneficial to all.

Cultural Sensitivity and Global Ethics

In an increasingly globalized world, negotiators must navigate different cultural norms and ethical standards. Cultural sensitivity, coupled with a commitment to global ethical principles, is vital. This includes being aware of different business practices and respecting cultural differences in negotiations while adhering to universally accepted ethical norms.

Long-Term Perspectives

Ethical negotiation is intrinsically linked to a long-term perspective. It recognizes that short-term gains achieved through unethical means are unsustainable and detrimental to long-term business goals. Building relationships based on trust, respect, and fairness paves the way for ongoing collaboration and success.

Creating tools to ensure ethical conduct in negotiations is essential for fostering trust, credibility, and long-term relationships. Here are a few practical tools designed to uphold ethical standards in negotiation situations:

- **Ethical guidelines checklist:** Develop a comprehensive checklist that outlines key ethical principles such as honesty, transparency, fairness, and respect for all parties involved. This checklist can serve as a reminder and guide to ensure that each step of the negotiation process aligns with these core values.

- **Stakeholder impact analysis:** Before entering a negotiation, conduct an analysis to understand how potential decisions and outcomes might impact all stakeholders. This tool helps to identify any ethical considerations and ensures that the interests of all parties are fairly represented and respected.

- **Cultural sensitivity framework:** Create a framework that provides information on various cultural norms and practices. This tool is particularly useful for international negotiations, ensuring that negotiators are aware of and sensitive to cultural differences, thereby avoiding ethical misunderstandings.

- **Conflict of interest declaration:** Implement a process where all parties in a negotiation declare any potential conflicts of interest. This tool promotes transparency and helps to build trust among the negotiating parties.

- **Negotiation reflection journal:** Encourage negotiators to keep a journal where they can reflect on their negotiation experiences, focusing on ethical dilemmas and how they were addressed. This practice promotes self-awareness and continuous learning in ethical negotiation practices.

- **Training program on ethical negotiation:** Develop a training program that covers the importance of ethics in negotiations, real-world scenarios, and strategies to handle complex ethical dilemmas. Regular training ensures that ethical considerations remain at the forefront of every negotiator's mind.

- **Feedback and evaluation system:** Establish a system where parties can provide anonymous feedback about the negotiation process, focusing on the ethical conduct of all participants. This tool helps to identify areas for improvement and reinforces the importance of ethical behavior.
- **Negotiation scenario simulations:** Use role-playing and simulations to practice handling ethical dilemmas in a controlled environment. This tool allows negotiators to develop and refine their skills in making ethical decisions under various negotiation scenarios.

These tools are designed to embed ethical considerations into every aspect of the negotiation process, helping negotiators navigate complex situations with integrity and respect for all parties involved.

Ethical negotiation is not just a moral obligation but a strategic necessity in today's business world. It is the foundation upon which lasting and successful partnerships are built. By adhering to ethical principles in negotiations, businesses can foster trust, enhance their reputation, and create sustainable value for themselves and their stakeholders. This approach to negotiation not only ensures compliance and reduces risk but also contributes to the creation of a more just and equitable business environment.

ELEMENT 97

Choosing a Strategy

More and more organizations are recognizing the critical importance of having a comprehensive negotiation strategy, placing it on par with other pivotal business strategies like sales, communication, R&D, and market strategies. In the dynamic landscape of modern business, negotiation isn't just a skill—it's a vital management strategy, pivotal to an organization's success.

Approaching negotiations with a well-defined strategy isn't just beneficial; it's essential. A structured approach to negotiation demonstrates initiative, boosts confidence, and provides a clear path to guide the conversation toward desired objectives. Within the realm of negotiation strategies, there are primarily two types: positional, or zero-sum, where only one party emerges victorious, and collaborative, which includes partnership and SMARTnership.

SMARTnership, or what I refer to as "Partnership 2.0," takes collaboration a step further by incorporating rules of the game, variables, NegoEconomics, and trust. This approach focuses on creating value for all parties involved.

Positional or Zero-Sum Negotiation

This is a traditional form of negotiation where the approach is often competitive. In a zero-sum scenario, the negotiators see the situation as a pie that cannot be enlarged. Any gain by one party is seen as a loss by the other. This approach is characterized by:

- **Fixed pie perception:** The belief that resources are limited and must be divided.
- **Adversarial approach:** Negotiators often adopt a confrontational stance, aiming to win as much as possible for their side.
- **Limited sharing of information:** Parties are less likely to share information openly, fearing it may be used against them.
- **Focus on positions:** Parties stick to their stated positions rather than underlying interests or needs.
- **Short-term gains over long-term relationships:** The emphasis is on immediate gains rather than building long-term relationships.

Collaborative Negotiation

This approach, also known as integrative or win-win negotiation, seeks to find solutions that are mutually beneficial. It is characterized by:

- **Expanding the pie:** Looking for ways to increase the resources or value available through creative solutions.
- **A focus on interests:** Understanding and addressing the underlying interests and needs of all parties, not just their stated positions.
- **Open communication:** Encouraging transparency and sharing of information to understand each other's needs and constraints.
- **Building relationships:** Emphasizing trust, rapport, and long-term relationships.
- **Problem-solving orientation:** Working together to find innovative solutions that satisfy everyone involved.

SMARTnership or Partnership 2.0

This is an advanced form of collaborative negotiation. SMARTnership takes collaboration to a deeper level by incorporating additional elements:

- **Rules of the game:** Establish clear, fair rules and protocols for negotiation to ensure a level playing field.
- **Variables:** Identify and leverage a wide range of variables beyond the obvious negotiation points. This could include timing, delivery options, additional services, and so on.
- **NegoEconomics:** Focus on the economics of negotiation. This concept involves understanding and optimizing the economic value for all parties, not just in terms of immediate cost but also long-term value creation.
- **Trust:** Build a high level of trust between parties. This goes beyond basic rapport to create a deeper understanding and reliability in relationships.
- **Creating value for all parties:** Create and maximize value for all involved, not just dividing existing value.

SMARTnership, by incorporating these elements, shifts the focus from competing over a fixed pie to collaboratively expanding the pie and creating additional value for all parties involved. This approach can lead to more sustainable and satisfactory outcomes in the long run.

Planning

Despite the clear benefits, many still rely on improvisation in negotiations, thereby missing opportunities to propose innovative offers or counteroffers. A structured strategy enables you to discern whether to make an all-encompassing offer or to address issues sequentially. Lack of preparation can lead to stress and mistakes, which are often costly in high-stakes negotiations.

A strategist in the realm of negotiation is not only aware of the benefits and drawbacks of making the first offer but also understands the risks of making one-sided concessions. However, flexibility remains a cornerstone of effective negotiation. As circumstances change, so must your approach. For instance, if faced with unexpected demands, like a longer warranty period, a skilled negotiator pivots swiftly to offer alternative value propositions such as expedited delivery, enhanced services, or alternative payment terms.

Exemplary negotiators are both structured and methodical. They approach each negotiation with a clear agenda, meticulously document discussions for future reference, and methodically address each point without unnecessary diversions. Summarizing key points ensures mutual understanding and sets the stage for the next phase of negotiation.

Time is a precious commodity in negotiations. Effective negotiators don't hesitate to alter their strategies if the current approach proves ineffective. This agility is vital in navigating the complex landscape of negotiation.

The choice of strategy and tactics is a critical preparatory step. Without a well-thought-out strategy, you risk ceding control to the other party and being forced to negotiate on their terms. Your strategy is your negotiation philosophy; it shapes your behavior and influences the negotiation's overall climate. Tactics, on the other hand, are the specific moves and maneuvers employed during the negotiation process.

It's surprising how many negotiators enter discussions without a concrete strategy, adjusting their approach reactively rather than proactively. This lack of planning often results in a disjointed and ineffective negotiation process. Your negotiation strategy is a reflection of your personality, shaped by your upbringing and experiences. It's often consistent with how you interact in other aspects of your life, be it with family, neighbors, or colleagues.

Expectations play a significant role in shaping your negotiation strategy. If you anticipate aggression from the other party, you might unconsciously prepare for conflict without considering more collaborative approaches. Similarly, perceived cooperation from the other party might lead you to adopt a more amenable stance. This dynamic is akin to a natural law, where pressure begets counterpressure.

An organization's culture and worldview also influence your negotiation strategy. Negotiators often align their approach with what they perceive to be the expectations of their organization and its leadership. However, those who recognize the significance of strategic choice in negotiations often take a more deliberate approach. They meticulously plan their strategy, adapting it to the specific context of each negotiation. These skilled negotiators understand the dual objectives of negotiation: creating and dividing NegoEconomics, and they adeptly navigate between various strategies to achieve the best possible outcomes.

A negotiation strategy is not a static blueprint but a dynamic framework that guides behavior, influences relationships, and shapes outcomes. The ability to adapt and evolve this strategy in response to changing circumstances is what distinguishes a proficient negotiator from an ordinary one. As you delve deeper into the intricacies of negotiation strategies, it becomes increasingly clear that a well-thought-out approach is not just beneficial; it's imperative for success in today's complex and ever-evolving business landscape.

ELEMENT 98

Brainstorming

"Y ou can't see the forest for the trees" is a saying indicating that sometimes people are too focused on the details to understand the overall situation or context.

This saying is highly relevant when discussing development in negotiations. If you always do what you have always done, you'll always get the same result. To change the outcome of a negotiation, you need to change how you perceive negotiations and how negotiations are conducted.

I recommend you invite somebody from the outside that you trust to evaluate your negotiation preparation and planning. Invite someone from a different industry—someone who is not familiar with the customs in your business and industry. Let them ask questions and challenge the way you handle negotiations and the variables you bring to the table.

I am fortunate to travel across various businesses and industries every year as an advisor and can compare their different approaches to negotiations. In our strategy work for a client, we always conduct a brainstorming session with the single purpose of developing variables. Your organization is not negotiating all the variables available to you. That is a promise I can give you.

As mentioned, invite someone from the outside or even your trusted suppliers and clients to participate in a mutual brainstorming session.

Set an agenda for what you want to achieve and spend three to four hours discussing new and different variables and ideas for your forthcoming negotiation. Don't let the typical comments prevent you from generating new ideas. The idea preventing comments you probably know is: "We don't have the budget." "We tried it before, and it didn't work." "The counterpart/management/team will never accept/understand this." And so on . . .

To run a successful brainstorming session in a negotiation that focuses on creating more variables, NegoEconomics, and SMARTnership, follow these steps:

1. **Preparing:** Before the session, inform participants about the key concepts of NegoEconomics and SMARTnership. Provide background materials or a brief overview to ensure that everyone is on the same page. Define the main objectives of the negotiation and the brainstorming session.

2. **Setting the stage:** Choose a comfortable, distraction-free environment conducive to creative thinking. Begin the session by reiterating the goals and emphasizing the importance of open-mindedness and nonjudgmental thinking.

3. **Defining the rules of engagement:** Establish ground rules that encourage free-flowing ideas, respect for all contributions, and an understanding that quantity of ideas is initially more valuable than quality. Emphasize that all ideas are welcome, and that criticism or evaluation of ideas should be withheld until later.

4. **Encouraging divergent thinking:** Encourage participants to think broadly and generate as many ideas as possible. Use techniques like mind mapping or free association to explore different aspects of the negotiation. Focus on creating variables that can add value for all parties, emphasizing the principles of NegoEconomics.

5. **Encouraging SMARTnership:** Foster an atmosphere where participants think collaboratively, not competitively. Encourage them to build on each other's ideas, creating synergies and exploring how different variables can work together in a mutually beneficial manner.

6. **Converging and evaluating:** After a substantial list of ideas has been generated, guide the group to categorize and evaluate them. Focus on the feasibility, potential impact, and alignment with the goals of the negotiation. Use criteria that prioritize SMARTnership and mutual gain.

7. **Developing an actionable plan:** From the evaluated list, select the most promising ideas. Develop these into actionable strategies and variables that can be used in the negotiation process. Ensure that these strategies are aligned with the principles of NegoEconomics and SMARTnership.

8. **Documenting and following up:** Record all the ideas generated and the strategies developed. Distribute this documentation to all participants. Plan a follow-up meeting to refine these strategies and prepare for their implementation in the negotiation.

Remember, the key to a successful brainstorming session in this context is to create an environment that values creative thinking, collaboration, and the pursuit of mutual benefits.

ELEMENT 99

Considering Gender

The subtle yet significant differences in how men and women engage can often shape the outcome. As an expert in SMARTnership negotiation, I've observed these variances not just as stereotypes but as diverse approaches that bring unique strengths to the negotiating table. This element explores these gender-based nuances, offering insights into harnessing them for more effective and collaborative negotiations.

The Art of Negotiation: Gender Perspectives

The way men and women step into the negotiation arena often reflects differing mindsets and strategies. Men typically enter negotiations with a competitive spirit, viewing the process as a battlefield where victory is paramount. This approach aligns with traditional negotiation tactics, where asserting dominance and securing one's interests at the expense of others is often the goal.

In contrast, women frequently approach negotiations with a mindset that leans toward collaboration. They tend to view the negotiation as an opportunity for all parties to win, a concept resonating deeply with the philosophy of SMARTnership. This approach is less about vanquishing an opponent and more about finding a harmonious solution that benefits everyone involved.

Communication styles also diverge along these lines. Men's communication in negotiations is often characterized by directness and assertiveness, while women usually adopt a more relational style. They excel in building rapport, understanding the counterpart's perspective and weaving emotional intelligence into their negotiation tactics. This skill in empathetic communication is a cornerstone of effective communicative competence.

Men in Negotiation

Men tend to be, and I am generalizing, more competitive and zero-sum focused in negotiation, often embracing the process with less empathy than women. They also tend to be more egocentric as negotiators and don't show the same understanding of the counterpart.

Men would benefit all parties by understanding the differences when negotiating with women. Such a difference can be as important as an American negotiating with a Japanese person.

The Dual Facets of Women in Negotiation

In my experience, most women exhibit remarkable prowess when negotiating on behalf of others. Their ability to empathize, understand various perspectives, and seek collaborative solutions makes them formidable negotiators in these contexts. However, a contrast emerges when women negotiate for their own interests. While generalizations are risky, it has been noted that many women can be less assertive in advocating for themselves compared to when they are representing others. This might stem from societal expectations, self-perception, and traditional gender roles.

To address this disparity, focused training and workshops aimed at boosting self-advocacy skills can be instrumental. Redefining what success looks like in a negotiation and cultivating a mindset where women see themselves as deserving and capable of achieving their own goals is crucial. This involves challenging existing stereotypes and encouraging women to embrace their negotiation strengths, whether they are negotiating for themselves or others.

Conclusion

Understanding the general differences in negotiation styles between men and women is a valuable asset in the negotiator's toolkit. However, transcending these differences to focus on adaptability, empathy, and collaboration is where the true art of negotiation lies. By empowering women to leverage their innate strengths in all negotiation contexts and encouraging men to understand other genders' perspectives, we can move toward a more balanced and effective negotiation landscape, reflecting the principles of smart partnership and communicative competence.

ELEMENT 100

Making Sure You Get Something in Return

The party that starts making unilateral concessions is most frequently the party that ends up with the poorest result. Concessions are perceived as a sign of weakness—a sign that you have lowered your level of ambition, or that you have considerable room for maneuver. The pressure on you will increase and start a chain reaction. You have to keep giving until you've given everything away.

A unilateral concession must be made with great caution at the end of the negotiation—to finalize it, or to unblock a negotiation that has become stuck. It must not be followed by further concessions until the other party gives you something or makes a counteroffer that you can decide about.

Let the other party make a major effort before you make a concession. Concessions at the beginning of the negotiation often go down the drain; no decisions are made, and the other party is only assessing how to negotiate. It's important, for psychological reasons, that the other party has to work hard to get a concession on the table. If not, they don't get to demonstrate their negotiating skills, and they feel no satisfaction at the result they have achieved.

Concession Must Be Linked to a Counterdemand

Normally a concession must be linked to the demand for something in return. In a negotiation you must avoid giving something without getting something. If you do, the negotiating position will shift adversely for you. If you forget your compensation, you must continue until you've given everything away. Something you could get in return for a longer warranty period could be a higher price, longer time off delivery, a service agreement, or something else.

When you are looking for an opening in the negotiation through concessions and compensations for these, you should always first think of compensation and only then of the concession you'll make. If you don't, the following can easily happen:

> *We might reduce our price by 5 percent, but then you must buy 20 percent of your annual requirements from us.*
>
> *5 percent, you say, what's the new price going to be then?*
>
> *$20.67 per unit.*
>
> *I'll round off the figure to $20.50 in your quotation. I suppose we can agree to a small adjustment to the conditions of payment. We want current month plus 30 days net.*
>
> *Yes, well, what do you have to say about the increase in quantity?*
>
> *I'll come back to that; do we agree about the payment conditions?*
>
> *Yes.*
>
> *Can you let us have this CPT? That's what your competitors are offering.*

The seller doesn't succeed in tying down the customer. They lose their grip on the negotiation. They show their cards much to plainly and have to make one concession after the other. A seller who is familiar with this trap works in a different way:

> *If you buy another 20 percent of your annual requirements from us, I can do something about the price.*
>
> *What price are you offering me, then?*
>
> *Do we have an agreement that you will buy another 20 percent?*
>
> *That will depend on the new price.*
>
> *Can we deliver 20 percent during the first quarter?*
>
> *That's okay, but what's the price?*
>
> *Are we agreed about all the other matters? Only the price is still outstanding?*
>
> *Yes.*
>
> *Can you make a decision now?*
>
> *Yes.*
>
> *What's a good price for you?*
>
> *About 20 euro.*
>
> *It would be difficult for me to go down so low. The highest I can give you is 3–4 percent.*

Already when preparing to negotiate, you must review all the counterclaims you can make and receive from the other party. When the negotiation is under way and the other party makes their demands, you will rarely have the time to think about what counterclaim would be reasonable.

ELEMENT 101

The Power of Habit

Negotiation, the backbone of all trade, is a powerful tool in creating wealth. In my interactions with various clients, I often hear a litany of reasons why adopting a new negotiation approach is challenging or seemingly impossible:

- "My counterpart won't engage openly."
- "Our company is too large for such strategies."
- "We are bound to e-auctions and tenders."
- "In my industry, it's always a zero-sum game."
- "There's a lack of trust in our field."
- "Can negotiation really be this straightforward?"
- "Everyone I deal with is aggressive."
- "We've tried similar methods, but they didn't work."
- "Our management wouldn't approve of this approach."
- "We attempted this before and it was unsuccessful."

The list continues, often filled with reasons for not even attempting a change, despite agreeing with the concept.

Let's try a small exercise. Cross your arms as you normally would. Now, cross them in the opposite way. Feels unnatural, doesn't it? That's the nature of habit. The way you cross your arms has been ingrained since childhood. Changing this habit requires conscious effort, but within a few weeks, the new way can become your norm.

Changing negotiation habits is similar. We're creatures of habit, and altering the way we've always negotiated can be daunting. It requires time, effort, and a strong will.

In your next negotiation, experiment with this approach: Start by telling your counterpart, "Today, my goal is to help you reduce costs, liabilities, and risks while increasing your profits and benefits. Are you interested in exploring this?" If they agree, continue with, "In return, I anticipate your support in reducing my risks, liabilities, and costs, while also enhancing my profits and benefits."

The change begins with you. You have the power to break away from traditional negotiation habits and pave the way for more collaborative, mutually beneficial discussions.

ELEMENT 102

Reflection: Essential Skills and Behaviors for Becoming an Accomplished Negotiator

In my extensive experience, conducting thousands of negotiation simulations with over 35,000 participants and participating in countless real-life negotiations, I have identified a range of skills that can be honed to enhance negotiation prowess. While these skills and behaviors vary among individuals, I've observed that most negotiators can benefit significantly from developing in the following areas:

- **Questioning technique:** Master the art of asking pertinent questions to unveil crucial information. (See Element 18.)
- **Balanced openness:** Maintain an optimal level of transparency without over-exposing your position.
- **Structured approach:** Employ a systematic method in negotiations to optimize time and resources.
- **Agenda setting:** Collaboratively design the agenda, as it serves as a guiding framework for both parties.
- **Persistence:** Persistently seek satisfactory answers and clarity where responses are lacking or vague.
- **Role definition in team negotiations:** Clearly define and adhere to team roles for effective collaboration.

- **NegoEconomics understanding:** Unlock additional value by recognizing and leveraging asymmetric values. (See Element 20.)
- **Creative thinking:** Embrace innovative approaches and introduce varied variables to enrich negotiation outcomes.
- **Appropriate mandate:** Ensure that both parties have the necessary authority to engage in meaningful negotiation.
- **Combativeness awareness:** Distinguish between combative and collaborative behaviors, and adapt accordingly.
- **Pre-negotiation of rules:** Set the rules of the game before negotiations commence.
- **Enhanced listening:** Focus on the underlying value conveyed in words, not just the words themselves.
- **Consideration of counterpart's position:** Contemplate your counterpart's costs, values, risks, and liabilities.
- **Group discipline:** The team should respect and adhere to their assigned roles.
- **Effective small talk:** Use casual conversation to build rapport and trust, and to gather valuable insights.
- **Initiative:** Being proactive often leads to gaining more value in negotiations.
- **Consistent honesty:** Truthfulness simplifies communication and builds credibility.
- **Utilization of visual aids:** Incorporate tools like flipcharts, PowerPoint slides, and whiteboards to clarify and enhance discussions.
- **Stress awareness:** Recognize personal stress triggers and develop strategies to manage stress effectively.
- **Communication proficiency:** Effective negotiation is rooted in clear, concise communication.
- **Emotional intelligence (EI):** Understanding and utilizing EI is crucial to becoming a skilled negotiator.

Developing these skills can significantly elevate your negotiation capabilities, making you not just a good negotiator but a great one.

ELEMENT 103

The Choice to Negotiate: Challenging the Obvious

In our day-to-day lives, we are often presented with situations, prices, and terms that seem set in stone. These "givens" are accepted without question, as if they are unchangeable truths of our world. But what if they're not? What if we possess the power to challenge and negotiate these so-called standards? This element serves as a wake-up call, urging you to recognize and embrace the often-overlooked choice to negotiate.

The Misconception of Non-Negotiability

Many of us labor under the misconception that certain aspects of our professional and personal lives are non-negotiable. Whether it's a price tag on a product, a salary offer, or the terms of a contract, we tend to accept these without question. This passive acceptance stems from a combination of societal norms, lack of awareness, and sometimes, our reluctance to step out of our comfort zones.

SMARTnership: The Art of Challenging the Obvious

SMARTnership, a concept at the heart of my negotiation philosophy, challenges this non-negotiable, passive approach. It's about recognizing that negotiation is not just a skill for boardrooms and formal deals but a valuable tool for everyday interactions. By adopting a SMARTnership mindset, you begin to see negotiation opportunities where you previously saw barriers.

The Price Is Not Just the Price

Take, for instance, the price of a product or service. The common belief is that prices are fixed, but in reality, they are often just starting points for negotiation. Retail environments, professional services, and even online marketplaces can have hidden flexibility in pricing. By initiating a negotiation, you might uncover discounts, better terms, or added value that was not initially apparent.

Standard Terms: Not So Standard After All

Similarly, the "standard terms" often presented in contracts and agreements are rarely as standard as they seem. These terms are usually set by one party and can be inherently biased toward their interests. By accepting these terms without scrutiny, you might miss out on opportunities to negotiate more favorable conditions—be it in a lease, a job offer, or a business partnership.

Negotiation as a Mindset, Not Just a Skill

Negotiating more in life isn't just about acquiring better deals or terms; it's about developing a mindset that questions the status quo and seeks mutual gain. It's about moving away from a win-lose paradigm to one where all parties involved can benefit. This is the essence of SMARTnership—creating value that did not exist before the negotiation.

A Call to Action

This final and 103rd element is a call to action. It's an invitation to start questioning the norms and to see negotiation not as a confrontation but as a collaborative process of exploration and problem-solving. By doing so, you open up a world of possibilities where you have the power to influence outcomes, create value, and forge stronger relationships.

Remember, every interaction is an opportunity to negotiate. It's time to awaken to the power you hold in challenging the obvious and embracing the choice to negotiate. Let this be your first step toward a more proactive, assertive, and ultimately more rewarding way of navigating the world.

Acknowledgments

I would like to express my sincere gratitude to the numerous individuals who have contributed to my development by showing me the ropes of right and wrong in negotiations since the mid-1980s.

To those who have taught, trained, and believed in me throughout this journey, I am deeply indebted. As negotiations are best approached as a team effort, it is impossible for me to recognize every person who has played a role in the formation of these ideas.

I want to extend my heartfelt appreciation to those who have entrusted me with the responsibility of sharing knowledge on one of life's most critical skills. I take this responsibility very seriously and have worked diligently to present the best possible information in this book.

I am also grateful for the late Mr. Iwar Unt's influence. He was a critical mentor to me, and the concept upon which my continued work is based was originally designed by him in 1976 in Stockholm, Sweden.

Several individuals deserve special recognition for their contributions to this project. My sincere thanks go to Jørgen Jacobsen, my loyal legal advisor for more than a decade, who is so much more than just a legal professional. I would also like to acknowledge the late Paige Stover, my first business agent when I moved to the United States, who was an inspirational lighthouse.

Throughout this journey, I have received support and wise counsel from numerous professional colleagues in Europe, Asia, and the United States. Among them are Tim Cummins from World Commerce & Contracting, Dan Shapiro of the Harvard Program on Negotiation, and the team at Wiley, especially my editor, Cheryl Segura. I am deeply grateful for their recognition of the importance of negotiation.

A special thank you goes to Mr. Per Holm, the CEO of BlueKolding in Denmark, whose company won the award for "Best Tender/Negotiation" of the year based on SMARTnership and NegoEconomics. I appreciate how well they have embraced the concept and encouraged others to follow their success.

I would like to acknowledge my lifelong and best friend, Antonis, for his loyalty through thick and thin.

The content presented in this book was inspired by presentations, training, meetings, advisory services, and writings of scholars and thought leaders in the fields of negotiation, behavioral economics, and conflict resolution. I have had many friendly debates with my peers, and breakthrough moments have occurred through research and debriefings following difficult negotiation sessions.

One individual in particular has been a dear friend and business partner and has been incredibly supportive throughout this journey. I would like to thank Mr. Werner Valeur, a successful entrepreneur with numerous exits and a great talent for negotiation.

Lastly, I extend my deepest appreciation to my wife, Keyanna, for her unwavering patience, love, and support. I also want to thank my two sons, Kruise and Kierland, for their love and affection.

About the Author

Keld Jensen is an internationally recognized and award-winning expert, TEDx speaker, author, and advisor on negotiation, celebrated for his profound impact in the field. In 2024, Keld added a significant milestone to his illustrious career by concluding his doctorate in negotiation and trust, further solidifying his expertise and commitment to advancing understanding in these critical areas.

He is the founder and head of The SMARTnership Negotiation Organization, a pivotal force in consulting and training for the private sector and governmental bodies, facilitating optimized solutions to complex problems. His notable clientele includes industry giants such as Vestas, LEGO, ConocoPhillips, Novo Nordisk, Johnson & Johnson, leading organizations like UNICEF and World50, as well as the governments of Canada, Denmark, and Great Britain.

Keld's extensive background in management and his role as a former CEO of PC Express AB, a publicly traded technology company, underline his leadership and strategic acumen. An associate professor, Keld teaches at top-ranked universities worldwide, including the Thunderbird School of Global Management at Arizona State University, BMI Executive Institute in Lithuania, BMI/Louvain University in Belgium, and Denmark's Aalborg University. He is the former chairman of the Centre for Negotiation at Copenhagen Business School.

With more than 200 international TV appearances, regular contributions to *Forbes* magazine, and hundreds of articles in major business publications across Europe, Asia Pacific, and the United States, Keld has established himself as a global thought leader. He is a prolific author of 26 books, which have been translated into 16 languages and have reached over 3 million readers worldwide. Several of these works have received awards, marking him as a significant voice in international business literature.

Keld was recognized as one of the world's 100 Top Thought Leaders in Trust in 2016, and he has consistently ranked in the Global Gurus Top 30, reaching #4 as a Global Guru on Negotiation worldwide in 2024. He is the creator of the world's most awarded negotiation strategy, which has received accolades from The Organization of Public Procurement Officers in Denmark and The World Commerce & Contracting Organization's Innovation and Strategic Award.

A dual citizen of The Kingdom of Denmark and the United States, Keld resides in the United States with his wonderful wife and two children, whom he humorously credits with improving his negotiation skills daily. His commitment to mentoring entrepreneurs and enhancing small and medium-sized businesses through vital negotiations has led to the creation and growth of numerous companies.

For more insights into negotiation and to access Keld's online training, visit **www.smartnershipclass.com**.

Index